# Qualitative Research Methods for Media Studies

Bonnie S. Brennen

Routledge
Taylor & Francis Group

NEW YORK AND LONDON

First published 2013
by Routledge
711 Third Avenue, New York, NY 10017

Simultaneously published in the UK
by Routledge
2 Park Square, Milton Park, Abingdon, Oxon OX14 4RN

*Routledge is an imprint of the Taylor & Francis Group, an informa business*

*Library of Congress Cataloging-in-Publication Data*
Brennen, Bonnie.
  Qualitative research methods for media studies / Bonnie S. Brennen.
      p. cm.
    Includes bibliographical references and index.
  1. Mass media—Research—Methodology. I. Title.
  P91.3.B74 2012
  302.23072—dc23                                              2012015011

ISBN: 978–0–415–89021–2 (hbk)
ISBN: 978–0–415–89022–9 (pbk)
ISBN: 978–0–203–08649–0 (ebk)

Typeset in Minion
by Keystroke, Station Road, Codsall, Wolverhampton

Printed and bound in the United States of America by
Walsworth Publishing Company, Marceline, MO.

# Qualitative Research Methods for Media Studies

Qualitative research: You may have heard it described as research-lite, an approach for the math-phobic that's less rigorous or even easier than quantitative research—but truth be told, qualitative research is actually just as challenging, time-consuming and difficult to get right as its quantitative counterpart. While qualitative research can be controversial, contradictory and ambiguous, it can also be inspiring, invigorating and enlightening. It can get you out from behind your desk and allow you to experience your research topic firsthand. And it can help you develop a more nuanced understanding of communication as a social and cultural practice.

*Qualitative Research Methods for Media Studies* provides students and researchers with the tools they need to perform critically engaged, theoretically informed research using methods that include **interviewing**, **focus groups**, **historical research**, **oral histories**, **ethnography and participant observation**, and **textual analysis**. Each chapter features step-by-step instructions that integrate theory with practice, as well as a case study drawn from published research demonstrating best practices for media scholars. Readers will also find in-depth discussions of the challenges and ethical issues that may confront researchers using a qualitative approach. Qualitative research does not offer easy answers, simple truths or precise measurements, but this book provides a comprehensive and accessible guide for those hoping to explore this rich vein of research methodology.

**Bonnie S. Brennen** is the Nieman Professor of Journalism in the Diederich College of Communication at Marquette University. Her research focuses on the intersection between labor and journalism history as well as on relationships between media, culture and society. She is author of *For the Record: An Oral History of Rochester, New York, Newsworkers*, and co-editor with Hanno Hardt, of three books: *The American Journalism History Reader*; *Picturing the Past: Media, History, and Photography*; and *Newsworkers: Towards a History of the Rank and File*.

# Contents

| Chapter 1 | **Getting Started** | 1 |
|---|---|---|
| | Quantitative vs. Qualitative Research | 3 |
| | The Development of Qualitative Research | 5 |
| | Conceptual Orientations | 7 |
| Chapter 2 | **Doing Qualitative Research** | 13 |
| | The Ethics of Qualitative Research | 16 |
| | The Qualitative Research Process | 18 |
| | Choosing a Research Topic | 18 |
| | Crafting Research Questions | 20 |
| | Gathering and Analyzing Evidence | 21 |
| | Crafting a Research Report | 22 |
| Chapter 3 | **Interviewing** | 26 |
| | Qualitative Interviews | 28 |
| | Ethical Considerations | 29 |
| | Using Qualitative Interviews | 30 |
| | Conceptualizing a Study | 30 |
| | Designing a Study | 30 |
| | Conducting Interviews | 31 |
| | Interviewing Techniques | 34 |
| | Transcribing Interviews | 36 |

|  | Analyzing the Information | 37 |
|  | Verifying Information | 38 |
|  | Writing a Research Report | 38 |
| **Chapter 4** | **Focus Groups** | **59** |
|  | The Development of Focus Groups | 61 |
|  | Contemporary Focus Groups | 62 |
|  | The Role of a Moderator | 63 |
|  | Facilitators' Communication Strategies | 64 |
|  | Recruiting Participants | 67 |
|  | Dealing with Difficult Participants | 69 |
|  | Ethical Considerations | 70 |
|  | Focus Group Research | 74 |
| **Chapter 5** | **History** | **93** |
|  | Traditional vs. Cultural History | 94 |
|  | Media History | 96 |
|  | The Method of History | 98 |
|  | Collecting Historical Evidence | 99 |
|  | Types of Historical Materials | 100 |
|  | Evaluating Historical Evidence | 101 |
|  | Ethical Considerations | 104 |
|  | Research Using History | 105 |
| **Chapter 6** | **Oral History** | **124** |
|  | Technique of Oral History | 126 |
|  | Interview Strategies | 128 |
|  | Learning to Listen | 130 |
|  | The Editing Process | 132 |
|  | Ethical Considerations | 134 |
|  | Research Using Oral History Transcripts | 134 |
| **Chapter 7** | **Ethnography and Participant Observation** | **159** |
|  | Thick Description | 161 |
|  | Ethnography in Media Studies | 161 |
|  | Participant Observation | 163 |
|  | Going Native in *Avatar* | 165 |
|  | Field Notes | 167 |
|  | Reflexivity | 169 |
|  | Analyzing and Interpreting Ethnographic Material | 169 |

|  | Ethical Considerations | 170 |
|  | Research Using Ethnography | 171 |
| **Chapter 8** | **Textual Analysis** | **192** |
|  | What Is a Text? | 193 |
|  | The Development of Textual Analysis | 194 |
|  | The Influence of Semiotics | 196 |
|  | Theory and Interpretation | 197 |
|  | Encoding and Decoding | 199 |
|  | Ideological Analysis | 201 |
|  | Genre Analysis | 203 |
|  | Rhetorical Analysis | 205 |
|  | Ethical Considerations | 206 |
|  | Research Using Textual Analysis | 207 |
| *Acknowledgments* |  | 232 |
| *Index* |  | 233 |

# CHAPTER 1

# Getting Started

*Value things not because of their worth but because of their meaning.*
— Gabriel Garcia Marquez

You may have heard it described as research-lite, an approach for the math-phobic, less rigorous or even easier than quantitative research, but truth be told, qualitative research is actually a messy endeavor that is challenging, time-consuming and difficult to get right. Qualitative research does not provide us with easy answers, simple truths or precise measurements. It can be controversial, contradictory and ambiguous. However, it can also be insightful, enlightening, emancipatory and fascinating.

*Qualitative Methods for Media Studies* provides you with specific instruction on how to undertake research using a variety of different qualitative methods. The methods addressed in this book are common qualitative methods that are particularly relevant to answering media-related communication research questions. The methods chapters include examples of and discussion about published scholarly research using the method being addressed. In addition, you will find activities and research exercises for each method to help you learn how to conduct research using qualitative methods.

Each qualitative method addressed in *Qualitative Methods for Media Studies* is grounded theoretically, culturally and historically. This text offers guidance on framing qualitative research questions, instruction on the interpretation of research findings and discussion on how to integrate theory with practice. It also discusses the implications of qualitative research in the field of media studies and considers ethical issues and challenges researchers confront related to specific qualitative methods.

As you will soon discover, full disclosure is always appropriate in the realm of qualitative research. This book is based on my personal experiences teaching qualitative methods to graduate students at Marquette University, Temple University and the University of Missouri, Columbia. My approach to qualitative research is influenced by my own research activity using a variety of qualitative methods as well as by discussions and debates I have had over the years with graduate students and research colleagues. My own research is based on the theoretical framework of British Cultural Studies. In my work I specifically draw on Raymond Williams' definition of theory as the systematic explanations of real-world everyday practices, and it is this understanding of theory that guides *Qualitative Methods for Media Studies*.

I agree with Williams' cultural materialist understanding of culture as a way of life, as well as his description of history as "a continuous and connected process" (Williams, 1983, p. 146). As a cultural materialist, I find that all documents of material culture, including newspapers, books, films, popular music, television programs, comic strips, current fashions as well as newer media such as Facebook, Second Life and Twitter, are produced under specific political and economic conditions, and that any or all of these cultural products can provide us with insights about our society at a particular historical place and time.

The cultural approach to communication that I take in *Qualitative Methods for Media Studies* understands the communication process as a means of production that is based on the discourse of individuals and groups and is produced within a specific cultural, historical and political context. It is through our use of language that we make meaning and construct our own social realities. Because language is a fundamental part of all qualitative analysis, I believe that it is important to use the correct words to describe aspects of the qualitative research process. Throughout this book I provide you with appropriate words and concepts that are particularly relevant to qualitative research.

I must be honest with you and tell you that I disagree with the belief that researchers can do qualitative research without using an explicit theoretical framework or that it is easy to mix qualitative and quantitative methods seamlessly. Instead, I agree with Cliff Christians and James Carey (1989) that there are important differences between qualitative and quantitative methods that are related to philosophical orientation, cultural traditions, research values and priorities as well as with specific worldviews or ideological positions.

In order for you to understand the theoretical orientation that guides *Qualitative Methods for Media Studies*, I feel it is important for you to get a sense of my views on key issues relevant to the field of qualitative research. Although the theoretical perspective that I incorporate into my work frames the content of this book, it is useful to understand that in a fundamental sense, all research is a collaborative effort. Throughout the process of writing this book I have bounced ideas off of fellow researchers, friends and family members. Through my discussions with others I have worked through a variety of conceptual issues, methodological puzzles and research concerns related to the process of qualitative research. I would like to thank my Dean, Lori Bergen, and my colleagues at Marquette University for their support of my research and give a special shout-out to my Provost, John Pauly, for writing the invaluable *Beginner's Guide to Doing Qualitative Research in Mass Communication* and serving as a wonderful sounding-board for this project. I have been fortunate to have a great research assistant, Colleen Moore, and I thank her for her thoughtful assistance on this project. In addition, I appreciate the insightful questions and thought-provoking comments from my children Annie and Scotty as well as their polite inquiries meant to keep this book on track. Finally, this book is dedicated to Hanno Hardt, who was a wonderful mentor and friend. I will miss his unfailing encouragement and guidance.

While I appreciate all of the help I have received throughout this project, clearly the buck stops here, and I take full responsibility for any errors or omissions that you may find in this text.

## Quantitative vs. Qualitative Research

When we think about quantitative social science research, we see that it strives to be systematic, precise and accurate as it tries to determine validity, reliability, objectivity and truth. Quantitative research attempts to isolate specific elements and it uses numbers and numerical correlations within value-free environments to measure and analyze the "causal relationships between variables" (Denzin & Lincoln, 1998a, p. 8). Because it uses numbers to quantify data, quantitative research is often considered more authentic, important and scientific. For some, numbers are seen as more reliable than thoughts. As one statistician suggests, some people "worship the statistician as someone who, with the aid of his magical computing machine, can make almost any study 'scientific'" (Blalock in McKee. 2003, p. 123).

In contrast, qualitative research is interdisciplinary, interpretive, political and theoretical in nature. Using language to understand concepts based on people's experience, it attempts to create a sense of the larger realm of human relationships. As Steinar Kvale (1996) explains, the subject matter of qualitative research is not "objective data to be quantified, but meaningful relations to be interpreted" (p. 11). Qualitative researchers consider alternative notions of knowledge and they understand that reality is socially constructed. They showcase a variety of meanings and truths, and draw on a belief in and support of a researcher's active role in the research process.

At this point you may be wondering how socially constructed realities are actually created through language. Several years ago I came across an *Utne Reader* article, "Stop Lights and Phone Sex," that provides us with a useful example of the construction of a language-based symbolic reality. The essay contrasts the socially constructed reality of a man named Charlie with the lived reality of Fido the dog. In the article, Charlie uses symbols to experience different cultures, learn about his environment and pass on the knowledge he has attained to future generations. Fido lives in the present, experiencing only what he sees, tastes and smells. While initially it might seem that Charlie's socially constructed reality is superior to Fido's, the essay maintains that in addition to the knowledge gained from symbolic reality, symbols can also alter our perceptions, and manipulate our feelings, our moods and our tastes. Offering examples from a misplaced zero in a banking transaction, a phone sex hotline and an unusual art museum exhibit made out of garbage, the article explains that "[s]ymbols can lead Charlie to do things he wouldn't normally do, buy things he wouldn't normally buy, and think things he wouldn't normally think; Fido is blissfully unaffected. Humans use symbols and symbols use humans" (Proctor, 1995, p. 50).

As we consider connections between a socially constructed reality and the qualitative research process, it is important to consider the notion of transparency. When researchers openly describe their theoretical foundations and research strategies, along with the basis for their decisions, intentions and motivations, readers become aware of the potential uses and implications of the research (Rakow, 2011).

Qualitative researchers tend to use a variety of different methodologies in their work. For example, in my own research I have used several types of textual analyses, including discourse analysis and ideological critique, as well as historical analysis, case studies and open-ended in-depth interviews. No matter what qualitative method researchers use, their choice of method is based on the questions they wish to ask, the specific historical context that relates to their research questions as well as the theoretical framework they plan to use for their research. In an effort to clarify the research process, each methods chapter in *Qualitative Methods for Media Studies* discusses research using a single qualitative method. However, as you begin your own research efforts you will come across qualitative research that combines two or more methods. This is because qualitative researchers often incorporate the notion of triangulation, which is the use of multiple methods, to increase the rigor of their analyses and to develop in-depth understandings of social experience.

In the realm of media studies, by which I mean research that looks at aspects of news, information and/or entertainment in mass communication, journalism, broadcasting, advertising, public relations, visual communication and new media, quantitative researchers tend to see communication as a behavioral science. They draw on scientific models of communication and use a variety of methodological strategies to measure the effects of different types of communication on various groups in society. For example, quantitative researchers consider topics such as the effects of television violence on children, the effects of race and ethnic identity on the evaluation of public service announcements, and the effects of political advertising on voters.

In contrast, qualitative researchers consider the diversity of meanings and values created in media. Rather than focusing on media effects or influences, they attempt to understand the many relationships that exist within media and society. For example, qualitative researchers who study media might look at how people understand advertising messages about cancer, how children are represented in online communities or how breaking news is framed in daily news photos. As John Pauly (1991) notes, the goal of qualitative research "is simply to render plausible the terms by which groups explain themselves to the world and to clarify the role that mass communication plays in such explanations" (p. 7).

## The Development of Qualitative Research

Just like 7 Up, the Un-cola, the use of qualitative methods in media studies research emerged as a viable alternative to challenge the status quo. When we look at the rise of qualitative research during the second half of the twentieth century, we see that it begins with a rejection of social science quantitative research ideas, procedures and protocols.

Although much of the early journalism and mass communication research was influenced by Pragmatism and framed from a cultural and historical understanding of communication, by the 1940s political scientists, sociologists and social psychologists were making important contributions to media research using quantitative social-scientific methodologies. As the field of mass communication research developed in post-World War II American society, communication researchers, who often saw science as a liberating force, embraced a scientific definition of mass communication and developed methodological techniques to measure the social effects of communication.

Preoccupied with the functional aspects of mass communication, researchers constructed scientific models that defined the field, illustrated its scientific nature and legitimated mass communication research as a social science endeavor. Critical cultural theorist Hanno Hardt (1992) suggests that the conceptualization of the field of communication as a behavioral science encouraged an emphasis on methodological concerns such as sampling, measurement, research design and instrumentation which tended to overshadow considerations of theoretical issues regarding the role of media and communication within society.

While quantitative social science research remained the dominant approach to mass communication research throughout much of the twentieth century, some researchers did not see the need for social science to "imitate the natural sciences in form or method" (Christians and Carey, 1989, p. 354). Scholars like Neil Postman suggested that attempts to understand human feelings and behavior should not be considered science because it was difficult to show cause-and-effect relationships within human behavior. Although researchers were unable to prove or disprove inter-pretations of human experience, Postman (1988) suggested that the more insightful research in media studies drew its relevance and strength "from the power of its language, the depth of its explanations, the relevance of its examples and the credibility of its theme" (p. 13).

Researchers who questioned the dominant social science perspective of mass communication often envisioned communication as a cultural prac-tice, through which issues of power, class and social identity could be nego-tiated. Like Postman, other researchers found that quantitative methods could not help them to answer central questions regarding the role of "communication as the social production of meaning" (Jensen, 1991, p. 18), and researchers began to turn to alternative theoretical perspectives and qualitative methods to understand communication as a social and cultural practice. Media studies scholars began drawing on the theoretical per-spectives of British Cultural Studies, Critical Theory, Political Economy, Feminism and Postmodernism among other alternative perspectives to frame their qualitative research studies.

The Qualitative Studies Division of the Association for Education in Journalism and Mass Communication (AEJMC) and the Philosophy of Communication Division of the International Communication Association

(ICA) were formed in the late 1970s to provide qualitative researchers with academic homes where they could present theoretically informed media-related research. While mainstream mass communication research journals tended to reject qualitative research that did not use an historical method, scholarly journals such as the *Journal of Communication Inquiry, Critical Studies in Mass Communication* and the *Journal of Communication and Media, Culture and Society* consistently published qualitative research. By the end of the twentieth century, qualitative methodologies had been fully integrated into the realm of communication and media studies; academic conferences regularly showcased theoretically informed qualitative research; and most of the scholarly journals in our field published qualitative research.

In the twenty-first century, qualitative research is an integral part of the field of media studies. However, you may be surprised to learn that there are still some social science researchers who remain hostile to the use of qualitative research methods in media and communication research. Some of these researchers see qualitative research "as an attack on reason and truth" (Denzin & Lincoln, 1998a, p. 7), while others maintain that their resistance not only reflects a desire to separate knowledge from opinion and to differentiate between "hard" science and "soft" research but also is framed from a belief that truth can be independent of politics (Carey, 1989, p. 99). Rather than take offense at the hostility of some social scientists, qualitative researchers often respond that because researchers are integral to the research process, offering insights, observations and evaluations of the evidence, at the most fundamental level all research methods are qualitative. As Vidich and Lyman (1998) note, "[W]e judge for ourselves on the standard of whether the work communicates or 'says' something to us—that is, does it connect with our reality? Does it provide us with insights that help to organize our own observations? Does it resonate with our images of the world?" (p. 44).

## Conceptual Orientations

While *Qualitative Methods for Media Studies* is not a book about theory, it is helpful for you to understand that researchers use theory to make sense of their findings and to orient their work within a larger conceptual orientation. Both qualitative and quantitative researchers like to draw on intellectual maps and models to help them represent their philosophical worldviews. These intellectual maps are often referred to as paradigms, and these paradigms provide a set of views and beliefs that researchers use to guide their work. An understanding of paradigms is of particular importance to qualitative researchers because they often find methodological questions of secondary importance to the larger philosophical issues and questions.

When we think about different research paradigms, there are three conceptual elements that quickly come to mind: epistemology, ontology and methodology. Denzin and Lincoln (1998b) clearly explain each of these concepts: "Epistemology asks: How do we know the world? What is the relationship between the inquirer and the known? Ontology raises basic questions about the nature of reality. Methodology focuses on how we gain knowledge about the world" (p. 185). For qualitative researchers, each of these elements influences the methods that they choose to use in distinct and significant ways.

And yet, since qualitative researchers pick and choose their theoretical positions from a variety of perspectives, some scholars find it difficult to create a single qualitative paradigm or intellectual map that represents a specific worldview and trajectory for qualitative research perspectives and traditions. These researchers prefer to see qualitative research not as a paradigm but instead as an interdisciplinary theoretical response to, and a reaction against, quantitative social science research. As David Hamilton (1998) suggests, the tradition of qualitative research is "a messy social movement, one that is structured as much by recombination of different activities as by their differentiation, divergence and continuity" (p. 113).

Guba and Lincoln (1998) maintain that qualitative research is not a unique paradigm but rather is influenced by several distinct paradigms, including Positivism, Post-Positivism, Critical Theories and Constructivism. Each of these paradigms is thought to provide specific values and principles that guide all of our research strategies and activities.

In contemporary society, Positivism remains the dominant paradigm of the physical and social sciences. Positivists consider reality to exist and scientific truth to be knowable and findable through rigorous testing that is free from human bias. The aim of inquiry of Positivism focuses on explanation, prediction and control while knowledge accumulates as factual building blocks in the form of "generalizations or cause–effect linkages" (Guba & Lincoln, 1998, p. 212). Within a Positivist paradigm the value of research is determined through internal validity, which is how findings correspond to the issue being studied, and external validity, which is the extent to which the findings can be generalized and related to similar studies. In addition, the reliability, or the extent to which the findings can be reproduced or replicated by another researcher, as well as the objectivity, or lack of bias, are also central considerations in evaluating the value of research. Researchers use experimental methods to verify hypotheses, and as you may have already figured out, these methods are primarily quantitative in nature.

The Post-Positivist paradigm is quite similar to Positivism. However, it responds to recent criticisms of Positivism in a few key areas. While reality is thought to exist, Post-Positivists consider that because people are flawed, they may not be able actually to understand it. Findings that can be replicated are thought to be probably true. While Positivists seek to verify their hypotheses, Post-Positivists use a variety of experimental methods, including some qualitative methods, in an effort to falsify their hypotheses. Post-Positivists also draw upon the concepts of internal and external validity, reliability and objectivity to evaluate the quality of their research.

The other paradigms that influence qualitative research are all non-Positivist alternative worldviews that blend research issues and theoretical positions, blur disciplinary boundaries and draw upon all types of qualitative methodologies. The term Critical Theories denotes a variety of theoretical positions, including (but not limited to) Neo-Marxism, Feminism, Cultural Materialism, Post-Structuralism and Postmodernism. Critical theorists consider reality and truth to be shaped by specific historical, cultural, racial, gender, political and economic conditions, values and structures; in their research they critique racism, sexism, oppression and inequality, and they press for fundamental and transformative social change.

Constructivism represents a theoretical shift regarding the concept of reality from realism to relativism. Constructivists lean towards an anti-foundational understanding of truth, rejecting any permanent "standards by which truth can be universally known" (Guba & Lincoln, 2003, p. 273). They work to build consensus and they favor negotiated agreements that are made by community members. Constructivists replace Positivist concepts of external and internal validity with notions of authenticity and trustworthiness.

Guba and Lincoln (2003) add an additional paradigm, Participatory/Cooperative Inquiry, to their list of paradigms influencing qualitative research. Participatory/Cooperative Inquiry is a transformative perspective that emphasizes the subjectivity of practical knowledge and the collaborative nature of research. While new paradigms are always interesting to consider, at this point it is not necessary for us to get bogged down debating the number of paradigms, if any, that influence qualitative research. What I would like you to remember from this discussion is that researchers who come from Positivist and Post-Positivist perspectives maintain a belief in a singular, big-"T" understanding of truth as well as a notion of a unified reality. Positivists and Post-Positivists try to exclude the influence of values from their work and they see ethics as being separate from their research concerns. Positivists and Post-Positivists see researchers as neutral observers who primarily rely on quantitative methods to test, verify, falsify or reject their research hypotheses.

In contrast, the alternative worldviews of Critical Theories, Constructivism and Participatory/Cooperative Inquiry, among others, all believe in multiple interpretations of a little-"t" understanding of truth and envision many constructed and competing notions of reality. All of these alternative paradigms consider values to shape their research and find ethical considerations essential to their work. They see researchers' subjectivity as integral to the research process and they draw primarily upon qualitative methods to answer their research questions.

There seems to be no clear consensus among researchers on whether qualitative methods actually constitute a paradigm in themselves or whether the field, instead, is influenced by a variety of other paradigms. Yet I think it is important to remember that it is the worldview, philosophy or theoretical framework that guides the questions qualitative researchers ask as well as the method or methods they choose to use in their research. Qualitative researchers do not pick a method they wish to use and then frame their research questions around their chosen method. For qualitative researchers, the choice of method comes from the questions they wish to ask.

You may wonder how you might go about selecting an appropriate theoretical framework, worldview or research paradigm to guide your work. I often tell my students that while researchers may try out a variety of perspectives, a theoretical framework usually picks you. What I mean by this is that each of you will develop a specific view of the world that makes sense to you. After some trial and error, each of you will discover a paradigm and/or conceptual perspective that fits with the specific way that you see the world.

What follow are some questions for you to consider to help you get started with your search for your own theoretical framework that will provide you with guidance for your media studies research.

- What does objectivity mean to you?
- What is neutrality?
- Do you believe it is possible for a researcher to be completely objective? Why, or why not?
- Do you see the field of media studies as a social science or as part of the tradition of humanities?
- What is your view of the role of science in contemporary society?
- Is human reality pre-set or is it shaped by specific historical, cultural and/or economic conditions?
- What is the goal of media studies research?

- Do you believe that truth is relative?
- What is a researcher's role in the research process?
- Do you think that researchers should try to bring about social change? Why, or why not?
- Do you think that we can measure people's opinions, feelings and/or concerns? Why, or why not?
- Are there cause-and-effect relationships that can be determined in people's behavior?
- Is there a single notion of truth that we can find out and/or know?
- Do you think that reality is socially constructed? Why, or why not?

While there are no right or wrong answers to these questions, your responses will help you to determine the type of research that is best suited to your own worldview and the particular qualitative methods that may best fit with your perspective. You may also wish to compare your answers with the earlier discussion of Positivism, Post-Positivism, Critical Theories, Constructivism and Participatory/Cooperative Inquiry. For those of you who embrace the relativity and fluidity of Critical Theories, Constructivism and/or Participatory/Cooperative Inquiry, you will find the multiple perspectives of qualitative research methods comforting and understandable. However, for those of you who reside comfortably within a Positivist paradigm, seeking precise answers, objectivity, neutrality and a knowable and findable Truth, the messiness of qualitative methods may test your worldview, common sense and patience.

## References

Carey, James W. (1989). *Communication as culture: Essays on media and society.* Boston, MA: Unwin Hyman.

Christians, Clifford G., & Carey, James W. (1989). The logic and aims of qualitative research. In Guido H. Stempel & Bruce H. Westley (Eds.), *Research methods in mass communication.* Englewood Cliffs, NJ: Prentice Hall.

Denzin, Norman K., & Lincoln, Yvonna S. (1998a). Introduction: Entering the field of qualitative research. In Norman K. Denzin & Yvonna S. Lincoln (Eds.), *The landscape of qualitative research: Theories and issues* (pp. 1–34). Thousand Oaks, CA: Sage.

Denzin, Norman K., & Lincoln, Yvonna S. (1998b). Major paradigms and perspectives. In Norman K. Denzin & Yvonna S. Lincoln (Eds.), *The landscape of qualitative research: Theories and issues* (pp. 185–193). Thousand Oaks, CA: Sage.

Guba, Egon G., & Lincoln, Yvonna S. (1998) Competing paradigms in qualitative research. In Norman K. Denzin & Yvonna S. Lincoln (Eds.), *The landscape of qualitative research: Theories and issues* (pp. 195–220). Thousand Oaks, CA: Sage.

Guba, Egon G., & Lincoln, Yvonna S. (2003). Paradigmatic controversies, contradictions, and emerging confluences. In Norman K. Denzin & Yvonna S. Lincoln (Eds.), *The landscape of qualitative research: Theories and issues* (2nd edn, pp. 253–291). Thousand Oaks, CA: Sage.

Hamilton, David. (1998). Traditions, preferences, and postures in applied qualitative research. In Norman K. Denzin & Yvonna S. Lincoln (Eds.), *The landscape of qualitative research: Theories and issues* (pp. 111–129). Thousand Oaks, CA: Sage.

Hardt, Hanno. (1992). *Critical communication studies: Communication, history and theory in America.* London: Routledge.

Jensen, Klaus Bruhn. (1991). Introduction: The qualitative turn. In Klaus Bruhn Jensen & Nicholas W. Jankowski (Eds.), *A handbook of qualitative methodologies for mass communication research* (pp. 1–11). London: Routledge.

Kvale, Steinar. (1996). *InterViews: An introduction to qualitative research interviewing.* Thousand Oaks, CA: Sage.

McKee, Alan. (2003). *Textual analysis: A beginner's guide.* London: Sage.

Pauly, John J. (1991). *A beginner's guide to doing qualitative research in mass communication.* Columbia, SC: Association for Education in Journalism and Mass Communication.

Postman, Neil. (1988). Social science as moral theology. In *Conscientious objections: Stirring up trouble about language, technology, and education* (pp. 3–19). New York: Alfred A. Knopf.

Proctor, Russell F. (1995, May–June). Stop lights and phone sex. *Utne Reader*, pp. 48, 50.

Rakow, Lana F. (2011). Commentary: Interviews and focus groups as critical and cultural methods. *Journalism and Mass Communication Quarterly, 88* (2), 416–428.

Vidich, Arthur J., & Lyman, Stanford M. (1998) Qualitative methods: Their history in sociology and anthropology. In Norman K. Denzin & Yvonna S. Lincoln (Eds.), *The landscape of qualitative research: Theories and issues* (pp. 41–110). Thousand Oaks, CA: Sage.

Williams, Raymond. (1983). *Keywords: A vocabulary of culture and society.* London: Fontana Press.

# CHAPTER 2

# Doing Qualitative Research

*Believing, with Max Weber, that man is an animal suspended in webs of significance he himself has spun, I take culture to be those webs, and the analysis of it to be therefore not an experimental science in search of law but an interpretive one in search of meaning.*

— Clifford Geertz (1973, p. 5)

Two very different understandings of the communication process emerged in Western cultures during the nineteenth century. Cultural theorist James Carey refers to these two perspectives as the transmission view and the ritual view of communication. The transmission view envisions communication as a process of sending, transmitting or delivering information in order to control others. Drawing on a transportation metaphor, and favoring technological advances within the communication process, the transmission view focuses on sending messages over distances in order to distribute common knowledge and ideas. In contrast, the ritual view associates the communication process with the ancient notion of communion. From the perspective of a ritual view of communication, people share customs, beliefs, ideas and experiences, a process that reinforces and maintains a common culture. As we compare the transmission view and the ritual view of communication, we can see that these perspectives also serve as metaphors that illustrate fundamental differences between qualitative and quantitative research.

Carey (1989a) illustrates differences between the transmission and the ritual views of communication through his analysis of a newspaper. From a transmission perspective a newspaper disseminates news and information, and "questions arise as to the effects of this on audiences: news as enlightening or obscuring reality, as changing or hardening attitudes, as breeding credibility or doubt" (p. 20). The transmission view questions that Carey raises are the same types of questions quantitative social scientists ask in their media-related research. Assessing a newspaper from a ritual view focuses less on news as information than on news as a dramatic ritual act that invites audience participation. Newspaper readers are thought to join in with the dramatic action to help make sense of their historically based cultural experiences and to socially construct their realities. As with qualitative scholars, from a ritual view readers do not focus on media effects, structures or functions; instead, the use of language in a newspaper provides readers with dramatic and engaging presentations of the world.

Language is a fundamental aspect of all qualitative research. It is through our discourse—or, in other words, our writing and speaking—that we communicate ideas and information, create communities and construct our social realities. At a basic level, qualitative research strives to understand the traditions, contexts, usages and meanings of words, concepts and ideas. As Neil Postman (1988) suggests, the purpose of research is "to rediscover the truths of social life; to comment on and criticize the moral behavior of people; and finally to put forward metaphors, images, and ideas that can help people live with some measure of understanding and dignity" (p. 18).

You may find that some of the qualitative research you come across is extremely complex, difficult to decipher and full of theoretical terms and discipline-specific jargon. Over the years, many of my students have expressed their frustration at trying to comprehend some of the qualitative research they encountered and they have wondered why it was presented in such a manner. Just as Andy Dufresne in *The Shawshank Redemption* asks Warden Samuel Norton, "How can you be so obtuse?" I too wonder why all qualitative scholars do not insist on crafting clearly presented, understandable research. Since the goal of qualitative research is understanding, I would encourage all researchers to write so that their work is accessible, allowing everyone who is interested to join in the conversation.

Given the crucial role of language in qualitative research, I believe it is important to use the most appropriate words to help us to explain our work clearly, precisely, carefully and correctly. When we look at social science research, we see that quantitative researchers draw on the denotative or explicit meanings of words in order to operationalize their research terms and create a precise coding system. In contrast, qualitative researchers understand that our everyday language "is lushly metaphorical, wildly contradictory, willfully connotative, and cynically strategic" (Pauly, 1991, p. 6), and in their work they focus on the denotative as well as the connotative meanings of the words that they use. If we think, for example, of the denotative definition of the word *mother*, we know that "mother" is defined as a female parent. This is the definition that quantitative researchers would use in studies involving mothers. However, the connotative meaning of a mother often signifies care, tenderness, compassion and love. Qualitative researchers understand that while words and concepts have important denotative meanings, they also have connotative interpretations that are important to consider. In their research they not only incorporate the denotative meanings of words but also embrace the variety of connotative meanings found within language.

Qualitative researchers do not identify variables, operationalize research terms, construct hypotheses, conduct experiments, measure data or replicate findings. Instead, they ask research questions, search for meaning, look for useful ways to talk about experiences within a specific historical, cultural, economic and/or political context, and consider the research process within the relevant social practices. What follows is a list of commonly used terms in both qualitative and quantitative research. When possible, try to use the terms that best describe the type of work that you are doing.

---

### Common Qualitative and Quantitative Terms

| Qualitative research | Quantitative research |
|---|---|
| Research question | Hypothesis |
| Subjective | Objective |
| Engaged researcher | Neutral observer |
| Transformative intellectual | Disinterested scientist |
| Research process | Operationalization |
| Critique | Predict |
| Experience | Experiment |
| Information | Data |
| Analysis | Measurement |
| Interpretation | Bias |
| Understanding | Explanation, prediction and control |
| Imbued with values | Value-free |
| Reconstructions | Cause and effect |

| Qualitative research | Quantitative research |
|---|---|
| Occurrence | Replication |
| Authenticity | Validity |
| Trustworthiness | Reliability |
| Context | Variables |
| Insights | Generalizations |

## The Ethics of Qualitative Research

Because of the active role of the researcher and the understanding that all inquiry is fundamentally subjective, qualitative researchers use a variety of strategies to develop ethical ways of dealing with the people they encounter during the research process. Of fundamental concern is the principle that all individuals who participate in qualitative research projects must voluntarily agree to participate in the studies without any psychological or physical pressure, manipulation or coercion. Qualitative researchers must provide potential participants with accurate information on the intention of their studies, and there can be no deception regarding the motives of the research. Individuals' agreement to participate in qualitative research must be an informed consent based on complete, accurate and open information. Participants must be told that they are part of a research project and should be explicitly informed about all aspects of the research. In addition, participants must be informed that they are able to withdraw from a research project at any time they wish. When appropriate, participants' privacy and confidentiality should be protected and secured, and all qualitative research should be based on authentic and accurate research. "Fabrications, fraudulent materials, omissions, and contrivances" (Christians, 2003, p. 219) are unethical and inappropriate for qualitative researchers.

Maurice Punch (1998) suggests that researchers are still trying to recover from the consequences of Stanley Milgram's 1960s-era obedience experiments in which participants were manipulated and lied to, without consent, to encourage them to administer what they thought were painful electric shocks to individuals who did not learn quickly enough. Milgram's "controversial research methods in laboratory experiments, allied to the negative reactions to revelations about medical tests on captive, vulnerable, and non-consenting populations, led to the construction of various restrictions on social research" (Punch, 1998, p. 168).

When researchers convince themselves that the use of deception is for a greater good and they maintain that deception ultimately results in little harm to the participants, they rely on manipulation, secrecy and lies to gather evidence. Ethicist Sissela Bok (1989) explains that lying easily becomes a way of life and she suggests that researchers seek alternatives to lying, deceiving and/or manipulating their research participants. Bok insists that researchers can use other, less invasive methods to gather evidence. She suggests that researchers can fully disclose the actual intentions of all of their research projects, or that if they are unable to gather information without producing harm, they can pick another research topic.

These days, most researchers understand the collaborative nature of qualitative methods and they strive to make sure that the concept of informed consent is taken seriously and fully realized. Given the nature of qualitative research, some ethicists have questioned whether any social research can be ethically correct (Ryen, 2011). Theorists have recently suggested that both quantitative and qualitative research may be seen "as a metaphor for colonial knowledge, for power, and for truth" (Denzin & Lincoln, 2008, p. 1). From this perspective, researchers offer representations of the Other that may be culturally, economically or politically motivated. At worst, these representations perpetuate stereotypical views of different cultures, which may result in additional ways to control others. Yet, Michelle Fine (1998, p. 139) reminds us that

> [w]hen we look, get involved, demur, analyze, interpret, probe, speak, remain silent, walk away, organize for outrage, or sanitize our stories, and when we construct our texts in or on their words, we decide how to nuance our relations with/for/despite those who have been deemed Others.

Fine maintains that, while there is no easy solution to "othering," researchers willing to "work the hyphen" can collaborate with research participants to construct interpretations that privilege their experiences and stories. Other researchers suggest that the concept of protecting subjects from harm is based on a positivist assumption of true knowledge existing in an untainted external reality. While Ryen (2011) acknowledges that qualitative researchers must accept their moral responsibilities, she reminds us that "the stories we get are produced *with* rather than *by* someone: they are contextually produced, designed for a particular audience, serve locally produced purposes and are embedded in wider cultural contexts" (p. 421). Ultimately, qualitative researchers should balance understanding the ethical challenges involved in protecting participants while supporting the freedom to do their own scholarship. Overall, a primary goal of contemporary qualitative researchers is to emphasize the collaboration and cooperation with research participants, as they work to build trust and empathy, while they strive to limit the exploitation of at-risk individuals, groups and cultures.

## The Qualitative Research Process

While each of the methods chapters provides guidance on how to conduct research using a specific qualitative method, this chapter now focuses on general aspects of the qualitative research process. Given the interdisciplinary nature of qualitative research, there are a variety of ways in which scholars present their work. Yet, the qualitative research process often consists of five distinct phases: (1) choosing a topic of study; (2) constructing a research question and picking a method of analysis based on an interpretive paradigm or theoretical framework; (3) gathering evidence; (4) analyzing and interpreting evidence; and (5) crafting a research report.

## Choosing a Research Topic

In the field of media studies, John Pauly (1991) notes that qualitative researchers often study mass communication as a product, as a practice or as a commentary. Researchers who consider aspects of mass communication as a product look at elements of media as texts that represent "integrated strategies of symbolic action" (p. 4). Unlike quantitative researchers who code distinct parts of messages found in advertisements, public relations campaigns, news stories or in other media artifacts, qualitative researchers look at media products in their entirety in an attempt to understand common practices, issues and concerns. Qualitative researchers also study elements of media studies as cultural practices through which people make meaning out of their lives, as well as considering media practices as a commentary on relationships between media and society. In some cases, researchers may combine two or more of these strategies to analyze media-related practices.

For example, perhaps you are interested in studying the roots of the Internet and you know that the technology we use for the Web began with the development of the telegraph. If you wanted to study the telegraph as a product, you might want to research the history of Western Union as a media company. Or, given that Western Union was the first communication empire, you could study the telegraph as a cultural practice, one that created, in Carey's (1989b) words, different production, organizational and administrative techniques

> that demanded a new body of law, economic theory, political
> arrangements, management techniques, organizational structures,

and scientific rationales with which to justify and make effective the development of a privately owned and controlled monopolistic corporation.

(p. 205)

However, the development of the telegraph not only allowed information to travel quickly over long distances but also changed news into a commodity that "could be transported, measured, reduced and timed" (Carey, 1989b, p. 211). The telegraph sped up the process of news; because each word sent across its wires was expensive, it also increased the costs of publishing a newspaper.

You could also study the telegraph as a commentary. From this perspective you might focus on changes in the nature of news that began with the development of the telegraph and evaluate the impact those changes have had on American society.

I believe it is important for each of you, understanding that as a researcher you will be an active participant in the qualitative research process, to consider what potential research topics, issues and/or concerns are of particular interest to you. Think about research studies you have read about, heard about or seen presented. Which ones did you find particularly relevant, interesting or important? Are there certain commonalities among these studies? Perhaps the research that resonated most with your interests all focused on aspects of sports coverage, or addressed different types of public relations campaigns or highlighted broadcasting pioneers. Thinking about past research that caught your interest will give you ideas for potential research topics that are well suited to your interests.

Once you have a research topic in mind, it is time to do some background research to see what has already been written on the topic. You can begin your background research by checking online search engines, research guides and databases, and looking through relevant academic journals and books. By the way, checking the references of a research study that you like will often lead you to similar published research in that area. Qualitative researchers routinely draw on existing research about topics of interest to gather relevant research for their literature reviews and to help them craft research questions.

The theoretical framework you choose for your study will also help you to frame the topic area and the method that you use, as well as your strategies of analysis. For example, perhaps you are a fan of the television show *Mad Men*, and watching its portrayal of advertising has piqued your interest in learning what it was actually like to work in an advertising agency during the 1960s and 1970s. If you decide to use a liberal feminist approach for your research, one key area you would focus on in your study is gender relations. In addition to learning about work responsibilities, types of clients and the creative process, you would want to consider the role of women working in advertising agencies during the 1960s and 1970s. You could research the positions they held, their work routines, their salaries as well as gender-related career challenges that they may have faced working in advertising agencies. Remember that a theoretical framework is not intended to limit your research but rather to help focus and guide your inquiry toward specific topics, issues and/or concerns.

## Crafting Research Questions

All qualitative research questions should be clearly stated, specific and researchable. When you are crafting a research question, the first step is to make sure that the question you want to research can be answered. While a question such as "What does God think about new communication technologies?" may be interesting to consider in a philosophical sense, there is no way such a question can be answered through qualitative research. Or perhaps you are interested in understanding the role of technology in contemporary culture. While this is an important area of media studies research, as a research topic it is too large for a single study and you would need to focus your interests more narrowly on one aspect of the topic. You might choose to research a specific communication technology such as Facebook, smartphones or Second Life. It is also helpful to narrow your research topic to a particular group of people, geographic region or era of inquiry.

Qualitative research questions should be open-ended in nature, encouraging you to understand a variety of potential responses, experiences and connections. They should also allow you to discover aspects of the topic that you may not have previously considered. Qualitative research questions should not yield a simple yes-or-no answer, because meaning is made and understanding is constructed from the reasons why people engage or do not engage with media. In addition, if you frame a question that results in a negative answer, your research project is usually over before it has started. For example, a research question such as "Has Second Life altered the way people communicate?" will provide you with minimal information about how people actually interact with Second Life. A more open question such as "How do disabled individuals use the computer-generated alternative reality of Second Life to communicate with others?" is a focused and researchable question, and one that can help you to understand how a specific group of people use Second Life to communicate with others.

Consider the following questions to help you get started crafting your research questions and choosing a conceptual framework for your qualitative research:

- What topic, issue or concern is of particular interest to you?
- What has been written on this topic before?
- What theoretical perspectives were previously used in research on this topic?
- What types of research methods have been used in other research on this topic?
- Are there any gaps in the literature that you would like to explore? If so, how might you fill in those gaps?
- What is the goal of your research?
- What types of methods do you think will help you to answer the types of questions you wish to ask?
- What types of insights can a theoretical framework give you with this research project?
- What conceptual frameworks provide you with guidance in crafting your research question?
- Which of these theoretical perspectives are you most comfortable using for your research project?

## Gathering and Analyzing Evidence

Once you have crafted a research question and chosen a theoretical framework and methodology to use, it is time to begin the evaluative process. While strategies for gathering, analyzing and interpreting evidence are often method-specific and are addressed more fully in each of the methods chapters in this book, in general the goal of qualitative analysis is "to contribute to a process of understanding, and to provoke other, probably contradictory, contributions" (Fiske, 1998, p. 370). Qualitative researchers try to gather all the evidence that they can find and they like to immerse themselves in all relevant materials related to their research. Unlike quantitative researchers, who rely on sampling techniques to generate statistical relevance, qualitative researchers generally consider that more is more.

However, they also understand that evidence may be significant even if it is not statistically relevant. Sometimes it is the outliers, the aberrations, the unusual findings that provide researchers with the most meaningful and significant insights. For example, Hanno Hardt's (2000) critical analysis of a bayoneted photograph album discusses the power and potential of photographs to disrupt and restructure cultural media history. Immersed in the conditions of war, the pierced images of a solitary photo album serve as a reminder of the destruction of lives and memories by an enemy as well as the role of images in constructing a social and cultural reality. Ultimately, the goal of interpretation, whether it is based on an advertisement, news report, photograph, website, press release or television show, is to help us to understand the essence of that media practice.

Qualitative research aims to understand the myriad meanings that people make. However, it is not enough for qualitative researchers to describe their observations, experiences and/or textual readings. Context is a central part of the interpretive process, and researchers must place their interpretations within the relevant historical, cultural, political and/or economic contexts. For example, if a person swings a club during a golf game, the meaning is much different than if that same person swings a club against an intruder.

Social practices and cultural traditions provide important context that qualitative researchers draw on throughout the process of analysis. As Clifford Christians and James Carey (1989) explain, "the interpretive process is not mysterious flashes of lightning as much as intimate submersion into actual traditions, beliefs, languages, and practices" (p. 363). Within the interpretive process, qualitative researchers do not take people's behaviors at face value but instead draw on the relevant contexts to help consider potential motives for their actions.

Qualitative researchers also attempt to reflect critically on their role as researchers, a process known as reflexivity. Reflexivity helps researchers understand how their interpretations of evidence are influenced not only by historical context, personal experiences and language but also by their race and ethnicity, class and gender. Reflexivity is discussed more fully in Chapter 7.

## Crafting a Research Report

In the field of media studies, qualitative researchers seek to understand aspects of the relationship between media and society and to interpret the multiplicity of meanings constructed in media. Qualitative researchers want to join in the ongoing scholarly conversation and they strive to provide thoughtful and insightful interpretations that will enlarge our understandings of important communication issues. While some qualitative research reports are primarily descriptive in nature, many are analytical, drawing on concepts and theories to analyze and interpret key findings. Still other qualitative reports are theoretical and philosophical discussions about important media studies issues and concerns. The individual methods chapters include examples of published studies that illustrate a variety of strategies for presenting qualitative research.

Pauly (1991) finds that scholars often present research based on one of three main strategies: "the realist tale, the confessional tale, and the impressionist tale" (p. 22). Researchers who opt for a realist tale write in the third person, a strategy that conveys a sense of neutrality, impartiality and objectivity. Researchers drawing on a confessional tale describe their own experiences, often in the first person, to help understand their personal cultural journeys. In contrast, researchers who craft an impressionist tale attempt to challenge readers' assumptions and expectations, and often focus on the text's role in our interpretations. No matter which presentation style a researcher chooses, ultimately it is important to remember that the stories qualitative researchers tell are shaped by their writing styles, personal histories, the theoretical perspectives they use, as well as considerations of race, ethnicity, class and gender, and the specific contexts surrounding their work (Denzin & Lincoln, 1998).

While there are a variety of ways in which qualitative research may be presented, many research reports include the following elements:

- Introduction
- Research Question
- Theoretical Framework
- Literature Review
- Methodology
- Analysis, Interpretations and Commentary
- Conclusion
- References.

However, although the above is a popular order for elements in qualitative research reports, it is important to remember that the order of the elements may vary. Some researchers interact with previously published literature throughout their reports, forming an extended conversation with other researchers. Other qualitative researchers begin with a discussion of their theoretical framework and literature review before they develop their research questions.

Qualitative research reports usually begin with an introduction, which provides relevant context and background for the study. The author may include a statement of why she or he chose to do this research. The introduction will also describe the research question or questions for the study.

Following the introduction is a section that addresses the theoretical framework used to guide the research project. This section defines the theoretical foundations for the study and it also explains the usefulness of key concepts that are drawn from the theory that the researcher uses in his or her research.

A literature review of all relevant scholarly research generally follows the theoretical framework discussion. Research that has been published on the same or a similar topic should be included. The literature review should not only give readers an understanding of what research has been done in this area but also describe how the new research project fits into the broader field of study and why it is important to pursue the study.

The methodology section begins with a general description of the methodology used in the research and a rationale for the choice of method. The methodology section also includes a detailed description of the specific research plan that will be used in the study.

While the introduction, research question, literature review and methodology offer important context for the study, the analysis section provides the concrete evidence of the research that is used to answer the research question. The author includes an analysis of the evidence he or she has collected, as well as commentary and interpretations of the evidence. This section is the most in-depth portion of the research, and the analysis should interact with conceptual issues and respond to previous studies addressed in the literature review.

The conclusion provides the author with an opportunity to summarize the findings, situate the research within a larger theoretical and/or philosophical context, and suggest areas of future research.

Finally, all research consulted and quoted in the research is listed in a reference section at the end of the study.

## References

Bok, Sissela. (1989). *Lying: Moral choice in public and private life.* New York: Vintage Books.

Carey, James W. (1989a). A cultural approach to communication. In *Communication as culture: Essays on media and society* (pp. 13–36). Boston, MA: Unwin Hyman.

Carey, James W. (1989b). Technology and ideology: The case of the telegraph. In *Communication as culture: Essays on media and society* (pp. 201–230). Boston, MA: Unwin Hyman.

Christians, Clifford G. (2003). Ethics and politics in qualitative research. In Norman K. Denzin & Yvonna S. Lincoln (Eds.), *The landscape of qualitative research: Theories and issues* (2nd edn, pp. 208–243). Thousand Oaks, CA: Sage.

Christians, Clifford G., & Carey, James W. (1989). The logic and aims of qualitative research. In Guido H. Stempel & Bruce H. Westley (Eds.), *Research methods in mass communication.* Englewood Cliffs, NJ: Prentice Hall.

Denzin, Norman K., & Lincoln, Yvonna S. (1998). Introduction: Entering the field of qualitative research. In Norman K. Denzin & Yvonna S. Lincoln (Eds.), *The Landscape of qualitative research: Theories and issues* (pp. 1–34). Thousand Oaks, CA: Sage.

Denzin, Norman K., & Lincoln, Yvonna S. (2008). Introduction: The discipline and practice of qualitative research. In Norman K. Denzin & Yvonna S. Lincoln (Eds.), *Collecting and interpreting qualitative materials* (pp. 1–43). Thousand Oaks, CA: Sage.

Fine, Michelle. (1998). Working the hyphens: Reinventing self and other in qualitative research. In Norman K. Denzin & Yvonna S. Lincoln (Eds.), *The landscape of qualitative research: Theories and issues* (pp. 130–155). Thousand Oaks, CA: Sage.

Fiske, John. (1998). Audiencing: Cultural practice and cultural studies. In Norman K. Denzin & Yvonna S. Lincoln (Eds.), *The landscape of qualitative research: Theories and issues* (pp. 359–378). Thousand Oaks, CA: Sage.

Geertz, Clifford. (1973). *The interpretation of cultures: Selected essays.* New York: Basic Books.

Hardt, Hanno. (2000). Pierced memories: On the rhetoric of a bayoneted photograph. In *In the company of media: Cultural constructions of communication, 1920s–1930s* (pp. 151–162, 177–178). Boulder, CO: Westview Press.

Pauly, John J. (1991). *A beginner's guide to doing qualitative research in mass communication.* Columbia, SC: Association for Education in Journalism and Mass Communication.

Postman, Neil. (1988). Social science as moral theology. In *Conscientious objections: Stirring up trouble about language, technology, and education* (pp. 3–19). New York: Alfred A. Knopf.

Punch, Maurice. (1998). Politics and ethics in qualitative research. In Norman K. Denzin & Yvonna S. Lincoln (Eds.), *The landscape of qualitative research: Theories and issues* (pp. 156–184). Thousand Oaks, CA: Sage.

Ryen, Anne. (2011). Ethics and qualitative research. In David Silverman (Ed.), *Qualitative research: Issues of theory, method and practice* (3rd edn, pp. 416–438). London: Sage.

# CHAPTER 3

# Interviewing

*Interviewing is rather like a marriage: everybody knows what it is, an awful lot of people do it, and yet behind each closed front door there is a world of secrets.*

— Ann Oakley (1981, p. 41)

What can be more natural than asking questions? Questions are a central part of the communication process, integral to our everyday conversations. We ask questions to gather information, evaluate opinions, establish common views and to understand key aspects of our lives. Interviewing has been used as a research method for thousands of years. The Egyptians surveyed people to determine their social and economic status. Romans used interviews with participants in the Peloponnesian Wars to gather source material in order to construct a history of the wars, and Socrates used dialogue to gather key philosophical insights (Kvale, 1996).

For many years, journalists, sociologists, political scientists, psychologists and clergy have drawn on interviews for their academic research, clinical counseling and diagnosis, and to try to understand people's social, economic and cultural conditions, as well as their political and religious views. These days, many researchers agree that because people speak from a variety of different backgrounds and perspectives, interviewing is a valuable method that may be used to gather a large amount of useful, interesting, relevant and/or important information. Some of the information accessed through interviews helps to broaden our knowledge base while other information may also help us to understand alternative points of view. In contemporary society, a variety of different types of interviews are routinely used in marketing surveys, legal interrogations, public opinion polls, job interviews, advertising surveys, medical interviews, therapeutic conversations and research questionnaires.

Recently, in just one week I was interviewed by a reporter about media labor issues, I participated in two research institute telephone interviews about my radio listening preferences and what I was doing to lower my carbon footprint, and I completed online surveys regarding various horse products, my grocery shopping habits and my perceptions of key political issues and concerns. As Gubrium and Holstein (2002b) suggest, in contemporary society interviews are widely used to obtain personal information and have become "an integral, constitutive feature of our everyday lives" (p. 11).

Simply stated, an interview is a focused, purposeful conversation between two or more people. Some interviews are only a few minutes long, while others last days, weeks or even months. Most research interviews are face-to-face conversations between one interviewer and one interviewee (also known as a respondent), with an interviewer asking questions and an interviewee answering them. However, interviews are also conducted online, in social networking sites, over the telephone as well as through mail-in surveys and telephone questionnaires. While this chapter focuses primarily on qualitative interviews, two additional types of interviews are also addressed in this book. Group interviews, known as focus groups, provide extensive information in a less costly format and are discussed more fully in Chapter 4. Oral history uses in-depth unstructured interviews to gather individuals' life histories and is the focus of Chapter 6.

In general, researchers use three basic types of interviews: structured, semi-structured and unstructured open-ended conversations. Structured interviews use a specific and standardized procedure, which includes pre-established questions that encourage a limited range of response and are open to a minimum of interpretation. For all participants in a given structured interview study, the same questions are asked in a predetermined order, using a consistent approach, format and words; interruptions, improvisations and/or deviations are not allowed with this type of interview. Structured interviewing is most often used for survey research; it focuses on gaining factual information from respondents with the goal of obtaining accurate and precise data that can be coded and may help "to explain behavior within pre-established categories" (Fontana & Frey, 1994, p. 366).

Semi-structured interviews are also usually based on a pre-established set of questions that are asked to all respondents. However, there is much greater flexibility with semi-structured interviews. Interviewers may vary the order of the questions and may also ask follow-up questions to delve more deeply into some of the topics or issues addressed, or to clarify answers given by the respondent.

Unstructured interviews focus on the complex voices, emotions and feelings of interviewees, as well as the meanings within the words that are spoken. Unstructured interviews are in-depth purposeful conversations that seek complex information about complicated issues, emotions and/or concerns in an attempt to understand the historical, social, economic and cultural experiences of individuals and/or groups. They strive to go beyond commonsense explanations to explore and reflect upon the "contextual boundaries of that experience and perception" (Johnson, 2002, p. 106). Unstructured interviews usually begin with a general list of topic areas, themes and/or open-ended questions that an interviewer draws upon.

## Qualitative Interviews

Surveys, questionnaires and other types of structured interviews emphasize the collection of quantifiable facts that can be used to generalize about elements of human behavior. In contrast, qualitative interviewing is less concerned with data collection and instead strives to understand the meanings of information, opinions and interests in each respondent's life. Through face-to-face, in-depth guided conversations using semi-structured or unstructured interview questions, qualitative interviewing explores respondents' feelings, emotions, experiences and values within their "deeply nuanced inner worlds" (Gubrium & Holstein, 2002a, p. 57). Qualitative interviewing is heavily influenced by a constructivist theoretical orientation which considers reality to be socially constructed; from this perspective, respondents are seen as important meaning-makers rather than "passive conduits for retrieving information" (Warren, 2002, p. 83). In recent years, with issues of representation becoming a central concern, we often see traditional research boundaries becoming blurred as qualitative interviewers and respondents collaborate to construct empowering narratives that allow diverse perspectives and multiple voices to emerge (Fontana, 2002).

Listening is central to qualitative interviewing. Researchers often start each interview with one introductory question and base their follow-up questions on the respondents' answers as well as on their own background research and other interviews they have conducted. Because qualitative interviews follow respondents' knowledge and interests, the interview process can take unexpected turns and detours. Interviewers must listen carefully to the conversation and remain open and flexible throughout each interview. In his conversations with people from all walks of life, Pulitzer Prize-winning oral historian Studs Terkel (1992) sought to present a feeling tone that combined intelligence with emotion in an attempt to explore the many possibilities in people that existed but had not yet been expressed. It is that feeling tone that helps to give qualitative interviewers access to, in Clifford Geertz's (1973) words, the "thick description" of our lives.

## Ethical Considerations

Because interviewers frame each research project, introduce issues and topics into the conversation, and influence the direction each interview will take, it is important to remember that imbalances may exist in the power relations between respondents and interviewers. Researchers using qualitative interviewing as a methodology should be sensitive to potential ethical dilemmas arising from the use of personal information. Qualitative interviewers should use their knowledge and experience to act with integrity, honesty and fairness (Kvale, 1996). All qualitative interviewers have a moral responsibility to protect their respondents from physical and emotional harm. There should be absolutely no deception about the scope, intention, goals or any other aspect of a qualitative research study. It is imperative to disclose the fact if there might be any potential harm to any respondents who are participating in qualitative interviews.

As a researcher, you should make sure when each respondent agrees to be interviewed that the consent he or she gives is an informed consent. It is crucial that each respondent knows exactly what your research study is about and how you plan for his or her interview material to be used. Be sure to explain how your research study will shed light on the relationship between media and society or how it will enhance some aspect of the human condition. Each respondent has a right to privacy and it is important to protect each person's identity when he or she requests it. Remember to ask each interviewee whether he or she is comfortable with his or her real name being used in the research project. If not, ask the person to choose a synonym in place of his or her real name. Once your research project is complete, you may wish to share your research findings with your respondents; they will be interested in your interpretations as well as what other respondents had to say.

## Using Qualitative Interviews

If you plan to use qualitative interviews as a methodology for your research study, there are several key research strategies that will help to guide your project. Kvale (1996) outlines seven research steps to be taken when using qualitative interviews, and this chapter now focuses on each of these steps: (1) conceptualizing a research question and outlining the theoretical framework guiding the research; (2) designing the research study; (3) conducting the interviews; (4) transcribing the interviews; (5) analyzing the information obtained from the interviews; (6) verifying the information from the interviews; and (7) writing up the findings of the study.

## Conceptualizing a Study

As with other qualitative methods, it is important to begin each research project by conceptualizing your study. Chapter 2 provides you with guidance that will help you to conceptualize your qualitative research study. However, I think it is important to remember to choose a topic that is based on your own interests, concerns or experiences. There is nothing worse than trying to complete a research project that you no longer find interesting.

## Designing a Study

When designing a qualitative interview study, you will want to consider the backgrounds of people you would like to interview, and how you will identify and gain access to them. You will need to craft a list of potential questions and/or topic areas to focus on, and you should also consider the time frame necessary to complete your research. You may be wondering how many interviews you will have to undertake to complete a qualitative interview research project. Unfortunately, there is no magic number of interviews that must be done. The right number of interviews will vary, depending on the length and depth of the conversations, the information obtained, the topic area and the focus of your research project. Ultimately, it is important to interview as many people as necessary in order to gather insights and understanding about your topic or issue. During the course of the interviews, when you hear the same information repeatedly and you feel that you are learning less and less from each new interview, you may feel that you have covered the topic thoroughly and it may be a good time to end the interview process.

It is also important to complete background research on each of your respondents so that you are knowledgeable about basic aspects of their lives, interests and activities. A Google search is a great place to begin, and be sure to consult Facebook, LinkedIn and other social networking sites. Gaining an interviewee's trust is an essential part of each qualitative interview. Fontana and Frey (1994) suggest that one way of establishing rapport is for an interviewer to see a situation from a respondent's perspective. It is also important for interviewers to understand the language, customs and culture of each person that they talk with.

Background research will provide you with key information about each respondent and will help you to ask informed and interesting questions. Learning as much as you can about the topic will also help you to gain access to key interview sources. Newcomb (1999) suggests that because media professionals do not have the opportunity or time to teach researchers about important aspects of their fields, access and rapport can be greatly enhanced when researchers have done extensive background research before the interviews and already have "specific knowledge of professional, organizational, and technical matters" (p. 100).

Once you have identified potential interviewees, you will need to persuade each person to participate in your study. In your initial email, phone call or letter to each potential respondent, outline the purpose of your study, mention your ideal research time frame and explain your rationale for interviewing the person. Be sure to follow up your initial contacts; it may take several attempts before some individuals will agree to be interviewed. When scheduling interviews, plan to meet in a quiet place that is comfortable and convenient for the respondent. Researchers must be flexible throughout the interview process and should understand that conflicts may arise with an individual that necessitate the rescheduling of an interview. It is also important to leave plenty of time for each interview so that you will not have to rush. It is embarrassing to be in the middle of an interesting conversation and realize that you have to cut the conversation short because you are late for your next appointment.

## Conducting Interviews

Once you have scheduled a few of your interviews, it is time to begin interviewing respondents. Barbara Walters, whose casual yet probing interview style has come to define the field of personality journalism, has excellent advice to keep in mind at the beginning of each interview. She notes:

> A conversation, even a brief one, should have all the best features of any functioning human relationship, and that means genuine interest on both sides, opportunity and respect for both to express themselves, and some dashes of tact and perception.
>
> (1970, p. xiv)

For both semi-structured and unstructured qualitative interviews, plan to bring a list of potential questions or topic areas as well as the background information you have collected on each respondent and your notes about the topic. I recommend taping all interviews. You may also wish to take notes during your interviews; it is helpful to jot down key concepts and topic areas to help keep the conversation flowing and to prompt follow-up questions. Some researchers recommend bringing photographs, newspaper articles and other cultural artifacts to the interviews. They find that discussing the materials is a great way to spark in-depth discussion about an issue or topic and they suggest that sharing elements of popular culture can be particularly helpful when discussing historical events.

At the beginning of each interview it is important to explain the purpose of your research study, help the respondent to see the relevance of the project and to express your genuine interest in her or his views and experiences. Be sure to refer to each interviewee by name and to pronounce each person's name correctly. The initial small talk and icebreaking questions that are used at the beginning of qualitative interviews help the interviewer get to know the interviewee, as well as to gain trust, build rapport and to establish the tone of the conversation.

While many different types of questions are used in interviews, qualitative interviewers begin primarily with icebreaker questions and then proceed with probing and follow-up questions.

## Icebreakers

Icebreaker questions are used to engage respondents in a conversation about key aspects of their personal lives, and they should begin to establish an environment where questions can be asked and answered in a non-judgmental manner. You may want to begin your interview by asking about your respondent's heroes, favorite sports teams, hobbies, favorite vacations or family activities. Feel free to comment on mutual interests, current events, the interviewee's fashion sense, musical tastes or even the weather. Walters (1970) suggests asking creative icebreaker questions based on a person's interests or career. Over the years she has asked artists what is the most intriguing or beautiful thing that they have ever seen, queried musicians on how they would inspire a child to play an instrument, and questioned news makers about recent experiences that have given them pleasure.

The background information you have gathered on each interviewee is especially helpful in framing icebreaker questions to get the conversation going. *New Yorker* writer A. J. Liebling recommends trying to understand enough about your interviewees' background to let them know that you appreciate their interests and want them to tell you more. Liebling (1963) explains that the icebreaker question he used to begin his well-known interview with jockey Eddie Arcaro was "How many holes longer do you keep your left stirrup than your right?" (p. 157). Arcaro responded that he could tell that Liebling had been around jockeys a lot, and in response to his question Arcaro spoke enthusiastically about his career and provided Liebling with great insights about his life as a jockey. Liebling writes that although he had only been around jockeys a week before the interview, he had learned from his research that on US racing tracks, jockeys ride with their stirrups longer on their left side.

## Probing Questions

Once trust has been established through your icebreaker questions, it is time to focus your questions more directly on the research topic. The questions you ask should be simple, sincere, direct and open-ended, encouraging respondents to explain and elaborate about their experiences. Open-ended questions offer respondents the freedom to respond with little influence from the interviewer. Try to ask questions that encourage personal opinions and commentary. Questions such as "How did you first get started in public relations?" or "Tell me about your first advertising position" will encourage a respondent to talk more openly about her or his career. Whenever possible, try to limit the number of specific factual questions and yes/no questions that you ask. While sometimes you will need to corroborate specific information, questions like "What year did you begin to work at JWT?" or "Did you major in broadcast journalism in college?" will do little to keep a conversation going. Thoughtful, well-crafted, open-ended questions will encourage your respondents to give you interesting, authentic, in-depth answers. Unfortunately, as Metzler (1977) suggests, the reverse is also true. When crafting interview questions, it is important to remember that "a superficial, insincere question will get you an equally shallow answer" (p. 132).

As you probe each topic, be sure to ask follow-up questions for clarification and to delve deeply into the experiences, emotions and feelings of each respondent. Questions such as "Can you tell me more about your first radio interview?" or "Can you give me an example of the types of stories you covered while you were on the science beat?" should help you to get in-depth information about your research topic.

## Asking Difficult Questions

During the course of an interview, you may need to ask a respondent a difficult question about a sensitive aspect of his or her life. Sensitive questions should be addressed carefully and respectfully, and should only be raised after you have established trust with an interviewee. One strategy is to depersonalize difficult questions by putting them in the third person and beginning the line of questioning by addressing the topic indirectly. For example, rather than asking a respondent, "Did you ever hire any minorities at your news station?" you might begin to explore the topic by asking, "What were the general hiring practices when you started in television news?" You might then mention that during other interviews, some respondents discussed racism in network broadcasting and, depending on the respondent's comments, you could follow up by asking a question such as "Have you observed or experienced any racism as a broadcaster?"

Perhaps you have reason to believe that one of your respondents is sexist. Rather than putting the individual on the spot by asking whether he or she thinks his or her views or actions are sexist, you might begin a discussion of this issue by saying something such as "During the course of my other research interviews, some respondents referred to you as sexist." On the basis of the respondent's response, you may be able to probe the sensitive topic more deeply. Walters (1970) finds that when addressing sensitive issues, it is helpful to ask respondents to comment on a well-known quotation, which may provide insight into the issue. For example, she suggests that instead of asking an individual to answer a sensitive question about how he or she feels about getting old in the media business, a better strategy is to ask the person to comment on a remark like the one credited to Brigitte Bardot: "The best years of my life were when I was 17."

## Interviewing Techniques

In qualitative interviewing, the interviewer's role is to encourage authentic, useful and in-depth responses from each respondent. Interviewers must learn how to assist respondents to freely share their stories, experiences and opinions. It is sometimes challenging to get access to the right respondents who are willing to speak openly and express their personal feelings about issues, topics and concerns. Not all respondents are able to provide meaningful, interesting responses to your questions. Some respondents will speak freely about the specifics of what they did but they remain uncomfortable explaining why they acted the way they did.

To become a skilled qualitative interviewer you should continually practice your interviewing skills. The best interviewers are creative, flexible and open to trying a variety of different strategies. It is helpful to adopt a neutral stance during your interviews and to refrain from influencing a respondent's commentary. Whenever possible, use non-threatening language and make sure that your non-verbal gestures, looks and body postures reinforce your interest in and support for the interviewee. Some journalists and law enforcement officers have adopted strategies that are intended to gain a psychological advantage over their interviewees. While they may position themselves so that the sun is in the eyes of a respondent, or they may stand while a respondent is sitting (Sontheimer, 1941), these strategies are inappropriate for qualitative interviewers, who should make sure their respondents are comfortable throughout their interviews.

I recommend that you consider the non-verbal cues that you give during the interview process. Make sure that you do not shake your head negatively, frown or gaze away during your interviews. Use silences in the conversation to help respondents gather their thoughts rather than to push them into speaking. Refrain from asking leading questions because they may influence a respondent's responses and can derail the conversation. It is important to avoid sexist, racist and/or demeaning questions as well as questions that illustrate your personal opinions, biases and/or prejudices.

For example, during the 2011 Miss Universe contest one of the finalists, Leila Lopes, was asked what has been called "the dumbest question in the universe" (Ravitz, 2011). Lopes was asked, "If you could change one of your physical characteristics, which one would it be and why?" Of course, the question asks Lopes to consider whether she measures up to the demeaning stereotypical standards of female beauty. Lopes, who responded that she was happy with her appearance and encouraged people to respect others, became the first Miss Universe from Angola. It is also important not to be over-solicitous, trying to ingratiate yourself with an interviewee. A statement such as "Some of my best friends are Muslim" is actually "patronizing —and bigoted" (Walters, 1970, p. 18).

Berger (1998) finds that during the course of each interview, research interviewers interact with respondents in at least one of four different ways: they primarily incorporate understanding responses, probing responses, evaluative responses and/or phatic responses. An understanding response is used to clarify information. The interviewer will repeat a statement made by the respondent and say something like "Correct me if I heard you wrong. Did you just say that crisis communication is the most important aspect of public relations?" Probing responses take the form of follow-up questions such as "Tell me more about your role in the AOL start-up." Probing responses are used to delve more deeply into a person's commentary, access how an interviewee feels about an issue or understand an individual's actions. Evaluative responses make value judgments about what an interviewee has said. Statements such as "I disagree with your opinion of the role of women in public relations" should be avoided because they can alienate a respondent and derail the conversation. Interviewers frequently use phatic responses to let respondents know that they understand what has been said and want respondents to keep talking. Comments such as "uh huh," "OK" or "Yes, I understand" are comforting phatic responses that let the interviewee know you are listening, and may also encourage a reticent respondent to speak more freely.

While qualitative interviewers focus on respondents' emotions and experiences, they must also maintain control of each interview; therefore, it is important for interviewers to avoid becoming the focus of the conversation. This can be challenging, because once trust has been established, it is only natural for a respondent to begin asking an interviewer questions. Fontana and Frey (1994) suggest diffusing the relevance of an interviewer's opinions by explaining that an interviewer's feelings, opinions and experiences are not relevant to the research project. In my own experience, a comment such as "I appreciate your interest in my views but what's important is your opinion and not mine" will help to refocus the conversation and remind a respondent of the purpose of the interview. One final interview strategy: be sure to ask all respondents at the end of their interviews whether they have anything else to add to the conversation. After many years of interviewing, I am still surprised at how much people will share with you when they feel comfortable and supported and know that you are truly interested in what they have to say.

The idealized interviewee is well-spoken, cooperative, knowledgeable, truthful, precise, motivated, coherent and focused, providing the interviewer with great stories, lively descriptions and wonderful examples (Kvale, 1996). Of course, no such a person exists. Many respondents have some of these characteristics and it is a qualitative interviewer's challenge to motivate and draw out the best stories from each interviewee. There are times when no matter how much background information has been acquired and how many skillful interviewing strategies are used, an interviewer is unable to establish trust with one of his or her respondents. The respondent does not open up, and replies with monosyllabic answers to all of the interviewer's creative questions. While the strategies discussed in this chapter as well as the chapters on Oral History and Focus Groups (Chapters 6 and 4 respectively) will help you to learn the craft of qualitative interviewing, it is important to realize that ultimately not everyone will be a good interviewee.

## Transcribing Interviews

It is much easier to work with a transcript of each interview rather than continually referring back to audiotapes. Therefore, you will want to transcribe each interview while the conversation is fresh in your mind. Transcribing interviews is a time-consuming process, and sometimes interviewers can become frustrated by the time it takes to complete a research project based on qualitative interviews. It generally takes between four and six hours to transcribe a one-hour interview. For his qualitative interviewing research project "Good Journalism: On the Evaluation Criteria of Some Interested and Experienced Actors," which is discussed later in this chapter, Risto Kunelius (2006) interviewed seventy-nine individuals. Each interview lasted approximately ninety minutes and yielded approximately 1,300 single-spaced pages of transcription. Clearly, Kunelius's time commitment was extensive for his qualitative research project. See Chapter 6, on Oral History, for additional information on recording, transcribing and editing interviews.

In general, qualitative researchers prefer not to edit interview transcripts apart from correcting spelling and removing false starts from the conversation. Most researchers caution against editing transcripts to improve upon a respondent's language or grammar because doing so can change the tone and meaning of the interview. For example, Rebecca Skloot (2010) wrote about how she learned the importance of understanding the meaning of a person's language while she was doing interviews for her book *The Immortal Life of Henrietta Lacks*. While Skloot notes that she was initially tempted to edit some quotations so that the respondents might sound better, Skloot was warned by a family member of Lacks that she should not change the quotations of people she interviewed to make them grammatically correct. Skloot was told, "If you pretty up how people spoke and change the things they said, that's dishonest. It's taking away their lives, their experiences, and their selves" (p. ix). After the conversation, Skloot writes that she realized that the way people spoke provided important insights into their backgrounds, customs and culture, and she decided not to alter any of the respondents' quotations for her book.

## Analyzing the Information

It is through a researcher's analysis and interpretation that issues, concerns and contradictions are brought into the open, discussed and sometimes even resolved. If relevant, it is useful to consider ways to assess each interview in order to enrich an aspect of our understandings of the relationship between media and society. The interpretation of interview information actually begins during the interview. It is helpful to attempt to verify each respondent's answers and clarify any initial interpretations that you might begin to have during the course of each interview. Comments such as "Are you saying that citizen journalism can coexist with mainstream journalism?" or "Do you mean that *American Idol* has altered the popular music business model?" are examples of questions that may help you to situate information shared with you by each respondent.

After an interview has been transcribed, you can work with the transcript to identify important insights and information, outline key concepts, opinions, patterns and themes, and make a note of interesting stories and experiences. The theoretical framework you use will provide you with contextual guidance that will help you to conceptualize the material you gather from your interviews. As Gubrium and Holstein (2002a) explain, "Each theoretical perspective implicates a set of procedures or ways of organizing, categorizing, and interpreting data. There is no single approach to qualitative analysis" (p. 673).

## Verifying Information

While Chapter 1 addresses basic differences between qualitative and quantitative research as it relates to the assessment of evidence, one potential issue with using qualitative interviews as a research method relates to the reliability of the information provided by respondents. Some researchers continue to worry that respondents' answers may be self-serving and that they may attempt to intentionally deceive the researcher. Some respondents' memories are faulty; others will lie or tell interviewers anything they can think of to end their interviews; and yet other respondents are a little too eager to please and they will attempt to tell interviewers what they think the researchers want to know (Berger, 2000). Newcomb (1999) suggests that researchers should examine all interviews for accuracy in detail as well as for basic truthfulness. While personal opinions and perceptions may be considered authentic responses from each respondent, specific factual information gathered from each interview should be verified from other research sources as well as corroborated by other respondents during subsequent interviews.

## Writing a Research Report

Researchers using qualitative interviews as a methodology will want to provide a contextual frame of reference from which the interview quotations are interpreted. Quoted material should be analyzed and interpreted, and researchers should keep a balance between the use of quotes and analysis of the insights. It's best to use shorter quotes or to use one or two quotes to illustrate a point rather than bombarding the reader with pages and pages of quotes.

The following research article, by Risto Kunelius, illustrates one way in which interviews are used in qualitative research. "Good Journalism: On the

Evaluation Criteria of Some Interested and Experienced Actors," first published in *Journalism Studies* in 2006, uses qualitative interviews with politicians, professionals and business leaders to explore their views on journalism in contemporary Finnish society. While the study focuses on media criticism regarding the practice of journalism in Finland, the research findings relate to contemporary journalistic issues and challenges throughout Europe and North America. Note how in the last paragraph of the introduction the author describes the focus of the study as well as the theories that he plans to use to frame his analysis of the interviews.

---

## "Good Journalism: On the Evaluation Criteria of Some Interested and Experienced Actors," by Risto Kunelius

From *Journalism Studies*, 7 (5), 2006, 671–690.

### Introduction

All living things are critics.

(Burke, 1954)

In recent decades, journalism has become an increasingly central social institution. This is evidenced by constant conflicts between journalists and other social actors (politicians, experts, non-governmental organizations (NGOs), etc.). Some analysts argue that these tensions are symptomatic of a more independent journalism, and of an increasingly healthier public sphere (cf. McNair, 2000). On the other hand, some think that journalism's "autonomous" conventions do not actually serve the critical functions they proclaim: journalism favors "top-down" communication (cf. Gans, 2003, pp. 45–68), and it has become increasingly subservient to economic and political pressures (cf. Bourdieu, 1998a, 2005). In professional circles the challenges of the profession are most often articulated as a threat to this autonomy. The self-image of journalism as an institution of public service is firmly founded on such vocabulary, and at moments of collapsing public credibility, the repair work of independent committees has usually underscored the value of autonomy.

The idea of journalistic autonomy has been an important device in carving out a social position for a journalism claiming to serve the "public." However, the very same idea also easily becomes an obstacle to thinking about the public purpose of the profession. Stress on professional independence makes it difficult to ask what good journalism would be like. After all, within the discourse of professional autonomy a good proof of the quality of journalism is often the very fact that a diverse set of other social actors is equally unhappy with its performance: if journalism serves nobody in particular, it must be serving the public in general.

This paper sets out from the idea not only that such autonomy is often an illusion but also that it does not serve us well in the effort to achieve a democratically useful press. I argue that in the changing economic, political, cultural and technological media landscape of late modernity, journalism and journalists need to listen to what kind of sense different people make of their performance. In order to elaborate this claim, I will draw on an interview study in which competent people outside the professional community evaluate journalism. I will use their definition of "good journalism" and their critique of the production practices of current journalism to illuminate both the potentials and the problems of journalism criticism. I will start from the empirical findings and work my way towards theoretical questions with help from both Pierre Bourdieu's field theory and Jürgen Habermas's theory of communicative action.

---

In the next section of the article, Kunelius explains challenges he had getting people outside of journalism to talk with him. He describes how interviewees were chosen to participate in the project, the type of people who were interviewed as well as the interview process that was used for the study. In case you are curious to learn more about the people Kunelius interviewed, endnote 2 provides demographic information on all seventy-nine respondents interviewed for the study.

---

## Competences in Being Critical

For journalism research, access to critical and useful views from outside the professional community of journalism is not easy. There are at least two problems.

First, it is difficult to formulate questions so as to enable people outside of journalism to exercise their critical faculties. The obvious idea of turning to the audience for innovative journalism critique suffers from the very conceptualization of the audience (cf. Ridell, 2000; Ward, 2005). For instance, surveys and focus groups often place respondents in the position of a "member of the general audience," and this move by itself deprives people of a large part of their critical capacities. After all, a member of the audience is an anyone or a no one— an abstract social being constructed by the messages of journalism. Michael Schudson (2003, p. 168) writes, "There is no news consumer apart from the news." On the other hand, market-driven research looks for audience segments, which, again by definition, only have a particular perspective to offer and little advice for journalism as practice for the general audience. Hence, existing journalism enjoys a strong position in setting the criteria by which it will be evaluated. Imagining what journalism might become is restricted by what journalism is. It is no wonder that many observers have been somewhat skeptical as to how usefully audience research might inform professional practice (cf. McQuail, 2003, p. 279; Schudson, 2003, p. 173).

Second, there is an institutional problem. In a recent effort to map the field of journalism research, Barbie Zelizer (2004), for instance, argues that academic perspectives offer important ways of making sense of journalism and taking its public purpose seriously. This is very true, but a problem remains: academic criticism of journalism has the disadvantage of keeping its distance from the actual production processes of journalism. Endless debates between "theorists" and "practitioners" all over the world are a frustrating testimony to the fact that the ability to articulate a critical stance often comes with a price tag of being also rather detached from the everyday professional practices of journalism. If in the case of the "audience" there is too little institutional base (the audience is nowhere) from which to argue for a different kind of journalism, in the case of more institutionalized critique the concrete realities of journalism are often out of reach (the institution is too remote, outside journalism).

Without claiming to solve these problems, the research design at hand[1] attempted to take them into account. Based on qualitative interviews, the study tried to offer its respondents a chance to use their concrete abilities and faculties of being critical about journalism. For this purpose, the people interviewed had two qualifications:

1. They were interested actors. They represented a particular field of interest or a sector of society. They were identified and interviewed as experts of their own particular perspective with a specific kind of knowledge. The aim, however, was not to list the particular concerns they had about journalism but to identify common dimensions of evaluation in their concrete, specific criticism.
2. They were experienced actors. Their talk about journalism was not only based on evaluating journalism from some particular perspective of expertise. In addition, it was based on concrete, personal lessons learned in situations of making the news. Thus, knowledge did not just spring from a discourse other than journalism; they also had practical knowledge about how quotes, facts and frames in journalism were produced.

The design was based on the idea that all critics are necessarily interested ones and that any effort to study criticism calls for a recognition and appreciation of these interests. The study design aimed both at choosing people with critical faculties and at accepting their particular, practical and concrete experiences as a source of valid knowledge about the performance of journalism.

Altogether, seventy-nine such interested and experienced "para-journalists," to borrow Schudson's (2003) apt coining, were chosen from various sectors in Finnish society.[2] The selection aimed at a diversity of relevant views, rather than any sort of statistical representativeness:[3] civil servants from different branches of the state/communal apparatus (teaching, social work, police, legal system), experts on various areas (technology, energy issues, genetics), people from the market sector (marketing professionals, investment bankers and professionals, publishers and public relations (PR) professionals), and civil society actors (NGO workers, foreigners living in Finland). Despite the quest for diversity, it is important to note that incorporating competence into the selection also meant incorporating a social/power bias into it: the interviewees were rather middle-aged, rather well educated and men outnumbered women.

---

In the next section, Kunelius specifically addresses the types of questions that participants were asked in order to gather information. He also explains his strategy for presenting the findings of his study.

---

The interviews were conducted individually. They followed a thematic structure that started with questions about the respondent's media use and went on to discuss the general responsibilities, and the explicit question of what "good journalism" should be like. Themes also touched on how the respondents evaluated the performance of journalism in their own field of expertise and what kind of memories, examples and problems they had regarding their cooperation with journalists.

The research design allows us at least to discuss two particularly interesting and important features of the idea of a (Finnish) "journalistic field."[4] First, the fact that respondents are outsiders to the professional community of journalism provides us with some insights into the importance and meaning of the journalistic field in relation to other fields of knowledge. The respondents approach journalism from different directions, with different forms of capital, and often with competences cultivated in contexts other than journalism. Second, interviews offer an actor's perspective on the journalistic field; they provide us with a sense of how people and ideas in practice enter the action. Since the interviewees are not major actors in the field of journalism, their criticism can help us to shed some light on the taken-for-granted, dominant practices of the field.

I will present the empirical findings from the interviews under three themes: First, the material provided an interesting inventory of what dimensions of evaluation the respondents mobilized. Second, on the basis of the concrete experiences of being part of the production process of journalism, the respondents offered robust critical views of the intellectual contribution of journalism to the public debate. Third, there were disturbingly interesting moments of self-reflexivity on the part of the respondents, which raises some concerns about the ability of journalism to function as a common and dominant form of public discourse.[5]

Kunelius begins to use specific quotes from his interviews in the following section of the research. Note how he presents his evidence in this section. He initially introduces each theme, includes a relevant quote and then offers commentary and discussion regarding each quotation.

## An Inventory of Criteria: Dimensions of Evaluation

### Cultural Self-Reflexivity in Interview Talk

In an interview, a respondent often starts from one idea but, after formulating it, begins to react to her own speech and moves to correct or expand what she has just said. These self-corrections provide an illuminating and rich sense of the respondent's cultural imagination about journalism. For instance, in judging good journalism, the usual starting point was that journalism should offer objective knowledge:

> . . . Well, I would say that firstly it is about transmitting knowledge, it is about providing accurate information, and I would like to stress the term "objective" here. On the other hand, I would leave the job of coming to conclusions more for the reader, listener, or consumer, you know, the stuff [journalism] should not be ready made. What I would expect, then, is factual knowledge, as trustworthy as possible.
>
> (A1:4, 5)[6]

This celebration of factuality often sounded like a chapter from a journalism textbook: journalism should offer the audience access to independently existing reality. However, this became problematic at the very moment it was voiced. Hearing themselves talk about "objectivity," the respondents suddenly felt that the view they were putting forward simply was not adequate or was not very credible. For instance, the respondent above continued:

> . . . [as trustworthy as possible]. Then, particularly from good journalism
> I would expect . . . that it respects humanity and humans and values
> and privacy. (- - -) I mean respect for values is needed . . . factual
> knowledge. . . . When things are reported, as many perspectives as
> possible are reported, a one-sided picture of issues is avoided.
>
> (A1:4, 5)

Respondents did not literally abandon the hard core of facts, but they quickly
moved on to other criteria that actually challenge the idea of general, common or
objective facts. Sometimes they argued that facts are not enough: ". . . But you
can't just live with facts, there is so much of them . . . there is so much
information nowadays . . . it's this big lump in your head that is not going to
open" (G7:7). Sometimes they realized that facts are in fact not common to
everyone: "Because we have our own religious background and so forth,
educational background and all that, cultural background. . . . You know, who
accepts a truth of what kind?" (G4:13). Sometimes a need for new and diverse
perspectives was deemed more important than factuality: "It should be touching
and interesting, it should go beyond the surface level of things. Oh, what a bunch
of clichés, but I think good journalism tries not only to repeat what other papers
have reported, it tries to find a new perspective or add knowledge, not just repeat
it . . ." (C3:7).

---

In the following section, Kunelius discusses three major themes in the
journalism critique that emerged from his interviews. Notice how
quotations are used to support the researcher's analysis and how he
continues to comment on his interpretations of information gathered from
his interviews throughout the research article.

---

## Concrete Experiences of News-Making

Another perspective on the question of "good journalism" opened when the
respondents talked about their own concrete experiences as participants in the
process of news-making. This version of journalism critique makes us focus on
three themes: framing, dramatization and the unpredictability of story production.

### Framing

Perhaps the most common denominator in the respondents' concrete criticism of
news-making was their experience of being framed. While none of them used the

fashionable communication research term, the concept captures many of the experiences of the interviewees.[7]

> . . . [I]t was extremely narrow, [the reporter's] point of view in that story, like a racehorse with those black things keeping them from looking aside.
>
> (K3:5)

> [T]here is [often in journalism] this particular storyline and a strong need to stick to it.
>
> (K5:7)

For the interviewees (i.e. for people who often provide the substance of which our public debates are made of), the practical terms of news-making seemed sometimes rather frustrating. From their point of view there seemed to be a ready-made frame for the forthcoming story they were involved in, and the frame preexisted the interaction with the reporter. They felt they were put into a position where they were largely expected to supply the necessary comments or play the role the storyline was in need of. Respondents also felt (particularly the NGO people) that journalism too easily used applied conflict frames and that journalists looked for those actors who were willing to present extreme views on a given issue. For the respondents, this looked like an easy way out of describing complex issues, and perhaps also a way out of the dilemma of providing a factual, objective view in the increasingly culturally diverse world.

Respondents also thought that journalists held a particularly clichéd conception about their (the respondents') organization: journalists think that the police want more hard-core action, that the state-owned company is bureaucratic and slow, that social security sector people are ineffective and hostile to ordinary people, that the medical industry merely looks for easy and fast profits, that gays think about everything through the lenses of sexuality, and so on. For the respondents, this gallery of stereotypes felt like a straitjacket for public performance and debate. Even if you said or did something contrary to the stereotypical expectations, the news would then be woven around the theme that you did not live up to your reputation.

## Dramatization

The respondents also talked about journalism's taste for dramatization. First of all, the attention paid by journalism to particular actors seemed to depend on something dramatic enough taking place. Second, the creation of news leads with a journalistically legitimate amount of exaggeration seemed to skew the picture of the world. Journalism was criticized for choosing and emphasizing the exciting over the relevant.

> Perhaps dramatic is the best word for it. On the one hand, it is good that it is there, because it attracts people's attention and gets them interested. (- - -) But I still think in journalism they usually cut the corners. . . . I mean no one has the patience for all the complexities (- - -) but sometimes it happens in a very bad way, so that people do not recognize themselves. It is usually not meant to be nasty, it is part of the journalistic process. But in issues where the general public is usually rather badly informed, for those the stories talk about it is somewhat unfortunate.
>
> (C2:3)

It is often said that journalism has problems representing "everyday life" or "ordinary people." The respondents, however, were not interviewed as "ordinary." Still, even in their view (the point of view of some of the routine institutional sources), journalism does not appear to capture the finer points of their action. Journalism seemed to be unable to see "inside" the institutions it works with. Instead, journalism is stuck with repeating particular, dramatized stereotypes.

Journalism's taste for the dramatic also pointed to an interesting question about the relationship between fiction and fact in the media: sometimes respondents sensed that journalists (perhaps unconsciously) tried to fit the real actors into roles possibly constructed elsewhere, even in popular fiction. This is how a young stockbroker talked about the tendency of journalism to dramatize:

> [W]e should really get rid of the [picture] that this [the stock market] is about young yuppies or about some fast investment sharks. We should get a more mundane, everyday picture across, because in reality the profits are far more modest and closer to the ground, so to speak. This is no rocket racket . . . you get good profit over a long period of time.
>
> (B5:8)

## Unpredictability

A third point of common criticism by the respondents was a sense of the unpredictability of working with journalists, a sense created by the interplay of framing and dramatization. Almost all the respondents had bad experiences of this, and, despite the many good or routinely acceptable experiences they had had, most of them remembered the bad ones vividly. Interestingly enough, many of them had dealt with the unpredictability of journalism by adapting to it. Here is an example from the respondents' ways to cope with problems of citation.

I have learned a little of how it is to be interviewed. For instance, for a TV reporter I never make statements that begin with saying "there are two things to consider here" and then say one thing in one sentence and the other in the next one. You just can't take the risk that on television you'll end up saying just either one of them.

(C1:11)

One of the most important skills that I try to develop is to try to talk TV in a manner that makes it difficult [for a journalist] to pick small things out of it and make weird connections. And I think that sort of thing is practiced rather often, and also rather deliberately.

(J5:21)

As a utopian counter-example for this strategic maneuvering, one can quote a respondent (a legal professional) who at the beginning of our interview commented on the tape recorder:

A:   Oh, so you have a tape recorder, then.
Q:   Yeah, the fun part of the research is to sit and prepare transcriptions.
     . . .
A:   I'm a little hesitant about taping, you know. In this place we have a lot of verbal negotiations, and I think it is extremely good that you can freely take up points and perhaps sometimes give up on those when you have heard the others. A kind of dialogue, you know. If you first say something and then come to another kind of conclusion, it is difficult if you are pinned down on it. Then [a journalist might] say that this is what the source said . . . although she might have put it differently after a while.

Framing and dramatization are closely intertwined, and from the perspective of our interested actors their combined effect is a degree of unpredictability (and sense of powerlessness) about how one is represented in journalism. These problems can be alleviated to a degree by investing in the skills the strategic power game requires: continuous contact with reporters, information packages prepared in advance for journalists, skill in giving interviews—all seem to help, but mainly by adapting to the rules of the game. The fact that unpredictability is managed suggests a practically negotiated balance of power between journalism and those who routinely deal with reporters. Nevertheless, this supposed level of satisfaction with the routine sources disregards the problems of those who are not routinely involved in the game and have less time and fewer skills (developed in the routines) to handle journalism.

News sources and journalists nowadays clearly meet on a field increasingly defined by journalistic criteria of professionalism: frames are chosen, news values are assessed and quotes defined by professional journalists, not by the institutional news sources they cover. For a professional journalist, the lament of the respondents is in fact a proof of professional development and the autonomy of the field. On the other hand, the fact that news sources have trouble recognizing themselves in the products they co-create (for which they have to take partial responsibility) is also disturbing. There seems to be an almost vicious circle of strategic action involved here: the journalists are armed with prejudices concerning the public actors and they frame the news according to these images. This, in turn, makes it very difficult for any public actor to act in a more broadly communicative manner. The fact that in an "autonomous" field of this kind public actors are losing control not only of their authority but also their authorship suggests that journalism may also be one of the institutional obstacles in public deliberation.

## The Politics of Style and Vocabularies of Responsibility

Critical talk about journalism was not easy, even for our interested and competent respondents. These difficulties were reflected interestingly in the styles in which the respondents talked about the social responsibilities of journalism. Focusing on the combination of styles and vocabularies of responsibility opens up yet another view of journalism criticism.

## Style: Critical Clichés, Irony, Overt Cynicism

Three relatively clear styles could be identified in the respondents' critical talk about journalism. First, respondents tended to use worn-out clichés about the corrupt, hopeless inner nature of journalism. This is an interestingly similar "counter-rhetoric" to that for which the respondents blamed journalists. If journalists have a stereotypical view of the respondents, the respondents, too, are using stereotypes. For instance, often respondents quoted the "old common sense" which suggests that journalists are really only "playing the tunes decided by owners and advertisers." Clichés and stereotypes of this kind functioned as ways of accomplishing two things at the same time. By referring to these "well-known facts," the respondents were able to talk about the ills of journalism but at the same time to present them as something that will hardly ever change. Framing the problems of journalism as somehow eternal (as the cliché talk allows and suggests) may be a necessary form of rhetoric to be able to present any criticism at all. However, it has a disadvantage: It separates the critic from calls for action to reform or improve matters. He can recognize the problem but also the mighty forces behind it. He can simultaneously be knowledgeable but not naïve.

Avoiding being seen as naïve is also a key to another style, namely irony. Irony is another way of accomplishing two things at the same time: it offers a chance to talk in a particular way while at the same time implying that you know that your criticism has certain limits. Irony was often mobilized when respondents tried to shift into a more ethical vocabulary of criticism. When respondents toyed with the idea that journalism should have social or ethical responsibilities, they often instinctively recognized that talking about this "higher" level sounded culturally implausible: This "instinctive realism" sounds like this:

Q: To whom is journalism responsible?
A: Well, that [laughter] is almost a moral and ethical question. (K6:2)
Q: To whom do you think journalism is responsible?
A: Well, we all have our responsibility to do more good than bad. At least I think that task is always there . . . listen to me, doesn't this sound really poor . . . (C2:7).

A third way of taking distance from one's own criticism was a technique of overt cynicism. This came close to using clichés but it lacked the explicit markers that cynical ideas were anything than the respondents' own. No old idiom was quoted; instead, we got a simplified and often hopeless view of journalism. "I think the whole media today is just one big business. Anyone who reads those papers [the Finnish tabloids] or watches television, you know the basic idea is very clear: to make money" (I5:1).

## Styles and Vocabularies of Responsibility

Describing how the respondents talked about the social responsibilities of journalism calls for two distinctions: First, respondents spontaneously wanted to distinguish between "what is" and "what ought to be." Second, they used a distinction between a mundane way of making sense of responsibilities (being accountable for concrete, material institutions or people) and a more lofty way of arguing for a link to higher and abstract values.

In the mundane constituency, journalism was seen to be responsible for real-life actors or institutions, such as citizens, consumers, readers, owners, etc. In this sphere, respondents saw the responsibility of journalism as pointing in two directions: First, they recognized that journalists in actual practice are to be responsible to the "market forces." For some respondents, these market forces were represented by the "readers/viewers/listeners" or the "clients," but behind these clients, respondents also saw the interests of the media owners and advertisers (investors, who would logically be implicated in this, were not mentioned at all). Some recognized the fact that journalism in this respect reflects the general development of consumer society. A second path of mundane responsibility was presented as an "ought to be" idea. This different chain of concepts led to the idea that instead of to "clients," journalism should be responsible more generally to the citizenry—that journalism should consider things from a broader perspective than merely the interests of those to whom it (journalism) is sold. There were slight tendencies among the respondents' talk as to who consistently favors either side of these worldly conceptualizations of responsibility (the NGOs and the civil servants tended to favor the latter path, the market people believed, logically enough, that the market served the general interest). However, a more consistent finding was that the distinction between these two paths or realms was often very fluid and vague.

Q:  [B]ack to journalism, then. To whom do you see journalism as being responsible?
A:  Oh, that's a good question. Well, it is, of course . . . how should I answer? . . . If I take a look at how, if I also genuinely think a journalist . . . well, in an economic sense this is business, of course, if we do not count YLE [the Finnish public service broadcasting company], there you have no problem, they are not responsible in an economic sense, they practice good journalism and people read and of course if you can make all that in a financially sustainable way. . . . Of course, they're responsible to the consumers, I mean I can't really figure this clearly now, but it is the Finnish people in a sense, if they do their work OK. They have this task we discussed, to do that, well, I mean the readers of papers, viewers of television and listeners of radio and others, to them they are [responsible]. It is of course a rather high-minded idea, that's all I can say.
Q:  What about . . .
A:  . . . And why not to the employer as well and to the community they are part of, yes, why not, but that is a factor, it reflects . . . the final responsibility is to the viewers (E2:7).

Such lack of clarity prompts a question. If the "general public" is equated with the "reading public," which in turn becomes synonymous with the "buying public," are we witnessing a fundamental (but logical) shift in the cultural resources of journalism criticism? What will this trend mean for the resources for ensuring legitimation for a public profession of journalism?

In addition to existing people and institutions, the responsibilities of journalism were also talked of in reference to a more lofty reference point of responsibility. Here, respondents recognized such things as (vaguely defined) "ethical values" or "principles." Another way of referring to such a materially non-existent constituency was to suggest that journalism should be responsible to the future.

> Now this might sound naïve, but it should be responsible to society or humankind or humanity or something like that, you know, what sort of people children see and what sort of models journalism offers to them and to people in general [journalism] offers.
>
> (C5:12)

Note how vocabularies of responsibility and moments of self-reflexivity are attached to each other. Indeed, when pointing to the "ought to be" direction or when evoking more lofty responsibilities, the respondents' talk was often framed with irony or other suggestions that the ideas are somehow utopian. In contrast to this, the "market path" was noted as realism or as cynicism. While this partly testifies to the ability of the respondents to think against the current trends of the media industry, it also might work as a further reminder of the direction of change we are witnessing. If it is true that the consumer frame of thinking about journalism is gaining credibility, this trend could be undermining important parts of the discourse surrounding journalism, a discourse that legitimizes but also serves as an important resource with which to publicly talk about the social responsibilities of journalism.

In relation to journalism, it appears that the definitions of citizenship may be in a state of flux: connotations of activity are perhaps shifting toward the notion of consumers and the concept of citizenship is more in danger of becoming a piece of empty rhetoric. If this trend continues, it can be bad news indeed for the public criticism of journalism. While it may serve as a way of intensifying the interaction between the producers of journalism and their customers, consumers or the "buying public," it is simultaneously based on an assumption that there really is no serious difference between citizenry and customers. Here, an important distinction of journalism criticism might be lost. Here, journalists themselves should also be worried about the vocabulary in which their profession is discussed.

---

The analysis of the interview material in the next section is based on research that debates the future of journalism, including some researchers envisioning an end to journalism. This concern is a prominent political-economic issue currently being debated in North American and Western European countries.

## Conclusion: Three Interpretations of Modern Journalism

What do the experienced and interested actors teach us? What do they tell us about the current role of journalism and its place in the social space of late modernity? As an attempt to make sense of these findings, I wish to present three interconnected readings. The respondents' talk around "good journalism" can be seen (1) as evidence of the emergence of late modern journalism; (2) as an inventory of some of the rules and conventions of its journalistic field; and (3) as potential moments of communicatively informed journalism criticism.

### The Emergence of Postmodern Journalism?

In recent years, communication scholars have produced an impressive amount of essays and studies talking about the "end of journalism" in some form or another (cf. Bardoel, 1996; Becker, Ekecrantz, & Olsson, 2000; Bromley, 1997; Hachten, 1998; Hallin, 1998; Hardt, 1996; Katz, 1992; Rosen, 1996). One way of making sense of our findings is to say that they partly support these readings.

For instance, it is striking to see how culturally fragile the "professional," core definition of journalism has become, albeit that it still persists as a starting point for a discussion. Our experienced and interested respondents clearly sensed that the "high modern" tradition of journalism has begun to sound somehow implausible. They also articulated a rich array of challenges to hard-core news journalism. The dimensions from which these challenges arise refer to a multitude of problems in the public role of journalism in "post-factual," "postmodern," increasingly "multicultural" and commercialized media societies. At first glance it is indeed questionable whether a common "public purpose" could be built on ideas that, on the one hand, call for more attention to ethical issues (or more support for the weak in public debates) but, on the other hand, demand better service for the particular needs of the commercially lucrative segments of the audience. One can also argue that journalistic framing and dramatization bear further witness to how the reputation of journalism as a fair and impartial mediator of public discussion is in jeopardy (despite or because of increasing "professionalism"). The ironic distance needed for articulating journalism with higher purposes is a further proof of the same: a sense of journalism becoming just one consumer product among others. To exaggerate and to sum up from this point of view, the respondents anticipate a cultural climate where the public professionals of modern news journalism will find it more and more difficult to function and defend their autonomy in the name of a "public" they represent.

The goal of Kunelius's interviews was to shed light on the contemporary role of journalism and its place in modern society. In the final section of his conclusion, Kunelius draws on his theoretical foundations to help interpret and frame his analysis of the interview material. He uses interview evidence to present support for the concept of good journalism as well as the importance of specific journalistic practices and conventions, and the potential for informed media criticism. Kunelius also uses the interview evidence to support the notion of a postmodern journalism and to illustrate and expand the relevance of Jürgen Habermas's theory of rationality. He concludes his study with the following commentary:

---

. . . Finally, the communicative framework also helps to put the ironic styles of journalism critique into perspective. Irony can be seen as symptomatic of respondents' sense that there are some "irrational limitations" to their expressions. Consequently, there is no reason to demonize irony itself. It is, after all, the very style that enabled any higher purposes of journalism to be spelled out. But in these interviews, and in the context of journalism, one can see it as a symptom of the systematically distorted nature of communication about journalism. It does not seem to be very realistic or rational to talk about journalism in the same breath as higher (democratic) values.

In conclusion, then, despite the cynical and problematic nature of much of the evidence, the findings also point to a common vocabulary of communicativeness. Concrete critical claims of the interested and experienced actors also articulated signs of a more general structure and criteria, perhaps a shape of a more (historically) quasi-universal pattern or framework of the critical discussion about journalism. Beyond the concrete criticism there may be a chance for a theory calling not for the autonomy, not for the credibility, not for the profitability, but for the validity of journalism.

---

## Interviewing Exercises

1. Interview someone you know, face to face, for thirty minutes on a topic of your choice. Before the interview, construct a list of questions that you plan to ask. During the interview, be sure to ask all of the questions on your list. You may also ask follow-up questions based on your respondent's commentary. After the interview,

discuss the interview process. Be sure to comment on your comfort level during the interview as well as what you learned from the conversation. Were there questions you wanted to ask but didn't? Did you find the list of questions helpful or hindering?

2. Repeat the interview outlined in the first exercise but this time choose someone you are not familiar with. After the interview, comment on the challenges of interviewing someone you don't know. How would background information have helped you prepare for the interview? Compare your experiences during this interview with those during the previous interview.

3. Interview someone about his or her work history. The interview should last between thirty and sixty minutes. In advance of the interview, outline a series of topic areas or open-ended questions to ask during your interview. Be sure to do some background research to help you frame your interview questions. After the interview is complete, comment on your comfort level during the interview as well as what you learned from the conversation. Compare this interview with one of your previous interviews. Did you find it more comfortable to conduct an interview with a set of pre-determined questions or did you prefer the more open-ended approach?

## Notes

1 The project was a joint venture of the Journalism Research Centre (University of Tampere, Finland) and the Finnish Journalists' Union. The Union provided a large part of the financial resources. In addition to the members of the Board of Communication Policy, I wish to thank the group of students and researchers, Marianna Laiho and Asta Rajala who were involved in the original project. The article at hand has gone through a number of revisions after several seminars and conferences, and I cannot trace all the contributions. However, the final version has greatly benefited from my visit to the University of Madison-Wisconsin and the lessons learned from Professors Lewis Friedland and Mustafa Emirbayer. The anonymous referees of *Journalism Studies* were also very helpful.

2 There were altogether seventy-nine respondents. Their average age was 45 years, the youngest being 24 and the oldest 61. Men outnumbered women by 47 to 32. Many respondents had a lower university degree or had spent some time in higher education. Geographically, the respondents were concentrated in southern Finland and in larger cities. Every effort was made to ensure that people in each (or most) sector included rank-and-file workers as well as people officially in charge of the organizations' policies (owing to the size of the sample, among other concerns, this was not always possible). The respondents' experiences in taking part in news production varied from being inter-viewed almost weekly to single experiences of being used as a source or being part of a

collective that was covered. The market sector (23 interviews) consists of interviews with marketing people in large or semi-large Finnish companies (6), with stock exchange professionals or kinds of Finnish journalistic outlets (5) and with PR professionals in various kinds of organizations and special PR companies (6). The civil society sector (18 interviews) consists of interviews with representatives from traditional NGOs (well integrated into society) as well as from newly emerged, more radical citizens' organizations (12) and with foreigners living in Finland and able to follow Finnish-language journalism (6). The sector of governance (24 interviews) consists of interviews with representatives from the education sector (6), with people from the social security and welfare sector (6), and with members of the police, judges at different court levels and attorneys (12). The experts sector (14 interviews) includes discussion with energy (8) and technology (2) experts in different institutions, and people with a special interest in and knowledge about genetically manipulated food (6). All the respondents were promised anonymity, although not all of them insisted on it. It should be said, though, that some were particularly concerned about it. The interviews usually lasted about 1.5 hours, and the total amount of material is about 1,300 pages of transcription (single spaced).

3 Very roughly speaking, these sectors correspond to a set of challenges for twenty-first-century journalism: the economic pressures of the market, the assumed crisis in the status of knowledge, the developing modes of political activity in civil society and the changing roles of public apparatuses in Western welfare democracies.

4 One way of making sense of the materials is indeed to say that they shed some light on the rules and boundaries of the Finnish "journalistic field." For Bourdieu (cf. Bourdieu & Wacquant, 1992, pp. 97ff.), a field is a configuration of objective relations between subjectively experienced actor positions. Despite this objectifying (sociological) emphasis, however, the very idea of the field theory is to suggest that action in the field must be seen through the metaphor of a play or a game (cf. Bourdieu, 1998b, p. 77). A field cannot be totally reduced to its conditions of existence, and the game metaphor suggests that there is meaningful action, unpredictability and even virtuosity in all fields. The skills and competences of playing "different forms and amounts of capital in a given field" are, in turn, collected and ultimately embodied in the habitus of the players. Thus, knowledge of how a given social field operates and how one acts there is contained not in theoretical knowledge but in a particular logic of practice (cf. Bourdieu, 1990, pp. 80ff.)—that is, in the internalized values and taste disposition of actors, or in the feel of the game (cf. Bourdieu, 1990, 1998b). It is this internalized sense of the journalistic field that the respondents help us to describe. As for the more "objective" conditions of Finnish journalism, some basic facts may be helpful. Finland has belonged firmly to the Northern European camp of "cooperative-democratic" media systems, characterized by a relatively strong professionalism on the part of journalists, a well-based and relatively stable public service broadcasting tradition and, internationally speaking, a widespread newspaper readership based on home delivery of mainly provincial newspapers (cf. Hallin & Mancini, 2004; Salokangas, 1999). The historical development of Finnish journalism follows, broadly speaking, the trajectory described in other Nordic countries (for instance, and particularly, in Sweden; see Djerf-Pierre & Weibull, 2001; Ekecrantz & Olsson, 1994), where the once relatively cooperative relationships between the news media and various structures and institutions of society have been turning into a more competitive one. At the same time, the once relatively closed sector of media ownership has been opened up, leading to ownership concentration. It is also noteworthy here to point out that recent economic success sectors within the media industry have tended to be based either on strategic audience segmentation (for instance, lifestyle or generations) or on more sensationalistic, popular rhetoric.

5  All the interviews were transcribed, and transcriptions were treated first as a large pool of interview talk. All three themes were identified in an interpretive collective of researchers and students with a number of close readings through the materials. After this, the material was thematically organized and the themes were analyzed in more detail in group meetings. The final interpretation here was made by the author.
6  The interview transcriptions have been slightly edited: some small sounds and repetitive words have been omitted; an ellipsis (. . .) signifies a sentence that the respondent him- or herself never finished; dashes in parentheses (- - -) signify a section I have omitted here for the sake of readability. The coding after the quotes is purely technical, referring to the interviewer, the interviewee and the page of transcript.
7  For varying uses of the term, see Ettema and Glasser (1998, p. 30), Gitlin (1980), Hackett and Zhao (1998), Jamieson and Capella (1997), Tuchman (1978) and Zelizer (2004, p. 140). In Goffman's (1974) original sense, some situations of story production have been somewhat paradoxical for the interviewees: they have not been able to answer the basic question of social interaction: "What is going on here?"

# References

Bardoel, Jo. (1996). Beyond journalism: A profession between information society and civil society. *European Journal of Communication, 11* (3), 283–302.

Becker, Karin, Ekecrantz, Jan, & Olsson, Tom. (2000). The events of journalism at four points in time. In Karin Becker, Jan Ekecrantz, & Tom Olsson (Eds.), *Picturing politics* (pp. 26–51). Stockholm: JMK.

Berger, Arthur Asa. (1998). Depth interviews: Favorite singers and recordings. In *Media research techniques* (2nd edn, pp. 55–62). Thousand Oaks, CA: Sage.

Berger, Arthur Asa. (2000). *Media and communication methods: An introduction to qualitative and quantitative approaches.* Thousand Oaks, CA: Sage.

Bourdieu, Pierre. (1990). *The logic of practice.* Stanford, CA: Stanford University Press.

Bourdieu, Pierre. (1998a). *On television.* New York: The New Press.

Bourdieu, Pierre. (1998b). *Practical reason.* Stanford, CA: Stanford University Press.

Bourdieu, Pierre. (2005). The political field, the social field and the journalistic field. In Rodney Benson & Erik Neveu (Eds.), *Bourdieu and the journalistic field* (pp. 29–47). Cambridge: Polity Press.

Bourdieu, Pierre, & Wacquant, Louis J. D. (1992). *An invitation to reflexive sociology.* Chicago, IL: University of Chicago Press.

Bromley, Michael. (1997). The end of journalism? Changes in workplace practices in the press and broadcasting in the 1990s. In Michael Bromley & Tom O'Malley (Eds.), *A journalism reader* (pp. 330–350). London: Routledge.

Burke, Kenneth. (1954). *Permanence and change.* Berkeley: University of California Press.

Djerf-Pierre, Monika, & Weibull, Lennart. (2001). *Spegla, granska, tolka: Aktualitetsjournalistik i svensk radio och TV under 1900-talet* (Mirror, criticize, interpret: Current affairs journalism in Swedish radio and television in the twentieth century). Stockholm: Prisma.

Ekecrantz, Jan, & Olsson, Tom. (1994). *Det regierade samhället* (The edited society). Stockholm: Carlssons.

Ettema, James, & Glasser, Theodore. (1998). *Custodians of conscience: Investigative journalism and public virtue.* New York: Columbia University Press.

Fontana, Andrea. (2002). Postmodern trends in interviewing. In Jaber F. Gubrium & James A. Holstein (Eds.), *Handbook of interview research: Context and method* (pp. 161–180). Thousand Oaks, CA: Sage.

Fontana, Andrea, & Frey, James H. (1994). Interviewing: The art of science. In Norman K. Denzin & Yvonna S. Lincoln (Eds.), *Handbook of qualitative research* (pp. 361–376). Thousand Oaks, CA: Sage.

Gans, Herbert. (2003). *Democracy and the news.* Oxford: Oxford University Press.

Geertz, Clifford. (1973). *The interpretation of cultures: Selected essays.* New York: Basic Books.

Gitlin, Todd. (1980). *The whole world is watching.* New York: The Free Press.

Goffman, Erwin. (1974) *Frame analysis: An essay on the organization of experience.* New York: Harper & Row.

Gubrium, Jaber F., & Holstein, James A. (Eds.). (2002a). *Handbook of interview research: Context and method.* Thousand Oaks, CA: Sage.

Gubrium, Jaber F., & Holstein, James A. (2002b). From the individual interview to the interview society. In Jaber A. Gubrium & James A. Holstein (Eds.), *Handbook of interview research: Context and method* (pp. 103–119). Thousand Oaks, CA: Sage

Hachten, William. (1998). *The troubles of journalism.* Mahwah, NJ: Lawrence Erlbaum.

Hackett, Robert, & Zhao, Yuezhi. (1998). *Sustaining democracy? Journalism and the politics of objectivity.* Toronto: Garamond.

Hallin, Daniel. (1998). A fall from grace? *Media Studies Journal, 12* (2), 42–47.

Hallin, Daniel, & Mancini, Paolo. (2004). *Comparing media systems: Three models of media and politics.* Cambridge: Cambridge University Press.

Hardt, Hanno. (1996). The end of journalism. *Javnost/The Public, 3* (3), 21–42.

Jamieson, Kathleen Hall, & Capella, Joe. (1997). *The spiral of cynicism.* New York: Oxford University Press.

Johnson, John M. (2002). In-depth interviewing. In Jaber F. Gubrium & James H. Holstein (Eds.), *Handbook of interview research: Context and method* (pp. 3–32). Thousand Oaks, CA: Sage.

Katz, Elihu. (1992). The end of journalism: Notes on watching the war. *Journal of Communication, 42* (4), 5–14.

Kunelius, Risto. (2006). Good journalism: On the evaluation criteria of some interested and experienced actors. *Journalism Studies, 7* (5), 671–690.

Kvale, Steinar. (1996). *InterViews: An introduction to qualitative research interviewing.* Thousand Oaks, CA: Sage.

Liebling, Abbott Joseph. (1963). *The Most of A. J. Liebling.* New York: Simon & Schuster.

McNair, Brian. (2000). *Journalism and democracy: An evaluation of the political public sphere.* London: Routledge.

McQuail, Denis. (2003). *Media accountability and freedom of publication.* Oxford: Oxford University Press.

Metzler, Ken. (1977). *Creative interviewing: The writer's guide to gathering information by asking questions.* Englewood Cliffs, NJ: Prentice Hall.

Newcomb, Horace M. (1999). Media institutions: The creation of television drama. In Klaus Bruhn Jensen & Nicholas W. Jankowski (Eds.), *A handbook of qualitative methodologies for mass communication research* (pp. 93–107). London: Routledge.

Oakley, Ann. (1981). Interviewing women: A contradiction in terms. In Helen Roberts (Ed.), *Doing feminist research* (pp. 30–61). London: Routledge.

Ravitz, Jessica. (2011, September 14). Dumbest question in the universe. *CNN Living.* Retrieved from http://articles.cnn.com/2011-09-14/living/living_miss-universe-question_1_beauty-pageant-miss-universe-pageant-miss-brazil?_s=PM:LIVING.

Ridell, Seija. (2000). Kuuliainen kuluttaja vai kiihkeä kansalainen? (Newspaper readers: Obedient consumers or passionate citizens?). In Risto Kunelius & Seija Ridell (Eds.), *Kaksi katsetta journalismiin* (Two perspectives to journalism) (p. 94). University of Tampere, Department of Journalism and Mass Communication, Series A. Tampere: University of Tampere.

Rosen, Jay. (1996). *Getting the connections right.* New York: Twentieth Century Fund.

Salokangas, Raimo. (1999). From political to national, regional and local: Newspaper structure in Finland. *Nordicom Review, 1,* 77–105.

Schudson, Michael. (2003). *The sociology of news.* New York: W.W. Norton.

Skloot, Rebecca. (2010). *The immortal life of Henrietta Lacks.* New York: Crown.

Sontheimer, Morton. (1941). *Newspapermen: A book about the business.* New York: Whittlesey House.

Terkel, Studs. (1992). *Race: How blacks and whites think and feel about the American obsession.* New York: The New Press.

Tuchman, Gaye. (1978). *Making news.* New York: The Free Press.

Walters, Barbara. (1970). *How to talk with practically anybody about practically anything.* Garden City, NY: Doubleday.

Ward, Stephen J. A. (2005). Journalism ethics from the public's point of view. *Journalism Studies, 6* (3), 315–330.

Warren, Carol A.B. (2002). Qualitative interviewing. In Jaber F. Gubrium & James A. Holstein (Eds.), *Handbook of interview research: Context and method* (pp. 83–102). Thousand Oaks, CA: Sage.

Zelizer, Barbie. (2004). *Taking journalism seriously: News and the academy.* London: Sage.

# CHAPTER 4

# Focus Groups

*Qualitative research is a contact sport, requiring some degree of immersion into individuals' lives.*

— Stewart, Shamdasani, & Rook (2007, p. 12)

Focus groups are a popular qualitative methodology, often used in political communication, advertising, public relations and marketing research. In fact, focus groups account for more than 80 percent of the qualitative market research currently being done (Stewart, Shamdasani, & Rook, 2007). Focus groups are used to provide inexpensive and timely information regarding consumer opinions of products, services, issues and policies, and they are also used to gather insights into voter reactions and behaviors. They can generate new ideas, help researchers understand how people use different services and/or products, and help marketers and advertisers to target consumers effectively. Focus groups are routinely used to identify participants' preferences, attitudes, motivations and beliefs, and they also provide researchers with interviewing flexibility and insights regarding group dynamics that product manufacturers and service providers find particularly useful. Considered a user-friendly and non-threatening research method, which participants find stimulating and enjoyable, focus groups are also used to help people express themselves openly about sensitive issues as well as to "bridge social and cultural differences" (Morgan, 2002, p. 141).

A focus group is a directed conversation among several people regarding a specific topic, issue or concern that is led by a trained moderator who facilitates group discussion. The goal of a focus group is to stimulate discussion in order to determine how people think and act individually and within a social group (Berger, 1998). Focus groups are usually audiotaped and/or videotaped, and while there can be from three to fourteen participants, eight to twelve members is considered the optimum size for useful group interaction. Participants are usually chosen on the basis of their having similar backgrounds, demographics, behaviors and/or attitudes and are brought together to discuss their opinions, practices, preferences and behaviors. Focus group participants are usually paid a small stipend to cover their time and travel costs, and snacks or a meal is often served during focus group sessions.

Most focus groups are face-to-face conversations. However, sometimes they are held via telephone calls or videoconferencing, or in online chat rooms. When focus groups are held through videoconferencing, participants usually gather at one location and the session is transmitted online to a different city, where some or all observers watch the focus group in real time on video monitors. While some moderators find it difficult to build a working relationship with clients who do not attend each focus group, videoconferencing can save money because observers do not have to travel to different locations in order to observe each focus group.

Focus groups have also been held on the Internet through blogs, bulletin boards and as web conferences in chat rooms. Although the use of online focus groups saves money, some researchers find a variety of security and research challenges with Internet focus groups. Stewart et al. (2007) suggest that with Internet focus groups a moderator has less control of the participants and cannot adequately assess non-verbal communication, which may reduce intimacy and spontaneity within the group. Greenbaum (1998) finds it difficult to stimulate authentic interaction and positive group dynamics in virtual focus groups, and he remains concerned that the security of the information and the authenticity of the participants may be compromised.

However, recent technological changes have led other researchers to consider the potential of virtual focus groups as a creative innovation that can aid the research process. For example, in the past few years, online focus groups have been held in the secure virtual environment of Second Life. Through the use of avatars, Second Life residents and researchers from all over the world have participated in a variety of focus groups: educators have discussed teaching at the college level, food enthusiasts have envisioned a restaurant of the future, visually impaired individuals have been consulted on ways online technologies may become more user-friendly, and self-identified gay participants have discussed gay spaces in Second Life. In 2007 the iAsk Center was constructed in Second Life to resemble a traditional focus group facility; the center includes a mirrored conference room and a client observation area. The iAsk Center recruits prospective focus group members, provides support during the sessions and saves transcripts from each focus group in an effort to broaden the use of chat room and other online technologies.

## The Development of Focus Groups

While coffee-klatches and sewing circles have been around for hundreds of years, the first media-related research using focused group interviews considered the persuasive appeals and effects of radio programming on audience members. This early focus group methodology was designed by Paul Lazarsfield, Robert Merton and their associates in an attempt to understand the effectiveness and likability of radio messages. From 1940 to 1945, Merton and Lazarsfield held focus groups at the Office of Radio Research at Columbia University to consider audience response to CBS radio programming. Lazarsfield understood the marketing potential of mass media research and had developed an "administrative research" perspective that envisioned communication research being carried out in service of media industries (Hardt, 1998). During these early focus group sessions, audience members were initially asked to press a red button if they heard anything in the program that angered, annoyed or bored them, or made them react negatively to the show. Participants were instructed to push a green button if they heard something that they agreed with or enjoyed, or if the communication messages encouraged them to react positively. Audience members' responses and the timing of those responses were recorded into a product analyzer, a device similar to those still used in media research today.

After the radio program, participants discussed the strengths and weaknesses of what they had heard with the researchers, who focused discussion on the audience members' reasons for their negative and/or positive responses to the radio program. The goal of the focus groups was to gather information from audience members to understand "the group dynamics that affect individuals' perceptions, information processing, and decision making" (Stewart et al., 2007, p. 9). In addition, the researchers gathered in-depth information on the participants' listening preferences, attitudes, interests and motivations. During World War II, Merton and his associates used focus groups to help train American soldiers and to develop propaganda films for the army, which were intended to boost soldiers' morale. Ultimately, Lazarsfield and Merton's focus group approach helped researchers to understand the effectiveness of persuasive media messages.

As was discussed in Chapter 1, after World War II, communication researchers began to emphasize a quantitative social scientific approach that emphasized numerical correlations and quantified objective data. The subjective individual experiences of focus group members, which did not yield statistical information that could be measured, became less useful to media researchers, and focus groups were rarely used in media and communication research during this era. However, by the late 1960s and early 1970s, with the rise of marketing and its emphasis on audience reception studies, focus groups began to become popular again. By the time qualitative research methods became an accepted alternative research strategy, focus groups were a useful method for many types of communication and media studies research.

## Contemporary Focus Groups

In contemporary media research, focus groups are regularly used to gather preliminary information, to aid in the development of products and to help researchers understand aspects of consumer behavior. Marketers often use focus groups to obtain feedback on services and products and to obtain consumer responses to business venues, advertising campaigns, branding and prices. Marketers particularly value the associations and connections that participants make using their own descriptions, and they also consider their direct interaction with consumers the most compelling aspect of focus groups (Stewart et al., 2007). Qualitative researchers often find focus groups appropriate for generating research questions, collecting general information about an issue or topic and identifying overarching themes and conceptual frameworks. Scholars often conduct focus groups as a preliminary research step that is later combined with at least one other qualitative or quantitative method.

More recently, qualitative researchers have used focus groups as a primary research methodology. For example, feminist researchers use focused group conversations to "provide women with safe space to talk about their own lives and struggles" (Kamberelis & Dimitriadis, 2008, p. 383), as well as to help raise women's political consciousness and empower them to reclaim their lives.

Focus groups play a pivotal role in contemporary political campaigns and are used to gain feedback about candidates and their platform positions. For example, during the 2004 presidential election campaign, public opinion polls repeatedly indicated that John Kerry was leading George W. Bush by a significant margin. However, from the in-depth conversations held in a variety of focus groups, researchers discovered that Kerry was not connecting with many voters, who were uncomfortable about his identity and uncertain about his policies. Although public opinion polls and media pundits repeatedly indicated that Kerry was winning the presidential debates, focus group members still felt they did not know enough about him to vote for him as president (Stewart et al., 2007).

In general, focus groups that address consumer attitudes or behavior are usually run by a trained moderator and held in a research facility that includes a one-way mirror and space for client-observers to watch each session. Client-observers are in direct contact with the moderator, communicating through an electronic earpiece or new media technology, or updating the moderator during quick briefings held while the focus groups are being run. Other qualitative researchers, who use focus groups for more general research purposes, often hold them in more casual settings such as at participants' homes, work spaces, conventions and coffee shops, and when client-observers are involved, they usually sit off to the side in the same room.

## The Role of a Moderator

A focus group moderator, who is also known as a facilitator, is a key part of each focus group. An experienced moderator manages the entire research process, conceptualizing the project, designing clear research objectives and presenting the research findings. A moderator provides the client or researcher with methodological guidance, helps craft discussion topics and questions, coordinates with the facility being used for the sessions and provides advice on specific logistical issues such as the geographical location for the sessions, the number and types of groups as well as the mix of participants in each group. Perhaps most important, a moderator facilitates the actual group sessions, prompts discussion and deals with group dynamics. Successful focus group facilitators should be personable, persuasive and energetic, have excellent listening skills, be organized and flexible, communicate effectively and have a great short-term memory. It is important for focus group moderators to be skillful enough to draw out shy participants and to handle difficult ones while encouraging discussion among all members of the group (Fontana & Frey, 1994).

In the fields of political communication, advertising, public relations and marketing, researchers often hire professional moderators who have considerable experience running focus groups. If you plan to hire a moderator to run your focus groups, you should consider the person a key part of your research team. It is important to draw on his or her experiences throughout the focus group process and to talk openly about your goals for the project. In other media-related fields, many qualitative researchers choose to serve as the facilitator for their own focus groups. Whether you plan to hire a professional moderator or intend to facilitate your own focus groups, it is important to consider several aspects of the moderator's role in the focus group process.

In order for a focus group to be successful, a moderator must be able to gain all of the participants' attention and quickly create a welcoming environment of openness and trust. The facilitator should also control the group dynamics so that everyone can share their experiences and interact effectively in a non-threatening environment. At the outset of each focus group, the moderator takes charge of the session, setting rules and procedures and explaining to the participants the topic under discussion as well as the research goals. Focus group facilitators should notify participants that the session will be taped and, if applicable, explain that observers will be watching through a one-way mirror in a separate room. It is also important that moderators explain that their role in the focus group is to facilitate discussion among members of the group rather than to share their personal opinions with the group members.

## Facilitators' Communication Strategies

Experienced focus group facilitators have both passive and active listening skills. Passive listening, which is also known as non-reflective listening, encourages participants to talk. When a moderator responds by nodding his or her head, or by replying "mm-hmm" to a focus group member's statement, it illustrates the moderator's interest in what the participant has to say and reinforces a sympathetic and nonthreatening environment. Active listening, or reflective listening, seeks to clarify what a participant is saying.

Fern (2001) notes that there are four different active listening responses that can aid the communication process: clarifying responses, paraphrasing responses, reflecting responses and summarizing responses. Clarifying responses encourage the participant to explain what she or he has said. Using the example of a focus group in which members are discussing the future of news, we can illustrate the four active listening responses. For such a focus group, an example of a clarifying response that a moderator might make is "I don't understand what you mean when you say that newspapers are dead." Paraphrasing responses restate key aspects of what a participant has said in order to make sure that the moderator fully understands what the person intended to say. For example, a facilitator might say, "When you say that newspapers are dead, you are talking about printed newspapers because you feel that most people these days get their news online." Reflecting responses are used to determine the feelings that people have regarding a product, issue or concern rather than focus on the content of the statement. For example, a moderator might say, "You seem to feel sad about what you see as the end of newspapers." Finally, summarizing responses reiterate the key statements and/or feelings of a participant in a focus group. A facilitator might say, "The main point I think you are making is that young people no longer have the newspaper habit and newspapers are finding it increasingly difficult to get new subscribers because the news is available for free online."

Focus group moderators pose questions that are clear and concise and encourage group discussion. Open-ended questions help participants to discuss a topic or issue rather than to respond with a simple yes or no. Questions such as "What did you think when you first saw the car ad?" or "How do you feel women are depicted in the music video?" or "What did you learn from the broadcast news story?" are all examples of open-ended questions appropriate to ask focus group members. Focus group moderators often begin with icebreaker questions that introduce all of the participants and get the conversation going. After focus group members are comfortable, a facilitator introduces the topic and begins to ask open-ended questions to encourage group participation. The initial questions are followed by probing questions that add depth to the conversation. It is important that facilitators avoid asking questions that may put participants on the defensive or make them feel embarrassed about their responses. For more information on framing interview questions, see Chapters 3 and 6.

If we use the example of a product-based focus group with cell phone users about iPhones, a moderator might begin general discussion on the topic with a question such as "What is your initial impression of the new iPhone 4S?" Depending on the group members' responses, the facilitator could follow up with some probing questions in order to gain additional information. The moderator might ask group members to explain why they feel a particular way about the iPhone, or to expand on their initial comments about the costs associated with the new iPhone 4S, or to clarify their feelings about using an iPhone. Asking follow-up questions based on the participants' comments will provide greater depth to the conversation and can help other members to join in. Moderators should not ask questions that reflect their personal perspectives on a topic. "Don't you just love iPhones?" is an example of the type of question that should be avoided because it illustrates a facilitator's personal opinion and can put pressure on a respondent to reply in a particular way. "I can't believe you don't want to own an iPhone" is also an inappropriate statement for a moderator to make because it singles the participant out and might put him or her in a defensive position.

Experienced facilitators are aware that their tone of voice and the way they word their questions can significantly impact the way participants will respond (Greenbaum, 2000). For example, in a focus group with teenage girls regarding their use of new media, a moderator might respond to a participant with the declarative sentence, "You don't feel email is a relevant communication tool for teenagers anymore." Such a comment is a neutral response that could be used to make sure the moderator understands what the teenager has said. Now if a facilitator's response is in the form of a question, "You don't feel that email is a relevant communication tool for teenagers anymore?" the moderator is asking the participant to explain why she feels the way she does about email. Responding to a participant's comments with a clarifying question is a good strategy moderators often use to aid discussion within a focus group. However, if a facilitator responds to the participant in a tone that indicates surprise, "You don't feel that email is a relevant communication tool for teenagers anymore!" a participant might feel that the facilitator does not like her response and she may feel that she has been put on the defensive.

Focus group moderators do their best to remain neutral and are careful about their own body language so that it does not influence the conversation. If they remain interested and engaged in the discussion, chances are the participants will too. Facilitators are also aware of the non-verbal responses of the focus group members. When participants are interested or enthusiastic about a conversation, they often sit toward the front of their chairs, bent forward as if attempting to get into the action. They often seem alert and enthusiastic and may nod in agreement with other members. However, if a participant sits with folded arms across his or her chest, looks up at the ceiling or makes disagreeable facial expressions, it is clear that he or she does not agree with what is being said. An alert facilitator will notice the disagreement and use it to engage the participant in the conversation. If a moderator notices that a group member is yawning frequently, repeatedly looking at his or her watch or has begun doodling, it is a safe bet that the person is tired and no longer interested in the discussion. A facilitator might take a break, walk around the room or even tell a joke to get all members refocused on the topic at hand.

Experienced moderators use a variety of techniques to encourage discussion and facilitate group interaction. Moderators often use prototypes for new products, advertising concepts and public service campaigns to get participants' first impressions and reactions to new items and services. Moderators may show group members photographs of individuals using a specific product and ask them to discuss their feelings about the people shown. In some cases, participants are asked to choose which of several pictures best relates to the topic being discussed. Greenbaum (1998) notes that when participants are asked to make "forced relationships" between a product and types of images the most commonly used categories "are automobiles, colors, and animals, since these appear to have a specific meaning to virtually all consumers" (p. 127).

For example, if a researcher is attempting to understand the reputation of an advertising agency, a moderator might ask focus group participants to write down the type of animal that they associate with the particular agency and to explain why they chose the animal. Greenbaum suggests that while some people may feel the exercise is silly, it provides a variety of perspectives about the issue or topic being addressed, and the choice of animal ultimately expresses a participant's feelings toward the agency. For Greenbaum, the choice of a bear is usually associated with a friendly, caring organization, while those participants who pick a lion see the organization as being powerful but not friendly. Conversely, a turtle references a slow-moving or backward organization, while the choice of a snake or other reptile or a rodent illustrates unpredictability and distrust regarding an institution.

## Recruiting Participants

Since the goal of focus groups is to gather information and understand group dynamics, it is important that all members of a focus group feel comfortable with each other and are open to engaging each other in conversation. One common strategy to help group dynamics is to create similar or homogeneous participant groups for each focus group. Bringing together people from the same backgrounds, perspectives and experiences can help focus group members to click. Depending on the research topic, it may be helpful to choose participants on the basis of age, income, education or occupation. Focus group members are also recruited according to their race and ethnicity, gender, socioeconomic status, religion and physical characteristics, including height, weight and attractiveness.

Most professional focus group firms prefer that all focus group members be strangers because they find that strangers tend to speak more freely than groups of people who know each other. However, some qualitative researchers construct focus groups from established special interest groups, work groups, clubs and organizations because recruitment can be easier and groups of friends can provide important context for the discussions. In some cases, one individual is recruited and then asked to encourage his or her friends or colleagues to participate in the focus groups. Stewart et al. (2007)

encourage researchers recruiting focus group members to also consider the issue of social power and how it may influence group dynamics. Those members with greater status and power based on their occupations, education, experiences or even because of the way they dress may be given special treatment by other participants in the group.

Bloor, Frankland, Thomas, and Robson (2001) maintain that homogeneous focus groups are more effective than heterogeneous groups with members who have diverse backgrounds, social or political views or experiences. Concerned with the dynamic interaction during a focus group, that even an innocuous topic may become unpredictable, damaging or even threatening, they explain that when diverse views and experiences are represented in a focus group, a great degree of conflict may occur which can "crush discussion and inhibit debate" (p. 20). For example, Bloor et al. would not recommend putting pro-choice and pro-life participants together in the same focus group, or even grouping Republicans, Independents and Democrats together. While group dynamics should be considered when constructing focus groups, it is also important to remember that some diversity of opinion is helpful. Sometimes when the focus group participants are too similar, there may be a lot of head-nodding in agreement with what one member says, and a moderator may find it difficult to get enough depth to the conversation.

I am often asked how to go about finding participants for focus groups. While there are a variety of databases available from market research companies, many clubs, organizations and political interest groups have membership lists that they are willing to share. You can also use social networking sites such as Facebook, Google+, BranchOut and LinkedIn to recruit participants. Online chat rooms and email list-serves can also provide you with potential focus group members. There are a multitude of online political, environmental, educational, social and cultural groups and organizations. For example, the US government lists online organizations at www.usgovinfo.about.com for a variety of issues, including health care, campaign policy reform, labor, immigration and taxes. There are also Internet clubs for sports enthusiasts, hobbyists, gamers as well as same-name clubs such as "The Bob Club," an online group started in 2003 that now has more than 3,000 members (Attoun, 2011, p. 6). You can also contact people through email and by telephone, and of course in person by visiting relevant community agencies and groups, local gyms and recreation centers, schools and businesses. A few years ago, some of my graduate students successfully recruited freshmen for their focus groups by posting flyers in the college recreation center locker rooms promising free pizza and cash prizes for those chosen to participate.

Focus group participants are usually paid anywhere from $50 to $200 to cover their time and expenses, and most focus group sessions also include snacks or a meal. Eight to twelve participants is usually considered the optimum size for a focus group. This is because it is difficult to get good group interaction when there are fewer than six participants, and when the group is larger than twelve, it is often difficult for a moderator to maintain control. Researchers usually recruit a couple of additional people for each session just in case there are people who cancel at the last minute. When recruiting focus group participants, it is important to tell them the research topic and to explain that their active participation in the group discussion is necessary.

## Dealing with Difficult Participants

Fresh from her 2011 Emmy win for Outstanding Lead Actress in a Comedy Series, Melissa McCarthy portrayed an overly enthusiastic focus group participant during the October 1 episode of *Saturday Night Live*. As Linda, a focus group member desperate to come up with a new slogan for Hidden Valley Ranch salad dressings, she is loud, obnoxious, disruptive and intent on monopolizing the conversation. Several times during the focus group, Linda shouts out, "There's a Hidden Valley Ranch party in my mouth," and she repeatedly asks the moderator, "Can you garlic ranch blast me now?" She even yells at another participant, "Shut up, Sue, we all hate you." After Linda begins to chug an entire bottle of salad dressing, which playfully cascades down her face, the frustrated moderator offers her $50 just to leave the group. While the skit is played for laughs, it also points out a variety of participant-related challenges that focus group moderators may encounter.

Moderators sometimes have to deal with a dominant focus group member who tries to control the group in any way he or she can. Such an individual may enthusiastically answer every question before others can respond, may interrupt other participants when they try to speak, or may even lecture other group members as to the correct responses to the questions. An overly enthusiastic focus group member can inhibit discussion and disturb group dynamics. Researchers consider the potential for a focus group member to dominate the conversation one of the primary disadvantages of focus groups. Given the potential for a dominant focus group member to destroy group interaction, it is imperative that a moderator respond to such a person quickly and appropriately.

Greenbaum (2000) suggests that moderators can use a variety of writing exercises as well as non-verbal and verbal cues to get all members to participate and to minimize the influence of an overly enthusiastic focus group member. Writing exercises, during which a moderator asks all focus group members to write down their opinions on a particular topic and then share them with the rest of the group, encourage all participants to consider how they personally feel about an issue. For example, a moderator for a focus group discussing press coverage of presidential candidates might ask participants to jot down how they usually learn about a candidate's political platform. The moderator would then go around the room and ask all participants to share with the group what they had written down.

Non-verbal cues such as looking directly at the person but not calling on him or her to speak, or holding up a hand to indicate that someone else is speaking, may also encourage a dominant person not to monopolize the conversation. In addition, a facilitator should remind focus group members that it is her or his responsibility to hear the opinions of each member of the group. Greenbaum (2000) notes that if none of the previous strategies works, a moderator should directly address the dominant group member by saying something such as "Bob, I can tell that you are very passionate about this issue, but we really need to hear how the others feel about it" (p. 148). As with the *Saturday Night Live* focus group skit, occasionally a participant is so difficult to deal with that he or she must be removed from the group. In such a case, it is helpful to work with client-observers, or professionals at the focus group facility, to remove the person from the focus group swiftly so that any negative group dynamics are quickly minimized.

Sometimes a focus group member may feel intimidated or become uninterested in the conversation and stop participating in the discussion. If this happens, the facilitator should remind the group that it is her or his job to make sure that everyone participates. If the focus group member still does not talk, the moderator should direct a question to the individual to help him or her become engaged in the discussion. If the participant still does not engage with other members of the group, another strategy is for the moderator to switch to a writing assignment and follow up by going around the table asking each participant to discuss what he or she wrote down.

## Ethical Considerations

Informed consent is pivotal to the focus group process. All participants must be told the topic of the study before the focus group begins. They must understand that their role in the group is voluntary and that they are free to answer or not answer any or all of the questions. It is also helpful to remind the participants that they may leave the focus group if they become uncomfortable with the process. When one participant is asked to recruit his or her friends or co-workers for a focus group, the use of informed consent can help participants not to feel guilty, or obligated to participate in the session.

The issue of confidentiality is more challenging in focus groups, particularly when a researcher chooses to use people in the group who know each other. If requested, a researcher can change the names of the group members and can also allow participants to review focus group transcripts before the sessions are analyzed and presented. Given the "unpredictability and dynamic nature of focus groups" (Bloor et al., 2001, p. 26), focus group discussions may go in many different ways. A moderator should be alert for any signs of discomfort among focus group members and should take action to maintain an open and comfortable environment. If a focus group member becomes hostile or belligerent, it is important for the facilitator to ask the person to leave the session.

As I mentioned earlier, most individuals receive payment to cover their time and travel expenses when they participate in a focus group. Apart from focus groups, qualitative researchers rarely pay people to participate in their research. While most advertising, public relations, political communication and marketing researchers support paying focus group participants, other academic researchers remain concerned at the implications of paying for participation. They worry that if money is the basis for participation, a study may be "susceptible to manipulation and dishonesty" (Lindlof & Taylor, 2011, p. 104). Other researchers wonder about bringing together a group of strangers to talk about issues and suggest that focus group conversations are less natural than other types of interviews. Yet, Morgan (2002) suggests that since all methods are shaped by specific historical and social contexts, a researcher's familiarity with traditional interview techniques may influence his or her response to focus group interviews.

---

### The Focus Group Process

Set research objectives and budget
Choose moderator
Determine criteria for participants
Set location, number of groups
Design interview questions
Recruit focus group members
Hold focus groups
Evaluate focus groups
Present findings

If you wish to use focus groups as a research method, you should begin by determining the research objectives, goals and a potential research question for your study. You will need to consider the use of a professional facilitator for the focus groups. If you plan to hire a moderator, it is important to pick one at the beginning of the research process so that you are able to work with the person throughout your research. You will also want to decide on the criteria that will be used to choose participants, and set a budget for the research project. In addition, you will want to determine the number of sessions that will be held, the geographic location for the sessions and the facility or place where the groups will be held. Quirk's Marketing Research Review (available online at www.quirks.com/directory/index.aspx) offers an international directory of market research companies that can help you to identify professional facilities and services, as does Greenbook: The Guide for Buyers of Marketing Research (accessed online at www.greenbook.org).

Because environmental factors may influence a focus group's dynamics, you will want to consider the size and composition of the room when choosing a facility for your focus groups. It is helpful to have a space that is large enough for all participants to sit comfortably around a table so that they can all see each other. Professional focus group facilities tend to be centrally located in popular places such as shopping malls or airports. They generally include state-of-the-art technology, rooms with one-way mirrors and a separate space for client-observers. If you plan to conduct your focus groups in a more natural environment, you should make sure the space is large enough for all members to sit comfortably and that there is a separate space for observers so that the participants do not feel they are being watched.

After these initial decisions have been made, you will work with your facilitator to construct interview questions and topic areas for the focus groups. Moderators should also be given the flexibility to ask follow-up questions and to revise or change any existing questions during the sessions.

The recruitment and selection of appropriate focus group members is crucial to the success of your focus groups. You will want to match your participants to your research objectives. While some marketing studies may only require focus group participants to have general knowledge or interest in a product, other research studies may require specific demographic characteristics. For example, for the study "US Teenagers' Perceptions and Awareness of Digital Technology: A Focus Group Approach," reprinted and discussed later in this chapter, the authors were specifically interested in young people's opinions and they recruited eighty middle-school and high-school students for their focus groups. Their initial plan was to compare the views of students living on the West Coast with those of students on the East

Coast, because they presumed that the locations alone would provide socioeconomic and ethnic diversity. However, they discovered that while the focus group members from the two locations were ethnically diverse, students from both regions were equally economically disadvantaged (Hundley & Shyles, 2010).

During each focus group session you will observe that the moderator poses questions to the participants in order to keep the conversation flowing. Focus groups are group discussions rather than group interviews; the moderator asks questions to facilitate the group dynamics and he or she uses a variety of strategies to encourage group members to fully interact with each other (Wilkinson, 2011). If you plan to serve as the facilitator for your focus groups, your topics and questions should be flexible enough to allow you to engage participants and encourage them to fully explore the issues and topics.

The evaluation of the focus group sessions varies, depending on the types of focus groups being held as well as on the researchers' goals for the research. In public relations, political communication and marketing research, as well as in other areas in which a professional moderator is used and clients usually observe the sessions, the evaluation of the focus groups is done by the moderator and presented to the client. The evaluation is based on the client's needs, and a moderator may craft a written report about the focus groups, or he or she may give an oral presentation to the client. Some moderators meet with client-observers immediately after the focus group is finished. Such a strategy allows the moderator to discuss any problems or concerns he or she has with the process, as well as to share initial observations about the group. Post-group discussions between the client-observers and the moderator may also help the research project to evolve and may result in changes to the questions asked to future focus group participants (Greenbaum, 1998).

Academic researchers who use focus groups usually transcribe the audio and/or video recordings of the sessions and then conduct a textual analysis of the focus group transcripts. For more information on textual analysis, see Chapter 8. If you plan to transcribe your focus group sessions, I recommend that you ask the moderator to introduce each participant by name at the beginning of each session. It is helpful for the moderator also to use participants' names whenever possible during the sessions. This is a strategy that will help to personalize the conversation and aid you with the transcription process. You should transcribe all conversation that occurs during the focus group sessions. As Bloor et al. (2001) explain, "[T]he transcript needs to reproduce as near as possible the group as it happened, so that anyone reading the transcript can really 'see' how the group went" (p. 61).

## Focus Group Research

At the most basic level the focus group transcript provides information for researchers to use in research reports and presentations. Some focus group analyses are descriptive in nature, summarizing the discussion, while others are analytical, identifying key themes, synthesizing information and interpreting key issues and concepts (Fern, 2001). The following research, "US Teenagers' Perceptions and Awareness of Digital Technology: A Focus Group Approach," by Heather L. Hundley and Leonard Shyles, illustrates an analytical analysis of focus group research. Note how the final two paragraphs of the introduction outline the research goals for the study.

---

### "US Teenagers' Perceptions and Awareness of Digital Technology: A Focus Group Approach," by Heather L. Hundley and Leonard Shyles

From *New Media and Society, 12* (3,) May 2010, 417–433.

Since the Internet's inception, media scholars have studied the impact and influence of this newest communication infrastructure on the media landscape. Researchers have studied users' time spent online (Jordan, Trentacoste, Henderson, Manganello, & Fishbein, 2007), what users do online (Subrahmanyam, Greenfield, Kraut, & Gross, 2002) and, more recently, online use and problem solving (Cheong, 2008). In the United States, Hargittai (2007) explored demographic aspects of both users and non-users; in the United Kingdom, attention has been given to analyzing Internet use by adults, while characterizing children as relative online experts (Livingstone & Helsper, 2007, p. 672).

More recently, scholars have begun focusing more closely on youth interaction with the internet (Cheong, 2008; Heim, Brandtzæg, Kaare, Endestad, & Torgersen, 2007; Jordan et al., 2007; La Ferle, Edwards, & Lee, 2000; Livingstone, 2008; Livingstone & Helsper, 2007; Bortree, 2005). As with studies of adult populations, research on younger people now seeks to learn in more detail who has online access, where that access is (i.e. home or school), how they spend their time online, and what they do there (i.e. chat, shop, email, download music).

One study indicates that teens are a unique audience; that is, their online usage patterns are distinctly different from those of other age groups (Jordan et al., 2007). However, Livingstone and Helsper (2007) note that while some differences are confirmed by research, little academic attention has been paid to understanding the motives behind teenagers' use of digital technology, specifically the internet. Despite the emerging literature, Jordan et al. (2007) claim that little effort has been made to explore teen media perceptions and awareness of digital technology. Indeed, while research on younger populations is increasing, many scholars agree that we still have a lot to learn about this demographic group.

Since "the very existence of youth, at least in the twentieth century, is intimately tied to the media and vice versa" (Grossberg, 1994, p. 26), this project set out to understand more about youth perceptions and awareness of digital devices. As Wartella (2002) suggests, attention should be focused on teenagers' exposure to and use of various media, specifically digital devices such as iPods, computers, cell phones and video game systems. One objective of such research is to learn what teenagers know and think about various digital technologies in order to extend research that has typically examined the amount of time spent with a particular medium. Our approach aligns with Mazzarella's (2006) observation that "youth scholarship . . . has sought primarily to understand ways in which youth incorporate mass culture into their lives" (p. 227).

This research continues this line of inquiry by listening to teenagers and gaining a perspective on what they think about emerging digital technologies and the functions various devices serve in their lives.

---

In the following methods section, the authors provide a rationale for their choice of participants and an explanation of how these young people were recruited. This section also explains the specific focus group procedure used for the research and the researchers' reasons for choosing focus groups as their research method. For this study, the researchers served as facilitators for the focus groups, asking structured and semi-structured questions that they felt allowed the students to speak freely about the topics.

---

## Methods

### Participants

Considering the diffusion of innovations theory, two geographic regions provided the potential for interesting regional comparisons; the eastern and western United States were used to locate participants for this research. Thus, while we were predominantly interested in learning about teenagers' perceptions and awareness of digital technologies, we also realized that new ideas spread at varying rates. Hence, we considered the possibility of digital devices that may not be implemented in one region but which may have reached our target population in another.

On the West Coast, teens from a high school in a predominantly Hispanic area in southern California participated, consisting of 75 percent Latino, 14.5 percent black, 7.3 percent white, 3.1 percent Asian and 0.1 percent Native American (MuniNet Guide, 2008a). On the East Coast, teens from a middle school participated, consisting of a predominantly white (66.2 percent) population followed by black students (28.5 percent), Latino students (3.8 percent) and, lastly, Asian students (1.5 percent) (MuniNet Guide, 2008b). Schools were chosen by convenience since the researchers had access through personal contacts. While the regions' ethnic compositions vary significantly, their economic standings are similar. Both areas selected for study are characterized as economically disadvantaged, with annual median household incomes of $41,000 (for the West Coast; US Census Bureau, 2000) and $37,000 (for the East Coast; MuniNet Guide, 2008c).[1]

Teachers provided access to their students during class time. For the East Coast location, 12- to 14-year-olds (6th- through 8th-grade students) were included; on the West Coast, 14- to 16-year-olds (9th- and 10th-grade students) participated. While we recognize that there can be quite a difference in maturity between a 12-year-old and a 16-year-old, we do not make age comparisons; we simply report and describe what a range of young teenagers do with digital devices and how they use them in their lives. A total of eighty teenage students contributed to the study.

## Procedures

The authors obtained human subject approval from their respective universities. Informed consent was granted by the participants' parents or guardians as well as the participants themselves.[2] In May 2007, arrangements were made with school officials ("contacts") to visit the schools and conduct focus groups with participants. When we arrived at our respective schools, the contacts instructed the students to get into groups (varying in size between five and nine students), allowing them to be with friends. Three focus groups were conducted in the East and eight were conducted in the West. The interviews took place in familiar locations[3] away from teachers, administrators and any other school authority figures. Among high-school students, extra credit was given for participation; the middle-school students did not receive any reward for their participation.[4]

The focus group sessions occurred over five days, and took between 20 and 30 minutes. All sessions were audiotaped, then later transcribed by graduate assistants.[5] The use of focus groups was found to be appropriate for the ages of the participants. One obvious advantage in collecting the desired information via focus groups was that they allowed researchers far removed from a demographic group in terms of age and other factors to tap into the participants' worldviews (Lindlof & Taylor, 2002). Further, focus groups enable a "cascading" or "chaining" effect, which encourages participants to feed off each other's ideas, producing a richly textured set of "complementary interactions" (p. 182). This was important since the researchers, acting as facilitators, were strangers to the participants. Therefore, we lacked a history or prior relationship with the students and thus had fewer preconceived expectations or opinions about the participants (and vice versa). The arrangement in this sense was viewed as advantageous to our goals both during and after the process of data collection.

During the interviews, both formally structured and semi-structured protocols were used (a copy of the protocol is available from the authors). The formally structured portion involved prepared questions, allowing for consistency across groups. These questions were designed to "serve comparative and representative purposes—comparing responses and putting them in the context of common group beliefs and themes" (Fetterman, 1989, p. 48). The semi-structured portion of the interviews allowed students to speak freely, elaborate, ask questions and join in group discussions. This approach permitted the researchers to gain access to "the fundamentals of a community from the 'insider's' perspective" (p. 48). Mazzarella (2006, p. 244) states that, typically, "adult culture does not give youth a chance to speak for themselves or does not listen when they do." To combat Mazzarella's concern, the procedures used in this research allowed for open conversation and richly textured perspectives.

## Instrument Development

Some focus group questions aimed at understanding what digital technology the participants possessed, used or wanted to own. Others asked specifically about various devices such as game systems, computers, cameras and cellular telephones, to develop an understanding of participants' familiarity with each piece of technology. Questions also inquired about how teenagers spent their time with various digital media devices and what they liked to do with them. For instance, in the case of game systems we wanted to know if they liked to play video games by themselves, with others or online. For cell phones, we wanted to know if they preferred talking on the phone, sending text messages, taking photos or emailing. We also asked about the amount of time they thought they spent with each device compared with the amount of time they spent doing other things like homework or other after-school activities.

Typically, the conversations were dominated by talk about the Internet, specifically social networking sites. Hence, questions arose regarding what they do on social networking sites, how many people are on their "friends" list, and how they control information on these sites. Interview sessions concluded by asking the participants if they had any questions or comments they wanted to add.

Hundley and Shyles identified four central themes from the transcribed audiotapes of the focus groups. Each of the four themes is discussed in this next section of the article. Notice how the authors use a variety of examples taken directly from the focus group conversations to illustrate each of these themes.

## Results

Several common themes emerged, along with some differences in the answers we received. It was clear that maturity and knowledge varied among respondents. For example, when asked about their favorite television networks or programs, one group discussed networks such as CNN, the Discovery Channel or the Food Network, while another mentioned the Cartoon Network and programs such as *Degrassi* or *The Simpsons*. One interesting difference between the participants also emerged: the younger, East Coast students were much more familiar with the website Facebook whereas the older, West Coast students by and large had not heard of it. All the participants, however, were familiar with MySpace. Overall, differences were far outweighed by similarities. Four dominant themes emerged in the data about teenagers' perceptions and awareness of digital technology: (1) an awareness of digital devices, (2) a sense of temporal displacement, (3) social functions, and (4) a palpable sense of risk associated with using digital devices.

### Awareness of Digital Devices

When asked what digital devices they owned or wanted, participants eagerly responded, in many cases almost boasting about their possessions. Items named in the first question included devices such as cell phones, iPods, computers (both desk and laptop), DVD players, game consoles such as PlayStation, Nintendo and XBox, cameras and various kinds of televisions. In fact, most of the participants possessed cell phones. For instance, in one group, four of the five participants had cell phones; in another group, seven out of nine teenagers had them. In one group, all eight participants had cell phones.

The responses revealed that the participants were keenly aware of devices and features even when they did not own them. In terms of technology they wanted, responses often matched the devices their friends already owned, and the respondents were highly specific. For instance, instead of mentioning the generic "video game," respondents named particular consoles (i.e. PlayStation), and some went further, frequently specifying the particular model (i.e. PS3, which is PlayStation 3). Others wanted laptops as opposed to the desktop computer they already owned. Students frequently clamored for improved technology (i.e. a better cell phone such as an iPhone, a faster computer or a more advanced digital camera). Additional items included iPods (a portable music- and video-playing device), CD players, WII (a physically interactive game system that connects to a television) and XBox 360 (a game system that connects to a television).

When asked what they would like to add to their possessions, one student said, "I can't think of anything right now." When prodded with examples, such as an iPod, she said she would like a green one in addition to the silver one she already owned. Thus, apparently when one has all the devices desired, the next best thing for some is to acquire various models, colors or styles of the same technology. When asked the same question, another respondent replied that she was "all set for right now." Another group appeared satisfied with what they currently possessed. When asked, "Do you have everything you want?" the group overwhelmingly responded "Yeah" in unison.

## Temporal displacement

While many respondents appeared to be quite conscious of digital devices, they seemed less aware of the time they spent with them. As for the amount of time spent online, on a computer, playing games (regardless of the device employed), responses ranged from less than one hour a day, between one and two hours a day, more than two or three hours a day, six hours on Saturdays, to all day in the summer. In more extreme cases, answers included:[6]

> F2: Probably at least five or six hours [a day].
> M2: . . . from the time we get out of school to the time we go to bed.
> F4: When my cousins come over mostly I play [games] with them like all day until like two in the morning or something from like nine in the morning till two.

In a few instances, participants disclosed parental control of their time spent with digital technology. For example, one respondent said:

> F3: My mom only lets me go [play video games] every other day.

Nevertheless, regardless of the amount of time these teenagers spent with digital media, it seems clear that several factors contribute significantly. For instance, one respondent explained:

> M1: Depends on the day.
> F3: Now that we are going on vacation it is going to go all day.

Her friend added:

> F1: During the day and night.

One respondent stated that she spent:

> F1: Like an hour a day [playing games and] sometimes less because of homework.

In describing the use of digital devices among teenagers, this study finds that time spent with digital media (i.e. video games, the Internet and MP3 players) often supplants time spent with older technologies, like television, radio and print. Of course, a few answers ran contrary to this finding:

> M3: Yeah, I watch like constantly.
> F8: TV is my life.
> F9: I love TV.
> M2: Nothing takes away from television time even if I have a wedding, graduation—nothing. Yeah. That's my life.

Nonetheless, most of the students we questioned said they watch television less:

> F6: I just go online [instead of watching TV].
> F7: Less TV. I do more radio.
> F3: I have like sport activities like track and stuff I come home like at five or six or something like that so I really have to do my homework, brush up, eat food, and basically go to bed. I don't really have time to like really watch TV or anything anymore.

Another interesting finding that emerged was the multitasking that takes place with respect to media use; that is, many respondents stated that they engaged in several media functions simultaneously (i.e. texting while watching videos while surfing the net while instant messaging, as evidenced by the following quotes:

> M3: I have my PSP [PlayStation Portable] next to me, then I have the computer, and then I have the TV on and I'm playing all at the same time.
> F5: Yes, Internet on and watching TV at the same time, and on the phone.
> F2: I use the computer once I get home. I'll be listening to music all day, like non-stop.

## Social functions

Another major theme that emerged from our study was the students' recognition that digital devices help them socialize. While there was some discussion about how cell phones connect participants to one another, and how video games are fun to use with friends, discussion about staying in touch and staying connected predominantly occurred via online social networking sites. While few of our West Coast participants even knew what Facebook was, all of our East Coast participants were familiar with it. MySpace, however, was an overwhelming favorite among all respondents, and the West Coast participants were more active with it than other respondents. For instance, in the East Coast group only five of the nine respondents reported using MySpace. While not all had created profiles, they nevertheless knew what it was. One West Coast participant was described as "an addict" by his classmate because of his level of interest in MySpace.

In addition to the students' awareness of MySpace, the number of people listed on the "friends" list was the topic of discussion during the focus group interviews. For instance, when asked how many people were on their "friends" list, responses ranged from as few as 6 to over 1,000. Most of the students claimed to have between 85 and 200 "friends."

When asked what they do on these sites, socializing and entertainment emerged as common themes. For instance, respondents said they "talk with friends," "stay in touch," "update [their] profile," "check other profiles," "check messages," "message friends," "meet friends" and "get in touch with old friends." The following excerpt was a typical response:

> F1: You look for your friends and stuff. You search them and then you add them and talk to them and stuff.
> F2: Chat with friends and make backgrounds, just entertaining. I use it when I'm bored.
> F3: Message people.
> F4: Yea, you leave them comments.
> F3: Like "hi, how is your day?"

## Risk

A fourth major theme emerging from the data was a palpable awareness of online risk. Respondents disclosed that they avoid such risk by altering or omitting sensitive information. Similarly to the socializing theme, this theme was only discussed in terms of online social network sites, despite the respondents' knowing that cell phones can threaten privacy and cameras' content can be stolen. When asked if they worried about their privacy on MySpace, the members of one focus group resoundingly stated, "No." The question was intended to increase our understanding of their awareness of or concern about hackers; however, their responses related back to who was on their "friends" list. So when asked why they were not concerned about their privacy, one respondent explained:

F2: I only have people who I know.
Researcher: You block out everybody else?
F2: Only people I know from school. If they ask me to be their friends and I don't really know them then I won't let them on.

Related to protecting themselves and deciding whether or not to add someone on to a "friends" list, one group of respondents answered as follows:

F4: You get those people who request you who don't even know you.
Group: Yeah, that's dumb.
F3: That's why you look at their page before you accept them. I don't accept them.
F1: Some people are stupid about it [adding people to their "friends" list].
F2: Like weird people will be like "Ooh, let me be your friend." Or some guy is like, "You're cute, let me talk to you." Stupid stuff like that.
F2: Deny.
F3: Deny, deny, deny.
F4: You have to be smart about it. You don't have to be stupid.
F2: Some people are stupid and they say, "Oh, he's [sounds] cute, let me talk to him" then you turn around and he's like 80 years old.

Such responses illustrate how these teenagers are aware of the need to be wary of whom they add to their "friends" list. Many showed concern for their privacy by adding only friends they already had from their actual social world. They appeared skeptical of online strangers who claim to be a "friend"; responses indicated a high number of overtures that are routinely blocked.

Associated with the desire to secure privacy is the practice of masking identity from hackers infiltrating computers or social network sites and appropriating personal information. Some teenagers we interviewed appeared to accept hackers as part of life online.

F2: It [getting hacked] could happen.
F1: Someone hacked into mine and started sending emails.
F2: They hack into it and they started messing with your MySpace.
M1: My cousin got into my page and I'm like how the hell did that idiot get into my page?

M2: Because he knew your password.

M1: He added people I don't even know. I just keep them there. I don't talk to them, though.

These four participants' responses were indicative of many others who disclosed that they know hacking occurs and that it is up to the individual to take necessary precautions against such privacy invasions by strangers.

While many respondents seemingly accept privacy threats from hacking as part of life online, one participant disclosed online vulnerability:

Researcher: Do you feel safe?

F2: Well, yeah, I mean you are never going to feel safe even if you have 100 million firewalls.

Despite this, some respondents treat their MySpace profiles as video games in that if they get hacked, they merely start over (this is similar to a video game character—if an onscreen character gets killed off, players can simply restart the game). Note the following passage:

Researcher: Are you ever worried about your privacy or people hacking in?

F1: Oh, they've done that before. I had to delete my profile.

Researcher: What did you do about it?

F1: I deleted my profile and I got a new one.

F3: Yeah, that's happened to me before but you just like redo it right over and it's fine. You can just change your password and it's not hard.

Another approach these students informed us about was their conscious limiting of information on their profile. For instance, one student stated:

F1: Well, I don't put things that are important on there, so there are not a lot of important things to be invaded.

As for limiting information on social network sites, the teenagers we interviewed were consistent in their responses as to what they would not post online. Overwhelmingly, they claimed they would not "put anything personal on it," which included their address, phone number, date of birth, "where we live," or "directions to my house." One student said:

F4: I don't even put the city where I live. They think I live in Ireland right now.

And another mentioned:

> M1: I don't put pictures of myself.

Yet another student sought privacy by not including her last name, only her first name. The student who claimed to live in Ireland was asked about lying on online social network sites and she justified her falsehood:

> F4: Everybody does that. It just sounds cool.
> F5: My boyfriend is 86 years old.

As discovered in the teenagers' responses, lying about one's age was common in these groups.

> Researcher: But on MySpace aren't you are supposed to be 18 and over to have an account?
> Group: No.
> F1: It was 16, then 15, now 14.
> F2: It doesn't really matter; you can lie about your age.
> Researcher: Do you lie about your age?
> F1: Yeah.
> F2: You can lie about everything.

The participants we spoke with were aware of the dishonesty they perceived that pervades social network sites. For instance:

> F3: Some people just do it [lie] to get back at people, like we had a friend where somebody made a MySpace about her telling her off, making stuff up about her. It wasn't her, it was the person who didn't like her, so people could be so cruel. Especially teenagers. They are cruel.

---

In the following section, the authors compare the evidence that they have gathered from their focus groups to other published research in this area to try to understand larger issues related to teenagers' use of technology. Note how the interaction between the examples from the focus group research with the published research in this area provides an ongoing conversation with other researchers related to issues of status, socialization, privacy and safety.

---

## Discussion

The findings in this research support the literature in this field. Responses indicate that these teenagers are generally happy with the spate of digital devices they currently possess and acknowledge the similarities and differences among technologies; that is, they are cognizant of capabilities each piece of technology brings to the market. With respect to particular media devices, these results suggest there is a clear and surprisingly stable desirable media technology hierarchy that exists across students. For instance, plain cell phones are the least desirable, followed by those with cameras and those that can record video; finally, those that can access the Internet are viewed as most desirable. The teenagers we interviewed did not speak much about cell phones with email and GPS capability. We suspect they are well aware of those developments by now, and we speculate that they would have ranked such capabilities as among the most desirable if they had been interviewed more recently.

The devices that appear to be most appealing are those perceived to make content easily accessible and shareable while being convenient and handy to use. For example, iPods, which make it possible to download, store and play thousands of songs and many videos, resonate as a higher social status item than CD players, which have relatively limited functionality in that they can only play audio. Thus, the students' acquisitiveness and the attractiveness of goods were largely based on the technological capability of each device.

Based on the data, the teenagers' acquisitiveness is obvious. Yet we wonder how these material possessions may relate to status among peers. The current literature reports that the mobile telephone, for instance, "is seen as a type of fashion accessory" (Ling, 2004, p. 85; also see Campbell, 2007; Fortunati, 2003). Digital devices can display that the owner is in demand (by the number of calls, texts, people listed in the address book or on the "friends" list, and by the number of people who want to use the device); they also confer status on their owner by showing others that the holder has the economic power to own and operate such devices, and they convey a level of user competence. As Ling (2000, 2004) details these elements of peer status for mobile telephones, we suggest that other devices serve the same purpose. Furthermore, we believe that cost, which may limit ownership, confers status, adding to a device's perceived desirability.

Jordan et al. (2007) reviewed the literature on the time teenagers spend with media and warn readers of the problems associated with this variable. Confirming some of these indicators, we find that indeed there are numerous factors, such as time of year, workload and demands from after-school activities, that function as predictors of teenage media use. Clearly, "as older teens expand their social lives, time spent online [or with other digital media] is displaced by time spent on other activities" (Livingstone & Helsper, 2007, p. 686).

Our data also reveal that teenagers often are unaware of (or unconcerned about) the amount of time spent using digital devices. Numerous factors compete daily for teens' time, which may explain their multitasking habits. Pendleton (2004) found that in the United States 80 percent of teenagers use more than one medium at a time. Rather than using their time exclusively interacting with computers or the Internet, most of our participants reported surfing the Net or updating their MySpace page while listening to music or having the television on in the background. They often reported doing their homework on the computer while listening to music (from a variety of sources such as the radio, their iPod or their computer) or having the television on in the background. Their disclosing of their multitasking abilities confirms research reporting that 70 percent of the respondents use two or more media simultaneously (Pan, 2004).

While multitasking appears popular, today's youths appear to take advantage of both face-to-face and digital forms of socializing. Scholarship reveals that media are powerful socializing agents (Aenett, 1995; O'Guinn & Shrum, 1997), and our focus group responses support the continued popularity of online socializing by participating in such activities as actively using social network sites like MySpace, text messaging and instant messaging. The majority of teenagers participating in our study are active on social network sites, especially MySpace. This is not surprising, given that "social network sites have become some of the most popular online destinations in recent years" (Hargittai, 2007; also see Lipsman, 2007a, 2007b) and "young people are known to be some of the most likely to participate on some social network sites" (Hargittai, 2007).

A strong majority of our focus group responses supported Hargittai (2007), who argues that "membership in an online community mirrors people's social networks in their everyday lives." Evidently, most of the students we spoke with disclosed that all those on their MySpace "friends" list were people they already knew. Therefore, it seems clear that the friends and relatives with whom they are familiar or have face-to-face contact with are the same people as their online friends.

La Ferle et al. (2000) report that teenagers concurrently learn from media to gain social skills, using media to satisfy their social needs. Ling (2004) extends the idea of social skills and claims that teenagers use digital devices, and in his example cell phones, to manage their social life. Our research confirms these findings. Teenagers we interviewed explained how much they depend on their phones and computers to keep connected with one another.

In terms of socializing and staying connected with peers with digital devices, particularly social network sites, a large "friends" list is a pride object with many of the teenagers we interviewed. Many suggested that the number of people on their "friends" list equates to popularity and perceptions of likability. This aligns with Ling's (2004) research examining Norwegian teenagers. Specifically, Ling posits that a "quantifiable measurement of popularity is how many names they have registered in their telephone" (p. 109). Ultimately, "it is important to be able to report a large number of names. It is a sign that the teen is successful socially" (p. 109). This also resonates in our data.

Finally, we discovered that our data coincide with research regarding online privacy and safety as well; boyd (2008, p. 14) states that privacy "is about the sense of vulnerability that an individual experiences when negotiating data" and Ling (2008, p. 14) claims that "it's about trust and group cohesion." Our respondents were aware of the perceived risks they take online; nevertheless, they nonchalantly accept being hacked or having their identity or privacy invaded. While "the ability to spread digital images or ill thought out words [sic] on the internet means that traditional issues of privacy and secrecy of the inner group are difficult to guard" (p. 3), our respondents reported that they do limit and/or alter information on their sites in order to protect themselves. In addition to controlling and limiting access to their "friends" list and restricting the kind of information they post, the teenagers we spoke with said that they often attempt to protect themselves by shading the truth about their identities, frequently misrepresenting themselves. This is not new, since "online internet interactions, in which players pretend to be someone else or at least stretch their own self-presentations, are common experiences of adolescents" (Calvert, 2002, p. 68). Indeed, distorting the self-image is a common practice among our respondents; what might be considered a misrepresentation was a natural part of online culture.

---

Hundley and Shyles address the strengths and weaknesses of focus groups as a research method in the following section. As I mentioned earlier in the chapter, most qualitative researchers prefer to combine focus groups with another qualitative or quantitative research method. It is this concern that the authors address in their comments.

---

## Limitations

As with any research, this project inherently has limitations. Rather than conducting traditional quantitative survey research to understand a population's perceptions and awareness of digital technology, this study employed a qualitative approach to examine the same phenomenon with another methodological lens. As a result, the findings are not broad and generalizable but, rather, focused and specific. However, these results enrich our current understanding of how teenagers perceive and use digital devices.

Of course, it is a commonplace that young people often feel put on the spot, embarrassed or uncomfortable in the company of older persons questioning them. However, these potential problems were ameliorated in a number of ways. For instance, the students were placed in a familiar and comfortable setting, surrounded by friends and classmates. The researchers, acting as facilitators dressed in casual clothing, were informal in speech and were often self-deprecating. Furthermore, rather than taking an authority role, we encouraged the students to help educate us on various digital games and social network sites. The East Coast researcher used the students' first names (name cards were provided). The West Coast researcher sat on the floor in a circle with the students.

As a result of these strategies, the student participation was very open, energetic and free-flowing. Hence, for this research we believe the focus group outcomes were successful. Most of the students spoke up, offered responses and opinions, and were enthusiastic in their demeanors and responses. Quieter students responded if asked directly; however, most of them worked off each other, reminded each other of stories, self-disclosed and eventually prodded others to engage. Indeed, despite potential methodological limitations, when conducted properly the focus groups conducted for our study functioned well.

---

In the concluding section of the research, the authors broaden the analysis of the focus group research to consider the ethical implications of teenagers interacting with each other through social networking sites. Because of the interaction between the group participants, the issue of lying emerges as a final concern Hundley and Shyles discuss in their article.

---

## Conclusions

The data garnered from these focus group sessions involving teenage participants were enlightening in several ways. First, they deepened what is known about teenagers' perceptions and awareness of digital devices. Teens' interaction with each other and the world through social network websites via their computers can be just as valuable as face-to-face encounters; their use of cell phones to connect to one another via texting enables teenagers not only to share ideas and make friends, but to plan and coordinate social time; their use of computers to download entertainment content as well as trade and share personal messages significantly shapes today's youth culture in broad, essential and significant ways, at times even trumping social contact itself.

The digital world may represent a cultural divide between some demographic groups based on age, race, education levels and other factors, but among teenagers it is more of a connection and an enabler that cannot easily be replaced. A major implication of our findings is our concern about the cavalier attitude our participants demonstrated regarding online risks and the idea that few, if any, repercussions are assumed for those who could potentially inflict harm. It also appears that there is little ethical concern about online lying. People in general are more apt to lie online (Calvert, 2002). This finding may easily extend to today's teen populations. Our data reinforce this notion and reveal that teenagers fully expect others to lie. We see this as a serious development that can have a potentially corrosive impact on traditional social cohesion and expectations about norms of acceptable behavior. While we do not view lying as something new, we see the justification of such behavior among teenagers on the Internet as a cheapening of social expectations. Better Internet security may reduce the validity of the rationale used to justify wholesale deceptive practices among users; yet trust eroded by such behavior is an unwelcome side effect. Silverstone (2004) urges that morality and ethics should be central to our media agenda. He calls for a social and just development of media civics that should be at the heart of our media regulation. Furthermore, regulation, Silverstone (2004) argues, is a private as well as a public matter. Thus, we concur that media civics should be integrated into our media literacy curriculum, with hopes that it will seep deeper into our culture.

---

### Focus Group Exercises

1. Observe at least three different groups of people in a restaurant or coffee shop. In particular, take note of the spatial relations, the non-verbal communication and the group dynamics. Explain how a facilitator might use this information to improve focus group interactions.

2. Craft a set of ten questions on a topic of your choice that will help you to learn more about some aspect of new media usage. Try each question out on a couple of your friends and see what types of responses you get. Did your friends understand the type of response you wanted from each of your questions? Ask each friend about the wording of each question—particularly if she or he did not respond to a question in the way you would have liked. Your goal is to make each question open-ended, clear, concise and accessible.

3. Volunteer to be a member of a focus group. Professional focus group facilities often recruit for participants at local malls. During the focus group, pay particular attention to how the moderator facilitates group interaction. If there were any challenging focus group members, explain how the moderator handled them. Did you enjoy being a focus group member? If so, what made the experience enjoyable? If not, what do you think could have made the focus group session more enjoyable?

## Notes

1  The schools were selected by convenience. Prior to the study, the researchers presumed the diverse ethnic composition because of location; however, they were unaware of the similar economic status between the two populations until after data were collected. Future research could target diverse economic areas.

2  Parental or guardian consent letters were required in Spanish and English for the West Coast participants. However, all the participants spoke English fluently and some were bilingual. The interviews were all in English.

3  For the East Coast, groups went to the library one at a time for the interview while the remaining student participants stayed in class. For the West Coast, groups met one at a time in the gymnasium while the remaining student participants visited with each other outside during the physical education class. Normally these high-school students would be busy with PE-related activities; however, it was the last week of the school year and they were not required to dress down or do work typically associated with the class.

4  The option for extra credit was at the teachers' discretion and was not a condition presented by the researchers. The West Coast researcher was informed of the extra credit offer after it was granted to the students. It was not part of the university human subjects' applications; however, we believe it is important to note in our study.

5  The authors appreciate graduate students Valerie Moses and Diana Reyes for transcribing the interviews.

6  In conversations during the focus groups, results are recorded by gender (M or F) and by speaker number to distinguish them. In this dialogue, M1, M2, M1, F1, M1 male #1 speaks followed by male #2, male #1 comments again, followed by female #1 and then male #1 says something again.

## References

Aenett, Jeffery Jensen. (1995). Adolescents' uses of media for self-socialization. *Journal of Youth and Adolescence, 24* (5), 519–532.

Attoun, Marti. (2011, October 23–29). Same-name clubs. Like-named members unite for fun, fellowship. *American Profile*, pp. 6–8.

Berger, Arthur Asa. (1998). *Media Research Techniques* (2nd edn). Thousand Oaks, CA: Sage.

Bloor, Michael, Frankland, Jane, Thomas, Michelle, & Robson, Kate (2001). *Focus groups in social research*. London: Sage.

Bortree, Denise Sevick. (2005). Presentation of self on the Web: An ethnographic study of teenage girls' weblogs. *Education, Communication and Information, 5* (1), 25–39.

boyd, danah. (2008). Facebook's privacy trainwreck: Exposure, invasion, and social convergence.

*Convergence: The International Journal of Research into New Media Technology, 14* (1), 13–20.

Calvert, Sandra L. (2002). Identity construction on the Internet. In Sandra L. Calvert, Amy B. Jordan, & Rodney R. Cocking (Eds.), *Children in the digital age: Influences of electronic media on development* (pp. 57–70). Westport, CT: Praeger.

Campbell, Scott W. (2007). A cross-cultural comparison of perceptions and uses of mobile telephony. *New Media and Society, 9,* 343–363.

Cheong, Pauline Hope. (2008). The young and techless? Investigating internet use and problem-solving behaviors of young adults in Singapore. *New Media and Society, 10,* 771–791.

Fern, Edward F. (2001). *Advanced focus group research.* Thousand Oaks, CA: Sage.

Fetterman, David M. (1989). *Ethnography step by step.* Newbury Park, CA: Sage.

Fontana, Andrea, & Frey, James H. (1994). Interviewing: The art of science. In Norman K. Denzin & Yvonna S. Lincoln (Eds.), *Handbook of qualitative research* (pp. 361–376). Thousand Oaks, CA: Sage.

Fortunati, Leopoldina. (2003). Mobile phone and the presentation of self. Paper presented at the Front State/Back Stage Mobile Communication and the Renegotiation of the Social Sphere Conference, Grimstad, Norway, June 22–24.

Greenbaum, Thomas L. (1998). *The Handbook for Focus Group Research* (2nd edn). Thousand Oaks, CA: Sage.

Greenbaum, Thomas L. (2000). *Moderating focus groups: A practical guide for group facilitation.* Thousand Oaks, CA: Sage.

Grossberg, Lawrence. (1994). The political status of youth and youth culture. In Jonathon S. Epstein (Ed.), *Adolescents and their music: If it's too loud, you're too old* (pp. 25–46). New York: Garland.

Hardt, Hanno. (1998). *Interactions: Critical studies in communication, media, and journalism.* Lanham, MD: Rowman & Littlefield.

Hargittai, Eszter. (2007). Whose space? Difference among users and non-users of social network sites. *Journal of Computer-mediated Communication, 13* (1). Retrieved from http://jcmc.indiana.edu/vol13/issue1/hargittai.html.

Heim, Jan, Brandtzæg, Petter Bae, Kaare, Birgit Hertzberg, Endestad, Tor, & Torgersen, Leila. (2007). Children's usage of media technologies and psychosocial factors. *New Media and Society, 9,* 425–454.

Hundley, Heather L., & Shyles, Leonard. (2010). US teenagers' perceptions and awareness of digital technology: A focus group approach. *New Media and Society, 12* (3), 417–433.

Jordan, Amy, Trentacoste, Nicole, Henderson, Vani, Manganello, Jennifer, & Fishbein, Martin. (2007). Measuring the time teens spend with media: Challenges and opportunities. *Media Psychology, 9,* 19–41.

Kamberelis, George, & Dimitriadis, Greg. (2008). Focus groups: Strategic articulations of pedagogy, politics, and inquiry. In Norman K. Denzin & Yvonna S. Lincoln (Eds.), *Collecting and interpreting qualitative materials* (3rd edn, pp. 375–402). Los Angeles, CA: Sage.

La Ferle, Carrie, Edwards, Steven M., & Lee, Wei-Na. (2000). Teens' use of traditional media and the internet. *Journal of Advertising Research, 40* (3), 55–65.

Lindlof, Thomas R., & Taylor, Bryan C. (2002). *Qualitative communication research methods.* Thousand Oaks, CA: Sage.

Lindlof, Thomas R., & Taylor, Bryan C. (2011). *Qualitative communication research methods* (3rd edn). Thousand Oaks, CA: Sage.

Ling, Richard. (2000). "'We will be reached': The use of mobile telephony among Norwegian youth. *Information Technology and People, 13* (2), 102–120.

Ling, Richard. (2004). *The mobile connections: The cell phone's impact on society.* Amsterdam: Morgan Kaufmann.

Ling, Richard. (2008). Trust, cohesion and social networks: The case of quasi-illicit photos in a teen peer group. Paper presented at the Budapest Conference on Mobile Communications, Budapest, Hungary.

Lipsman, Andrew. (2007a). comScore Media Metrix releases top 50 web ranking for July. Retrieved from http://www.comscore.com/press/release.asp?press=1582.

Lipsman, Andrew. (2007b). Social networking goes global. Retrieved from http://www.comscore.com/press/release.asp?press=1555.

Livingstone, Sonia. (2008). Taking risky opportunities in youthful content creation: Teenagers' use of social networking sites for intimacy, privacy and self-expression. *New Media and Society*, *10*, 393–411.

Livingstone, Sonia, & Helsper, Ellen. (2007). Gradations in digital inclusion: Children, young people and the digital divide. *New Media and Society, 9*, 671–696.

Mazzarella, Sharon R. (2006). Constructing youth: Media, youth, and the politics of representation. In Angharad N. Valdivia (Ed.), *A companion to media studies* (pp. 227–246). Malden, MA: Blackwell.

Morgan, David L. (2002). Focus group interviewing. In Jaber F. Gubrium & James A. Holstein (Eds.), *Handbook of interview research: Context and method* (pp. 141–159). Thousand Oaks, CA: Sage.

MuniNet Guide: Your Hub for Municipal Related Research. (2008a). Retrieved from http://www.muninetguide.com/schools/.

MuniNet Guide. (2008b). Retrieved from http://www.muninetguide.com/schools/.

MuniNet Guide. (2008c). Retrieved from http://www.muninetguide.com/states/.

O'Guinn, Thomas C., & Shrum, L. J. (1997). The role of television in the construction of consumer reality. *Journal of Consumer Research, 23* (4), 278–284.

Pan, G. (2004, March 24). Seventy percent of media consumers use multiple forms of media at the same time, according to a study for the Media Center at API. Media Center at the American Press Institute. See http://www.prnewswire.com/news-releases/seventy-percent-of-media-consumers-use-multiple-forms-of-media-at-the-same-time-according-to-a-study-for-the-media-center-at-the-american-press-institute-72195562.html.

Pendleton, Jennifer. (2004). Multitaskers: Kids quick to master myriad choices in media but marketers question effectiveness of ad impact in their fast paced lives. Special Report: Marketing to Kids, Tweens and Teens. *Advertising Age, 75* (3), S1.

Silverstone, Roger. (2004). Regulation, media literacy, and media civics. *Media Culture and Society, 26* (3), 440–449.

Stewart, David W., Shamdasani, Prem N., & Rook, Dennis W. (2007). *Focus groups: Theory and practice* (2nd edn). Thousand Oaks, CA: Sage.

Subrahmanyam, Kaveri, Greenfield, Patricia M., Kraut, Robert, & Gross, Elisheva. (2002). The impact of computer use on children's and adolescents' development. In Sandra L. Calvert, Amy B. Jordan, & Rodney R. Cocking (Eds.), *Children in the digital age: Influences of electronic media on development* (pp. 3–33). Westport, CT: Praeger.

US Census Bureau. (2000). American Fact Finder. Retrieved from http://censtats.census.gov/data/US/01000.pdf.

Wartella, Ellen A. (2002). Introduction. In Sandra L. Calvert, Amy B. Jordan, & Rodney R. Cocking (Eds.), *Children in the digital age: Influences of electronic media on development* (pp. xiii–xv). Westport, CT: Praeger.

Wilkinson, Sue. (2011). Analysing focus group data. In David Silverman (Ed.), *Qualitative research: Issues of theory, method and practice* (3rd edn, pp. 168–184). London: Sage.

# CHAPTER 5

# History

*He who controls the past controls the future. He who controls the present controls the past.*

— George Orwell, *1984*

History is about the achievements, challenges, failings and mysteries of our lives. Using stories to provide glimpses into the past, historians help us to understand what it means to live at a particular place and time. They offer us guidance about what to value, what to avoid, how to spend our time and how to make sense of our world. Contrasting the past with the present, historians focus on the context associated with people, events and issues in an effort to explain the human experience. Some historians see that their job is to bring an authentic recounting of the past to life through the crafting of accurate narratives that are based on the most relevant historical evidence. Others maintain that while historical evidence is created in the past, we can only evaluate this evidence in the present. What this means is that we cannot comprehend the past as it actually was; at best we are able to understand aspects of the past from a contemporary perspective.

History is the oldest qualitative method, and ancient cultures drew on historical evidence to create social narratives about their lives. For example, the Greek historian Thucydides, who is generally regarded as the father of history, crafted a detailed political and military account of the Peloponnesian

War in the fifth century BCE. One of the earliest Chinese historians, Confucius, introduced ethics into history and suggested that discussions about the past could teach people how they should conduct their lives (Donnelly & Norton, 2011). For thousands of years, historians have crafted oral and written stories to explain, enhance and justify the actions of a culture.

These days there are all kinds of historians who do many different types of history. There are researchers who focus on the history of a particular subject or field such as journalism history, military history or economic history. Some researchers do history from the top down, focusing on the lives of kings, presidents, industry leaders or other elites, while other researchers do history from the bottom up, stressing the role of everyday people in the historical process. Other historians specialize in a specific time period, like American Civil War history or 1920s social history. There are comparative historians, who study different societies that existed at a similar time; labor historians, who focus on the labor movement; and intellectual historians, who address the development of ideas in human thought. There are also antiquarians, who narrowly focus on historical periods and facts to evaluate ancient objects of science and art, and there is even a field of study known as historiography that deals with the actual writing of history as well as the philosophical issues related to the craft of history.

Historian John Tosh (2009) suggests that contemporary researchers are motivated by four somewhat contradictory attitudes toward history. Some historians aspire to learn what it was like to live at a previous time and place, envisioning historical research as a type of "detective enquiry, or a venture in resurrection" (p. 2). Some historians seek to uncover the progress of human destiny, while other researchers showcase history within the political or ideological interests of a society. Finally, there are historians who draw on the historical record as a "cautionary tale" (p. 8) to help us to learn from the past.

## Traditional vs. Cultural History

In this chapter I distinguish between two different types of historians; while they are known by many different names, I refer to them as traditional historians and cultural historians. Traditional historians study the past from a positivist or post-positivist understanding of evidence as elements of reality. In contrast, cultural historians who come from a constructivist or critical theories philosophical orientation focus on "the domain of the lived" (Hall, 1989, p. 26), which is the way people actively engage with, experience and interact within elements of culture within the historical process. As I discuss in Chapter 1, during the twentieth century, scientific research protocols and procedures influenced all types of research, including the study of history. Some historians began to envision the stories of the past as generalizable facts while others reacted against a scientific focus, critiquing the influence of culture and ideology within the narrative structures of history (Brennen & Hardt, 2011).

Although Thucydides was one of the first historians to differentiate literature from history (Donnelly & Norton, 2011), to this day researchers continue to debate the relationship between history and literature. Cultural historian Hayden White sees the writing of history as a type of fiction that is more like literature than science, because of its content and narrative form. Yet, he suggests that most historians choose to ignore the fictional aspects of their work, believing that by following specific guidelines and rules to evaluate their evidence, historians are somehow transcending fiction. For White (1978), while historians often focus on events with "specific time-space locations" and novelists rely primarily on "imagined, hypothetical or invented" (pp. 121–122) events, they both use the same forms and techniques in their narratives, striving to provide an image of "reality" that corresponds with authentic human experience.

Traditional historians often incorporate a commonsense understanding of history as the story of the past, presenting historical evidence as chronological reconstructions that address names, dates and places. Focusing on the quantity of facts rather than the quality of information, this type of historian addresses catastrophes, crises and ruptures that are measured and evaluated as outliers from the norms of continuity and progress. While traditional historians attempt to reconstruct the past by emphasizing the collection and description of evidence, their evidence often remains untouched by theory, analysis or interpretation. Yet other historians refer to this type of history as "pseudo-history," and, as political theorist Fredric Jameson (1971) sarcastically suggests, it is characterized as an "obsession with historical rise and decline, the never-ending search for the date of the fall and the name of the serpent" (p. 324).

Traditional historians present their narratives as fact-based objective explanations of events, issues and problems. However, cultural historians maintain that researchers cannot remain neutral about historical evidence—that they interpret the past using relevant concepts and theories in order to understand the evidence that they are able to access. Cultural historians suggest that researchers must go beyond reconstructions of the past to consider people's experiences in culture. For cultural historians, connections are drawn between historical figures, events and issues and the relevant social, political and economic developments in society. Rather than emphasizing facts alone, they evaluate evidence as it interacts with the relevant historical context, looking at the challenges and struggles and envisioning progress as a contradictory notion. They see history as a living process, including issues of continuity and discontinuity as well as instances of evolution and of revolution. In addition to placing an emphasis on crisis, catastrophe and oppression, cultural historians also address the challenges, changes, oppositions and regenerations that occur within societies (Williams, 1989).

## Media History

The development of media history began with the invention of the printing press and other communication technologies. Journalism historians initially focused on crafting stories about famous editors and publishers, whom they saw as working to ensure the fourth estate function of the press. These biographies were augmented with institutional histories that recounted the development of newspapers in the United States.

In 1974, cultural theorist James Carey called for the creation of cultural media history as an alternative to traditional journalism history. Carey (1974) found the existing Whig or progressive view of journalism history, with its emphasis on progress, "something of an embarrassment" (p. 3). He suggested that its accounts of the struggles between good and evil and its focus on the growth and progress of freedom, democracy, liberalism and knowledge had become an exhausted genre. At that time, traditional media history emphasized a search for facts, yet historians often excluded the interpretation and contextualization of those facts. Critical theorist Hanno Hardt (1989) suggests that historical facts were usually presented chronologically as a linear tale providing "overwhelming evidence" (p. 119) to support the growth of newspapers as well as a particular notion of freedom of the press within American democracy.

In contrast, Carey noted that cultural history, with its emphasis on the emotions, motivations, values, attitudes and expectations of people involved in historical events, could offer journalism history a fresh perspective. Cultural media history emphasizes the collective process of people connected with communication within specific economic, political and cultural environments. From this perspective a consideration of media will address the development of specific technologies as well as viewing them as social practices and cultural forms. When media history focuses primarily on the specific technological inventions, it privileges the tools, making the technologies seem more important than those who use them. Understanding how people accept or reject new technologies, along with considering the reasons for their incorporation and how they use them, reinforces human agency in the communication process (Williams, 1974).

Carey's call for cultural media history prompted considerable debate about the field of journalism history. While some researchers have embraced Carey's suggestions, others suggest that the field of journalism history should be expanded further to consider all aspects of media and communication history. Communication historian David Paul Nord maintains that an emphasis on individuals and how they interact with elements of communication neglects important structures of power within mass media institutions. Noting that a focus on history from the bottom up is difficult, since media messages are constructed from the top down by those in charge, Nord (1988) maintains that it is important to remember that the "'consciousness' embedded in the language of journalism is the product of large institutions" (p. 10).

More recently, sociologist Michael Schudson (1991) outlined three contemporary approaches to the study of communication history: institutional history, macro-history and history proper. Institutional history focuses specifically on the development of media properties. This is a popular approach: there are many historical studies of newspapers, advertising agencies, broadcast stations and public relations firms as well as biographies and memoirs of publishers, editors, reporters and photographers that have been published. Relying on the availability of organizational and government archives and records, institutional histories rarely address larger issues regarding the role of communication in human experience or social change. As Schudson (1991) explains, institutional media histories "too often become a parade of personalities and organizational reshufflings" (p. 179). Nord (1989) refers to this type of history as "hagiography," which is the study of the "saints" of journalism like Joseph Pulitzer and William Randolph Hearst, who helped to build media empires. Nord suggests that institutional media history remains primarily atheoretical in nature apart from "a vague faith in progress" (p. 309).

Schudson's second approach to communication history, macro-history, considers the relationship between communication and human nature. Often focusing on issues of development, progress and modernization, macro-history has helped to legitimate communication as a relevant field of study. History proper is Schudson's third contemporary approach to media history. Akin to Carey's understanding of cultural history, history proper considers the relationship of media to the larger social, economic and/or political history. It seeks to understand how changes in media influence society, as well as how changes in society impact the communication process. As Schudson explains, while macro-history focuses only on what communication illustrates about some aspect of human nature, history proper looks at what media say about society or what society reveals about the communication process.

## The Method of History

As with other qualitative methods, historians pick their topics and craft their research questions on the basis of their interests, receiving guidance from their theoretical frameworks and conceptual orientations. See Chapter 2 for more information on the crafting of qualitative research projects. After historians have chosen their topics, they gather as much documentary evidence as possible and evaluate that evidence for reliability and authenticity. They interpret the significance and meaning of the evidence and finally craft stories about their findings.

Historians maintain that it is important for all researchers to immerse themselves in the general history as well as the published research in their area of interest before crafting their research questions. For example, if a researcher is interested in the development of the blurring of news and entertainment on television, it is important for him or her to gain background knowledge about how the conception of news began to change during the nineteenth century, as well as to understand the larger issues of media conglomeration and concentration. It is also important for the historian to immerse him- or herself in general broadcast media history and to be knowledgeable about theories of communication and society. Once a researcher is familiar with the general history in his or her interest area and has a good grounding in the relevant theory, the crafting of research questions should follow naturally. Historical research questions should be open-ended and flexible, allowing a researcher to revise a question if needed during the research process. Research questions should also be clearly stated, unambiguous and precise. In recent years, some media and communication historians have begun to consider relational questions that address the complex interactions between aspects of media, culture and society.

There is a huge amount of historical evidence available on some media history topics, and if you pick one of these, you will find it necessary to narrow your topic and research question so that you are able to immerse yourself in the literature. However, you may find that there is very little evidence for some historical topics that you might be interested in researching. If this is the case, you may need to broaden your topic and/or consider collecting different types of evidence or conducting oral history interviews, which are discussed at length in Chapter 6. For example, if you were interested in a historical research project on the development of

Edelman Public Relations during the 1950s and 1960s, you would quickly be able to find many different types of evidence for your research project. As one of the world's largest PR firms, Edelman has been written about extensively. Its website alone includes six decades of information about its offices, clients and campaigns. However, if you were interested in learning about labor issues in public relations firms during the 1950s and 1960s, you would have to get creative and consider using novels, films and memoirs, or even doing your own oral history interviews with PR professionals, because there has been only limited historical research done in this area.

## Collecting Historical Evidence

Until recently, doing historical research usually meant traveling to historical archives that were housed on university campuses, in libraries or at historical societies. These days, considerable historical material is available online through electronic archives, databases, organizations and a variety of other publications. For example, the Electronic Records Archives (ERA) houses approximately 10 billion US federal government records online at the National Archives at www.archives.gov/era/.

This searchable archive includes photographs, videos, films, interviews, letters, news articles, federal agency records and many other types of historical material. The archive also promotes a variety of featured exhibits in its Digital Vaults on significant historical events such as the American Revolution, the influenza epidemic of 1918 and the Civil Rights March on Washington. The ERA includes many types of historical materials, including World War II propaganda posters, images of Americans working from the mid-nineteenth century throughout the twentieth century, online copies of the Declaration of Independence, Edison's light bulb patent, Apollo 11's flight plan and even a letter from Jackie Robinson to President Dwight D. Eisenhower. The site also includes an online Archival Research Catalog, searchable by name and number, referencing all types of collections held by the National Archives.

There are also a variety of newspaper archives currently available online; many are fully indexed and searchable. For example, the *Chicago Tribune* historical archive is a fully searchable online newspaper resource, and the Los Angeles Public Library has online newspaper databases dating back hundreds of years. Many state historical societies have uploaded a variety of different types of historical documents and digital photograph collections, and community libraries often include online county historical archives. There are online archives for many different types of history, including women's history, labor history, presidential history, military history, and ancient and medieval history.

Considerable biographical material on many public figures is also now available online, and more documents are being uploaded every day. For example, the Hebrew University of Jerusalem is currently digitizing and posting its entire collection of 80,000 items related to the life of Albert Einstein. As of March 19, 2012, its web portal included about 7,000 pages of material from Einstein's public and private life. The searchable archive, available at http://alberteinstein.info/, includes scientific and non-scientific documents, correspondence, travel diaries, personal materials, photographs, films and sound recordings. The research portal offers many of Einstein's commentaries on his physics research, including his theory of relativity, as well as private correspondence with family members and friends, fan mail he received, and letters regarding his commitment to social issues ranging from nuclear disarmament to civil rights (Estrin, 2012).

Even when historical materials are not available online, many archives have uploaded searchable indexes that researchers can use to get a sense of their holdings. Archivists are also available to talk with researchers about their collections. Several years ago I was writing a book chapter on the development of the American Newspaper Guild and I worked with a wonderful archivist from the Archives of Labor and Urban Affairs at the Walter Reuther Library who helped me to locate key historical documents for my study.

## Types of Historical Materials

In their research, historians evaluate many types of primary and secondary source material. Traditional historians define primary sources as "eyewitness testimony" (Smith, 1989, p. 321) by a person, video or still camera, or other recording device that was present at an event and documents it for the purpose of leaving a historical record. The format or presentation style of an eyewitness record is of less importance to historians than its time frame and content. While some primary sources include commentary regarding an event or issue, other primary sources do not. Traditional historians also distinguish eyewitness testimony about an event from historical documents that were created for other purposes. They use the term records to define primary source material about a topic that was intentionally produced and was intended to be seen and distinguish relics as primary source materials that are relevant to a study but were actually created for some other reason. Records include news accounts, memoirs, autobiographies, letters, diaries, films, photographs, oral testimony, and some industry and government documents, while relics are things like business financial records, treaties, tools and equipment, local customs, and some government documents. Historians also evaluate paintings and sculptures, advertisements, cartoons, pamphlets, maps and other cultural artifacts to help us understand the social customs and values.

Unpublished primary source documents can provide historians with a more detailed record of an issue or event than published reports or official documents. Historians draw on unpublished papers, memos, letters and email correspondence to help them understand people's motivations and intentions for their actions. They understand that published materials often document decisions that were taken, rather than discuss the reasons behind the decisions (McDowell, 2002). For example, the unpublished minutes from a corporate media board meeting might provide additional context and information regarding the reasons the board instituted a new international news policy than would be available in the company's published annual report.

While traditional historians remain wary of using poems, novels, songs and other fictional materials as primary sources of evidence, cultural historians, who see history as a creative endeavor, reject distinctions between history and fiction based upon differences between real evidence and imagined material. Instead, they focus on the relevance of the evidence to their specific research projects.

Secondary sources of evidence are created after an event has happened and they often involve the restatement of primary sources of information that have been presented somewhere else. Individuals who craft secondary sources rarely witness the actual events, yet they are important sources of evidence providing historians with contextual information about the topic. Most secondary sources include interpretation of the evidence, and these accounts and interpretations tend to change over time. Books, recordings and journal articles on the topic are usually considered secondary sources of evidence. While many traditional historians primarily use secondary sources to begin their research projects, drawing on the existing research to provide context and to help them frame their research questions, cultural historians tend to draw on a mixture of primary and secondary sources through their research.

## Evaluating Historical Evidence

On November 22, 2011, to commemorate the forty-eighth anniversary of the assassination of President John F. Kennedy, filmmaker Errol Morris created a short documentary, *The Umbrella Man*, in which he addresses the interpretation of historical evidence. The film highlights an interview with the author of *Six Seconds in Dallas*, Josiah (Tink) Thompson, who discusses the story of the one man who stood under an open black umbrella at the time and place where President Kennedy was assassinated. The question of why a man stood holding an open black umbrella on a lovely warm day in Dallas initiated numerous theories of an assassination conspiracy. Some maintained that the umbrella man was the real assassin, while others insisted that his opening of the umbrella, as the motorcade approached, signaled the actual marksman or marksmen. As Thompson explains, the umbrella man became a sinister fact that signaled conspiracy. No one was able to interpret the open umbrella as anything but peculiar and evil.

In 1978 the umbrella man, Louis Steven Witt, came forward and testified before the House Select Committee on Assassinations. Witt said that he had held the open black umbrella as a visual protest against Kennedy's father, Joseph P. Kennedy, and his support for Britain's appeasement policies when he served as ambassador to the Court of St. James's in London in 1938 and 1939. For Witt, the umbrella represented the former prime minister of the United Kingdom, Neville Chamberlain, who was known for carrying a black umbrella.

Thompson finds Witt's explanation wacky enough to be true and he suggests that the umbrella man offers a cautionary tale regarding the way we interpret information. When we try to understand seemingly sinister things that occur in life, it is important for us to remember that there may be a logical or reasonable interpretation. The umbrella man also reminds us of the active role that researchers play in the interpretation of historical evidence. Historians do not merely record the names, dates and places of events that occur. Through their selection of information, their evaluation of documentation, their analysis of facts and their interpretation of evidence, researchers construct specific historical narratives.

After historians have collected all relevant source material, they analyze the evidence they have obtained for its authenticity and credibility. While most documents held in archives and depositories have already been authenticated, other historical information will need to be evaluated for intentional and accidental errors which might indicate that the documents are forgeries. Historians also assess the credibility of historical information, considering personal letters, photographs, diaries, interoffice memos and other historical artifacts to be more credible than memoirs, news reports and unsigned memos. The credibility of historical material is often enhanced when it can be corroborated by several other independent sources.

In their evaluations of historical evidence, historians consider the type of information they have obtained and when and where the evidence was produced, and they assess the creator of the evidence as well as his or her intention, original purpose and intended audience. They evaluate evidence for inconsistencies, omissions, contradictions and/or distortions and attempt to verify the information from other sources. In addition, historians also consider the language used in the historical evidence. Because the definitions of words change over time, it is important for researchers to consider the meanings of words within their proper cultural and historical contexts.

Traditional historians evaluate evidence for its reliability and integrity. They look for accidental and intentional errors of fact, forgeries, and cases of plagiarism, and worry about the misuse of evidence and information that is taken out of context. Traditional historians also consider the loss and/or suppression of evidence and problems with identity, motives and the origin of documentary evidence. In their evaluation of evidence they privilege the original over the copy and value the expertise of the document's author and the level of confidentiality, suggesting that government documents and official sources often provide the "best" evidence (Nevins, 1963).

However, historical research is based on more than the collection of factual information; it involves the interplay between the evidence and the evaluation, and interpretation of this evidence by historians. In their efforts to understand the past, it is important for historians to consider the relationships between one event and a broader pattern of events. Unfortunately, there is not one definitive text on history, or a standard compilation of historical facts or even one interpretation of key historical events. The past is no longer fully available to us; the observations that survive may have misrepresented or misunderstood elements of the past, or taken them out of their proper context. Firsthand observers may have documented some events considered of minor relevance when they first occurred. If the documentation was saved, historians may have studied these events, and their historical narrations may have increased the events' significance. In their efforts to understand the relevance of past events within a society, historians systematically evaluate evidence of the past, doing their best to distinguish authentic from inaccurate reports. While historians cannot completely reconstruct the past, they can provide "penetrating insight into snapshots of past events" (McDowell, 2002, p. 29).

Cultural historians see evidence not merely as facts but also as cultural practices, created by people at a distinct place and time, that may provide insight into the values, beliefs and experiences of a society. Finding that all types of cultural products may contain relevant historical evidence, cultural historians go beyond surface evaluations to consider the style, language, structure and absences and other latent meanings of the evidence.

While traditional historians usually evaluate evidence as "particles of reality" (Kellner, 1989, p. 10) from which a factual story of the past can be constructed, cultural historians encourage researchers to consider historical materials as cultural artifacts that can help us to make sense of how people lived their lives at a particular place and time. In addition, cultural historians attempt to study their own cultures as "alien" cultures and to see those who lived at a particular place and time as the "other." As cultural historian Robert Darnton (2009) explains, "We constantly need to be shaken out of a false sense of familiarity with the past, to be administered doses of culture shock" (p. 325).

After historians have evaluated historical evidence for its authenticity, integrity and significance, they select relevant evidence, compare it with other information gathered from primary and secondary sources, and they analyze and interpret the evidence. Finally, they craft stories and attempt to understand the significance of their historical research.

## Ethical Considerations

The assessment of historical evidence raises some ethical challenges for historians. Researchers find it challenging to understand people's motivations for their attitudes, beliefs and actions. They also find it difficult to determine the accuracy of historical sources and to determine which information is based on observation, which is grounded in opinion and which evidence has been created or fabricated. For example, Ira Glass, host of the National Public Radio program *This American Life*, recently pulled one of its shows after he learned that key evidence had been fabricated. The thirty-nine-minute radio episode was based on Mike Daisey's one-man theater show depicting Apple's manufacturing processes in China. Daisey justified his invention of some events and characters by insisting that theater was not journalism and that his fabrications were created "in service of a greater narrative truth" (Carr, 2012) about people's suffering in China. However, Glass noted that although the goal of the show was to raise people's consciousness about offshore manufacturing, it was important to share accurate information with the American public.

Historians craft stories that are meant to be interesting, well written, dramatic and compelling, and it is this narrative emphasis that may lead to "simplifications or exaggerations" (Berger, 2000, p. 135) of the historical record. While most historians see history as "part art and historians part artist" (Nerone, 1993, p. 150), it is important for researchers to do their best to present the historical evidence they obtain accurately, clearly, completely and within its proper context.

## Research Using History

Historical research is usually presented in narrative form, recounting one or more stories that are built from a researcher's interpretations of historical evidence. Some historians use a chronological framework for their narratives, tracing a variety of themes over time, while others tell their stories thematically. In the following research study, Matthew Ehrlich uses a chronological approach to showcase the poetry and politics in a 1947 radio documentary. Ehrlich sees his historical research as a response to Carey's call for researchers to use cultural media history. In his study, note how Ehrlich also responds to Nord's caution regarding the role of institutional power in assessments of the communication process.

---

## "Radio Utopia: Promoting Public Interest in a 1940s Radio Documentary," by Matthew C. Ehrlich

From *Journalism Studies, 9* (6), 2006, 859–873.

### Introduction

Historical studies can be powerful means for enhancing the critical understanding of journalism. They shed light on journalism's "lessons" and "triumphs" and also on its "contradictions and problems" (Zelizer, 2004, pp. 11, 96). James Carey (1997a, pp. 88–90) famously declared that historians should move beyond "Whig"-like accounts of journalism's inexorable progress and instead try to reveal "historical consciousness" by showing how it felt "to live and act in a particular period." Rather than reducing all consciousness to ideology or viewing journalism as the transmission of information and expertise, scholars should see journalism "as an exercise in poetry and utopian politics" (Carey, 1987, p. 14). In response, David Nord (1988, pp. 10–11, 14) argued that historians ought not to get so caught up in utopian views as to overlook the fact that "the 'consciousness' embedded in the language of journalism is the product of large institutions" and "the exercise of power." In brief, press history should retain a "focus on powerful individuals and institutions."

This study examines a historical episode, the production and nationwide broadcast of an acclaimed 1947 American radio documentary, as an example of poetry and utopian politics aligning with the interests of powerful individuals and institutions. *The Eagle's Brood* was written by Robert Lewis Shayon, later a communication professor at the University of Pennsylvania. The program was produced by the CBS Documentary Unit, founded by Edward R. Murrow and declared by its director, Robert Heller (1952, p. 383), to be "a virtual Utopia for craftsmen who believe in radio's usefulness as a social force." The documentary advocated as a solution to juvenile delinquency the grassroots organizing philosophy of Saul Alinsky (1946), author of *Reveille for Radicals*. If in that way *The Eagle's Brood* aimed at promoting the public interest, its producers also sought to promote and gauge interest in the program itself. Heller (1952, p. 386) asserted that documentaries "should be tested by radio research" to measure their hold and effects on the audience. Thus, the tools of Paul Lazarsfeld and motivation researcher Ernest Dichter were applied to the program. Finally, *The Eagle's Brood* promoted the image of CBS and its chief William Paley as serving the public interest at a time when broadcasting faced increased regulatory scrutiny, with others such as film producer David O. Selznick also benefiting from association with the program.

Ultimately, *The Eagle's Brood* pointed to a familiar lesson consistent with Nord's view of history, as power eventually trumped idealism. Once CBS came to see the radio Documentary Unit as less vital to its public image and the network shifted its attention to television, and after blacklisting befell both Shayon and Heller among others, "radio utopia" vanished. Nevertheless, *The Eagle's Brood* is significant in that it offers a historical example of corporate media presenting an optimistic, community-oriented vision via an alternative journalistic form.

---

In the following sections Ehrlich details the types of primary source materials that were used in his historical research study. He also discusses the interpretive framework he uses to analyze the evidence he has compiled and he provides the reader with important context for understanding the radio program.

---

## Interpretive Framework and Method

A growing scholarly literature has called attention to the network television documentary as the "product of converging social, economic, political, institutional, and discursive forces" (Curtin, 1995, p. 7). Curtin (1995) shows how a series of documentaries in the early 1960s emerged from a consensus among government officials and broadcasters that television ought both to raise its standards and to promote America's image as a bastion of freedom during the Cold War. Similarly, Raphael (2005) analyzes how muckraking documentaries of the 1960s and 1970s were enabled by government regulation that encouraged such programs even as they sparked government investigations into their reporting methods.

The American radio documentary has received much less scrutiny. Bluem (1965), Bliss (1991) and Lichty (2004) briefly trace how the documentary evolved from dramatizations of reality such as *The March of Time* in the 1930s into poetic, patriotic wartime works such as Norman Corwin's *On a Note of Triumph* and finally into postwar programs including *The Eagle's Brood*. Lichty (2004, p. 474) notes that some of those programs today "are still remembered as the pinnacle of radio writing and production," whereas Bluem (1965, p. 71) praises them for creating "an authentic and dramatic form of journalistic documentary" that served as a model for television. However, Bluem and Lichty both note that radio documentary declined with television's ascendancy, and Sterling and Keith (2006) argue that historians since then have overlooked much of the serious radio work of the earlier era.

On the other hand, a new wave of audio documentary has recently attracted notice for "telling stories that can't be told on film" and introducing listeners to those with "lives that are different than theirs" ("Radio Documentaries," 2001, pp. 13–14). Documentary's revitalization parallels a rise in radio history studies (Hilmes & Loviglio, 2002; Lenthall, 2007). Douglas (1999, p. 24) argues that radio played a role "in constructing imagined communities" more powerful than that of print, even as it also allowed listeners to experience "multiple identities" both consistent with and opposed to "prevailing cultural and political ideologies."

The present study draws and builds upon those strands of research. It fills a scholarly gap by focusing on the 1940s program *The Eagle's Brood* that Bluem (1965, p. 48) says helped show "that radio had finally reached its goal of making documentary a force to influence a vast listening audience." The postwar spate of socially minded radio documentary was fostered by a convergence of institutional interests. Those included the Federal Communication Commission's efforts to raise radio's standards via the "Blue Book" and the networks' attempts to respond in a way that avoided significant alteration of broadcasting's commercial structure. At the same time, the postwar documentary gave voice to a specific historical consciousness and political sensibility that embraced both cultural consensus and difference. Documentarians exploited radio's perceived ability to promote those ends through a journalistic form that combined factuality and dramatization. In due course the institutional and cultural context shifted, and the brief heyday of programs such as *The Eagle's Brood* passed.

In addition to an original broadcast recording and a script of *The Eagle's Brood* (Shayon, 1947, 1952), the primary source materials for this study are the Robert Lewis Shayon Papers at the Howard Gotlieb Archival Research Center, Boston University. They offer extensive background on the documentary's writing and production, and the context from which it emerged. The study also draws upon Shayon's (2001) autobiography and Saul Alinsky's papers in the Industrial Areas Foundation Records, Daley Library Special Collections, University of Illinois–Chicago. Additional sources include the day's trade and popular press and histories of the period, as well as materials provided by the CBS News Archives in New York City.

## Shayon and His Times

Robert Lewis Shayon was born in 1912 and began writing for radio in the mid-1930s. Shayon (2001, p. 12) later said that the Depression "made a host of us sensitive and sympathetic to justice, social 'causes,' and reform," a sympathy that was sharpened by the wartime fight against fascism. A cadre of writers emerged who held a vision of "a world without prejudice, brutality, political oppression, or economic deprivation" and who sought to produce radio programs that "challenged Americans to reform their own country" (Lenthall, 2007, pp. 192–193).

Shayon moved to CBS as a writer-director in 1942. Under head William Paley, the network was known as an innovator in "sustaining," or non-sponsored, programming. It used such programs to demonstrate public service and discourage attempts to stiffen government regulation (Barnouw, 1968, pp. 55–73). Shayon worked on many such programs during the war. In one 1945 show he recounted the misery he had witnessed during an overseas tour of war zones. "My country, you're young and you're brave and you've got power and wealth," said Shayon's narrator. "But the world is closing in on you fast. We must roll up our sleeves and dig into our hearts and our pockets . . . to clean out the swamps of the world." At about the same time, Shayon publicly chided the radio industry in *Variety*: "Keep on selling soap, boys, that's right and proper, but for God's sake give a little thought and network time to selling peace" (Shayon Papers, box 14, folder 72).

In 1946, Shayon wrote *Operation Crossroads* under the oversight of Edward R. Murrow, CBS's new vice president of public affairs. The show advocated United Nations control of atomic energy at a time when America alone possessed the bomb. Shayon and CBS recruited a cast including Albert Einstein (Shayon, 2001, pp. 91–100). Archibald MacLeish concluded the show by asserting that the people's collective will should be determined not "by reading the papers" or listening to "an advertising slogan," but "by talking and listening and thinking." That way, Americans could best learn how to live "in a new and greatly threatening, greatly promising world" (Shayon Papers, box 6, folder 34).

Soon after *Operation Crossroads*, CBS announced a new Documentary Unit to produce programs "dealing with major domestic and international issues and involving extraordinary research and preparation" (CBS News Archives). Unit head Robert Heller (1947, p. 11) declared that such ventures represented "the birth of a new kind of journalism, more ambitious, comprehensive and vital than any other effort in print or sound." It quickly generated praise. Charles Siepmann (1947, p. 697) credited the new radio documentaries for showing "us our responsibility for the inhumanity in our society."

Siepmann's approbation was especially significant. He had authored a sharp critique of radio (Siepmann, 1946) and been a consultant for the "Blue Book," the 1946 FCC report that outlined new public service standards to curb radio's rampant commercialism. The report sparked a firestorm of criticism from broadcasters, with Siepmann and others being branded as leftist (Meyer, 1962a, 1962b; Socolow, 2002). At the 1946 National Association of Broadcasters convention, William Paley said the Blue Book represented "the most direct threat made yet by Government to interfere with programming." However, he also acknowledged that broadcasting had engaged in "advertising excesses" and needed to do a better job of policing itself. To that end, he called for "new and sparkling ideas in the presentation of educational, documentary and controversial issues" (Rosen, 1946; Variety, 1946).

Paley's speech came just after the announcement of the new CBS Documentary Unit. The unit offered a riposte to broadcasting's critics: a "new and sparkling" way of addressing "controversial issues," commercial-free and in prime time. Robert Shayon would write and direct the unit's first true production (Bluem, 1965, p. 68). It focused on a subject of controversy both in radio and in the country at large.

## Juvenile Delinquency and Saul Alinsky

One criticism aimed at postwar radio was that it glamorized crime and contributed to juvenile delinquency (Gould, 1947b; New York Times, 1946a). Broadcasters responded by adopting a new code and adding socially conscious storylines to children's programs (Gould, 1947a; Lohman, 1946).

*The Eagle's Brood* was another radio response to widespread concerns about juvenile crime. Attorney General Tom Clark convened a national conference in November 1946 after declaring that the country potentially faced "a wave of delinquency such as never before experienced in its history" (New York Times, 1946b; also Furman 1946). The press amplified such alarms. *Life* published a photo-essay of youths loitering, vandalizing, fighting, stealing, and landing in prison. The magazine asserted that "prevention rests with the parents" (Life, 1946, p. 92).

In *The Eagle's Brood*, Shayon would adopt a broader viewpoint that was heavily influenced by G. Howland Shaw, the chair of an anti-delinquency committee formed out of Attorney General Clark's national conference. Shaw was also on the board of the Industrial Areas Foundation (IAF) of Chicago. Rather than primarily blaming parents for delinquency or relying on child experts to dictate solutions, the IAF advocated the neighborhood council approach of Saul Alinsky (Furman, 1943; Gilbert, 1986; Horwitt, 1989).

Alinsky had co-founded the Back of the Yards Neighborhood Council in one of Chicago's most crime-ridden districts, with the IAF extending the council's work.

Alinsky argued that to fight juvenile crime, one must also fight "the crime of economic insecurity; the crime of poor housing; the crime of inadequate medical care; the crime of prejudice and man's inhumanity to man" (Shayon Papers, box 3, folder 12). That fight had to happen at the grass roots, with community members directing "all of their efforts and collective skill towards the solution of their common problems" (Horwitt, 1989, p. 105). To that end, Alinsky (1946, p. 73) called for additional "people's organizations" like the Back of the Yards council, which he boasted had "bridged all of the economic, social, religious, and political cleavages" in the neighborhood while promoting "responsibility, strength, and human dignity."

Although Alinsky proclaimed himself a radical in his best-selling *Reveille for Radicals*, many found his approach reassuring. The solidly Republican *New York Herald-Tribune* commended the IAF for promoting "uncoerced self-improvement . . . that no government paternalism could supply" (New York Herald-Tribune, 1940). Similarly admiring stories appeared in *Reader's Digest* (Palmer, 1946) and *Woman's Home Companion* (Smith, 1946). In a six-part *Washington Post* series, Agnes Meyer (1945) praised the IAF for promoting "the most powerful upsurge of organized individualism yet to come into being in the U.S.A."

Regardless, according to his biographer (Horwitt, 1989, p. 108), Alinsky's philosophy was consistent with a "left liberal, New Deal agenda"; it stressed that "one questioned authority" and "took the initiative to address community problems." Howland Shaw guided Robert Shayon toward the same philosophy in the making of *The Eagle's Brood*.

## Program Preparation

Shaw organized a nationwide fact-finding trip for Shayon in fall 1946. Shayon visited New York, New Orleans, San Francisco, Los Angeles, Denver, Boston, and Washington, DC; he also toured Alcatraz, a death row cell in the South, and other correctional facilities where he learned of children routinely being flogged. "What I saw and heard cast me deeper and deeper into despair of ever finding a way out of the abysmal social mess," recalled Shayon (2001, p. 103). That changed when he arrived at the final stop that Shaw had arranged for him: a visit with Saul Alinsky in Chicago's Back of the Yards neighborhood. "I lit up like an electric tree," said Shayon, "because in his neighborhood council I saw a vision of hope, of democracy solving its own problems" (Horwitt, 1989, p. 205).

He returned to New York determined to "stir the listener, to unsettle him, to shock, to enlighten, and finally to inspire" (Shayon Papers, box 3, folder 12). Although Shayon (2001, p. 103) had taken "careful, copious notes" while touring America, he had not used a tape recorder; portable audio recording technology in 1946 was still crude and bulky. Furthermore, CBS and NBC still banned airing recordings in most cases, fearing that recordings could undercut their uniquely powerful position as nationwide purveyors of live entertainment (Barnouw, 1968, pp. 109–10, 216–219; Ehrlich, 2006). Programs such as *The Eagle's Brood* were thus akin to what today would be called docudrama. "Reality was simulated and transformed," said Shayon (2001, pp. 101–112), with actors playing real people. The technological limitations could be liberating, encouraging radio writers to "convey socially charged messages" in storylines that "leapt across space and time" (Lenthall, 2007, pp. 178, 197).

Shayon (2001, p. 103) fondly recalled that he had all the time and funding he needed to create *The Eagle's Brood*. However, he was not free of corporate oversight. In a memo to William Paley, Edward R. Murrow said that a few pages of the script had been rewritten to eliminate any "specific reference to press, radio, advertising and other stimuli," thus avoiding implicating the media in fostering delinquency (Shayon Papers, box 3, folder 12).

CBS lawyers similarly directed Shayon to delete critical comments toward radio soap operas and not to mention the names of the cities he had visited (Shayon, 2001, p. 104). When CBS recruited actor Joseph Cotten to play the lead role, producer David O. Selznick excused him from filming a movie on the condition that there would be nothing "attributing juvenile delinquency even inferentially to the effect of motion pictures." At the same time, Selznick acknowledged "the great [publicity] value to me to a gesture on our part towards a juvenile delinquent program" (Shayon Papers, box 3, folder 12).

CBS also seized upon *The Eagle's Brood*'s publicity potential, saying it would present a "picture of civic indifference, official impotence and economic short-sightedness that is destined to shock the average hearer by its straightforward statement of authenticated facts." Network president Frank Stanton wired the mayors of every city with a CBS-affiliated radio station and asked them to listen, and Murrow recorded promotional spots to air on the stations. CBS also announced that the General Federation of Women's Clubs was arranging "town meetings and forums to listen to the broadcast and to discuss, immediately afterward, ways of implementing the program's conclusions" (Shayon Papers, box 3, folder 12; CBS News Archives).

Shayon (2001, pp. 104–105) recruited actor Luther Adler at the last moment to play a character modeled on Saul Alinsky. The live broadcast was scheduled for March 5, 1947.

## The Broadcast

*The Eagle's Brood* was preceded by an announcement that *Information Please*, a commercially sponsored quiz show, would not be heard that evening. Then dramatic music was interspersed with the reenactment of a crime: "three husky

American youngsters on the prowl," who were beating and robbing a drunk on a city waterfront. "From Boston to Butte, Hartford to Houston, Savannah to Spokane, more and more children are climbing the crescendo of a wave of crime, brutality, violence, and murder," an announcer intoned. "This is what is happening to all of us and to our children—today."

Joseph Cotten then assumed Shayon's role and retraced his nationwide journey, with frequent and at times intentionally jarring shifts in time and location. First came a youth canteen in "the Negro quarter in an East Coast city" at Halloween. A 15-year-old gang member related how he already had survived two shootings and how the local gangs arranged "rumbles." At heart, however, the youths were "just like any other American youngsters" in "wanting normal fun," according to a recreation worker. Next there was a visit to another Eastern city and a 20-year-old mother who had deliberately burned her 3-year-old son with an iron. The local press had made no effort to probe the woman's unhappy background and honed in only on the most sensational details of the case. "A good witch hunt now and then is like a bloodletting," an official said. "If you ask me—it's a good deal."

Cotten's narrator then recounted a grim series of experiences across the South: a juvenile court judge who "plays God with children's lives for votes," a prison farm of "unspeakably filthy camps and dungeons" where youths mixed with "murderers, thieves, dope addicts, [and] perverts," and, worst of all, a death row with four teens awaiting execution. Over the voice of a deputy describing how the county was investing in "the most modern improvements" to its death chamber, Cotten's narrator expressed his thoughts with mounting fury: "It didn't matter that this was America. . . . Nothing mattered except this man's blind, stupid, blasphemous, incredible pride in his plaster paint and portable electric chair."

It was little better out West. A visit to the penitentiary at "the Rock" revealed that some of the nation's worst criminals were barely out of their teens. Cotten's narrator ticked off a host of maladies: "ignorant, careless, or incapable parents, rich or poor," "lack of jobs," "indifferent citizens," materialistic social values. There seemed to be no solution: "It's a merry-go-round. Where do we get off?"

Finally, the narrator arrived in a "city in the Midwest," where he "met a man who answered my question." That was Luther Adler's Alinsky-inspired character, who declared that to make change happen, "we're going to have to do it with our own hands, brains, money and imagination." A merchant, Mexican immigrant, union organizer, teacher, police captain, and war veteran took turns praising the local neighborhood council. "That's why we've got to have Neighborhood Councils everywhere in America," said Adler. Not only could Americans attack the root causes of delinquency, they also could recognize their common lot and mission. "Our children are our only REAL assets," Adler concluded as music swelled underneath him. "Our FUTURE is 'THE EAGLE'S BROOD'" (Shayon, 1947, 1952).

Note how the author uses a variety of different primary and secondary sources of evidence to construct his argument and interpretation of *The Eagle's Brood*. The following section also addresses several types of responses that were received to the radio broadcast.

## Response

Shayon (2001, p. 105) recalled the immediate impact of *The Eagle's Brood* as being "theatrical," with CBS's switchboard flooded with calls. Edward R. Murrow said the network received "in the vicinity of 3,500 to 4,000 letters" and reports of several neighborhood councils being formed ("What should be," 1947, p. 84). Alinsky wrote to a friend that it was "as fine and as outstanding a public acknowledgement of our work and philosophy as we can ever expect to get" (Alinsky Papers, folder 173).

*New York Times* critic Jack Gould (1947c) proclaimed of *The Eagle's Brood* that "the art of broadcasting found its voice and lifted it as one truly come of age." *Time* commended CBS for preempting commercial shows and showing "that when radio has something to say about an important problem, and says it intelligently—people will listen" (Time, 1947, p. 93). Others similarly praised the network for employing "radio's supreme capabilities for dramaturgy, sound effects, and musical compulsion" in making important issues "vital and significant" (Williams, 1947, p. 62), and for demonstrating public-spiritedness on the part of a "radio industry [that] has not been notable for providing such leadership" (Frankel, 1947, p. 304). A magazine executive wrote to CBS's Frank Stanton that *The Eagle's Brood* had done "more for radio to win over its most severe critics than almost anything I can remember in the last decade" (Shayon Papers, box 3, folder 13).

The praise was not unqualified. Some who otherwise liked the program demurred that it "over-sentimentalized" delinquency (Crosby, 1947), and that its neighborhood councils agenda alone would not eliminate the problem (Rosen, 1947). One critic noted that "to realize the utopia described in 'The Eagle's Brood' would take more money than citizens are now spending" (Shayon Papers, box 27, folder 132). The liberal *PM* went further in scolding the program for not delving more into the systemic inequities underlying delinquency (Peck, 1947).

CBS's scheduling of *The Eagle's Brood* also raised some eyebrows. It achieved a 6.4 audience rating, which compared favorably with what CBS's commercial shows had received in the same time period and especially with the numbers that past documentaries had earned (Williams, 1947). However, the program aired against Bing Crosby's popular show, and one critic said those who should have heard the documentary were instead listening to Crosby (Shayon Papers, box 115, scrapbook). Edward R. Murrow and CBS countered such criticisms by asserting that the program still had aired in prime time and that 42 percent of those who had tuned in did not ordinarily listen to the network's programs during that time slot ("Radio production," 1947; Wilson, 1948).

Nevertheless, the concern remained that, as Charles Siepmann (1947, p. 698) put it, "Much of the best in radio today goes down the drain, unheard and unappreciated." CBS's Robert Heller was determined to prevent that. "Every documentary should be tested by radio research," Heller (1947; 1952, p. 386) declared; otherwise, there would be "no blueprint for improvement" in the documentarian's task of "extending the horizons of constructive citizenship." So it was that CBS employed such tools in studying *The Eagle's Brood*.

### Ernest Dichter and "Big Annie"

The Documentary Unit had been formed during what *The New Yorker* called a "frenzy" surrounding radio research, with CBS a key player (Taylor, 1947, p. 32). Robert Shayon would work with both motivation researcher Ernest Dichter and with "Big Annie," the "Program Analyzer" invented by CBS president Frank Stanton and Paul Lazarsfeld.

In time, Ernest Dichter would be acknowledged as a pioneer in applying psychoanalytic techniques to marketing while also being branded as part of a dangerous breed of "hidden persuaders" (Packard, 1957; Stern, 2004). In 1946, however, he was still a little-known CBS researcher from Vienna. Shayon (2001, pp. 92–93) hired him to conduct interviews with ordinary citizens during preparation of *Operation Crossroads*. The findings were that "the American mind was schizophrenic on the subject of the atom bomb," fearful of its destructive force but intrigued by atomic energy's potential. Shayon thus designed the program as "a national therapy session on radio." In Dichter's words, it aimed to bring the listener "face to face with the inescapable facts of reality and offer him not only the tools with which to solve his problem, but also the encouragement to solve it" (Klein, 1946).

As Shayon began work on *The Eagle's Brood*, he again turned to Dichter, who suggested that no "remedies in the forms of clubs and agencies, etc., no matter how helpful and realistic, should be suggested as final means." Instead, the program should impress upon the listener that delinquency was "proof of the wrong reality of your own life. It is unreasonable and unrealistic to assume that you are not your brother's keeper" (Shayon Papers, box 3, folder 12). Eventually, Shayon (2001, p. 102) decided against using Dichter's "therapy" approach for *The Eagle's Brood*, believing it "too abstract" and "not dramatic enough." Its "no remedies" recommendation also was not consistent with Shayon's advocacy of neighborhood councils.

Once *The Eagle's Brood* aired, Shayon again came into contact with CBS's research department in the form of the Lazarsfeld–Stanton Program Analyzer. Frank Stanton had come to CBS as a researcher himself and quickly risen through the corporate ranks. He met Paul Lazarsfeld through the latter's association with what would become the Bureau of Applied Social Research at Columbia University. The two invented an instrument to measure listener response to radio, and by 1940 CBS was using it to study a wide range of programs (Levy, 1982; Sills, 1996).

The Program Analyzer provided two buttons to each member of a panel of listeners. The listeners pressed green buttons upon hearing anything they liked in a program and red buttons for anything they disliked. Their collective responses were recorded on a sort of polygraph from the program's start to its finish. The bigger version of the Analyzer could track 100 listeners at once and was dubbed "Big Annie" (Hallonquist & Peatman, 1947). On the basis of their studies, CBS researchers asserted that educational programs "must be built with real show-manship" (Katz, 1944, p. 266). Certain content could be dangerous; unlike with a movie or play, "very rarely will anyone continue to listen to a radio program once he has become confused or annoyed" (Hallonquist & Suchman, 1979, p. 292).

CBS used "Big Annie" to test a recording of *The Eagle's Brood* soon after the show aired. The researchers reported that it "was very successful in arousing listener concern about the problem of juvenile delinquency"; the Program Analyzer score was "exceptionally high for both sponsored and sustaining pro-grams." In the minute-by-minute tracking of responses, however, "the out-standing low point" came in the description of the teens awaiting execution in the death chamber (Shayon Papers, box 3, folder 12; Wilson, 1948).

"I had deliberately written that scene to shock the audience," recalled Shayon (2001, p. 108). When he asked the researchers whether he should have omitted it, they replied that the decision was up to him. Still, Shayon said it pointed to "a bone of sharp contention between the psychologists and the artists who said, 'Very often I want the audience to hate somebody.'" There also was the concern that CBS and the other networks were using research more to promote themselves than to improve their programming. Looking back at his partnership with Ernest Dichter, Shayon lamented that more had not been done to "bring together the world of the creative broadcaster with the social scientist" in studying programs' impact on audiences (Shayon Papers, box 77, folder 2).

## Aftermath

Radio documentarians and social scientists did continue collaborating in the immediate aftermath of *The Eagle's Brood*. The CBS Documentary Unit produced additional programs on subjects ranging from atomic energy to race relations, and they again were tested by the network research department (Wilson, 1948). A Michigan sociology professor (Kercher, 1947) examined the reaction of Kalamazoo listeners to *The Eagle's Brood* and another CBS documentary, and Charles Siepmann and a colleague studied a civil rights program that aired on the Mutual Broadcasting System (Siepmann & Reisberg, 1948–1949).

Those studies reported positive findings, including "almost universal expressions of approval" regarding *The Eagle's Brood* (Kercher, 1947, p. 408). However, Kercher (p. 410) noted that stations seemed to air documentaries only to "lessen the public pressure for this sort of thing." Siepmann and Reisberg (1948–1949) found that fewer than half of Mutual's affiliated stations had both aired and promoted the civil rights documentary. Critic Saul Carson (1949, pp. 73–74) similarly observed that the "CBS Documentary Unit was never given a regular time and a definite cycle on the basis of which to build an audience." With the documentary appearing at irregular times and intervals, "it will most often be just another catch-as-catch-can entry in the broadcaster's 'public service' dossier."

In fact, the radio documentary soon declined precipitously as a priority at CBS. Writer Norman Corwin recalled that by 1948 William Paley was urging him to write for a broader audience; otherwise, said Paley, "we're not really making the best use of our talent, our time and our equipment." Paley also warned Corwin of a growing "wave of reaction" against the network's perceived liberalism. Not long afterward, Corwin left CBS (Barnouw, 1968, pp. 241–242). Robert Heller also soon was gone. As for Robert Shayon, he had moved on to develop the CBS historical radio series *You Are There*. In July 1949, however, the network fired him, along with some 175 others, in a budgetary move (Billboard, 1949; Variety, 1949). The following year, Shayon, Heller and Corwin all were branded as communist sympathizers in *Red Channels*, along with Luther Adler from *The Eagle's Brood*. Heller left the country (Barnouw, 1968, pp. 265–273; Sperber, 1986, pp. 366–377).

Shayon was stunned at his *Red Channels* listing and subsequent blacklisting. He had addressed an October 1947 Progressive Citizens of America conference where he defended the freedom "of minority opinion to criticize, to challenge, to experiment in its proper quest for new phases of political, economic and cultural truth" (Shayon Papers, box 18, folder 83). Such episodes proved his undoing. He pleaded his case to an author of *Red Channels*, and by 1953 he had removed himself from the blacklist. A long tenure as critic and professor followed. Nevertheless, Shayon (2001, pp. 143–145) said he experienced "torment" for decades, believing that *Red Channels* had led directly to his ouster from CBS and destroyed his broadcasting career. It was only years later that he realized that the Red-baiting book had not appeared until the year after he was fired and that William Paley simply "had made a routine business decision" by cutting costs in radio to help underwrite the transition to television. "I was neither victim nor hero," Shayon concluded. "I was a human being, as all of us were, trapped in the tangle of peculiar times."

---

In the final section, Ehrlich goes beyond the recounting of historical evidence to evaluate and interpret the meanings of the information he has gathered. In his conclusion, note how he returns to a discussion of Carey's call as a way to help make sense of the evidence.

---

## Discussion

The postwar era of American broadcasting both made and unmade the "radio utopia" that *The Eagle's Brood* epitomized. As was observed at the time, ventures such as the CBS Documentary Unit were "a partial answer to the insistence of the Federal Communications Commission, enunciated in the so-called 'Blue Book,' that radio devote more and better time to programs in the public interest" (Siepmann & Reisberg, 1948–1949, p. 650). According to Shayon (2001, p. 144), such programs "made a good impression on opinion leaders. Radio could be touted as a public service medium—the losses in commercial time sales were sustainable." However, the postwar consumer boom, the expensive shift from radio to television, and the increasingly reactionary political climate soon meant that "documentaries could be thrown overboard." That is consistent with other historical studies that have noted the key influence of government regulation and other institutional pressures on journalism and network documentary (Curtin, 1995; Nord, 1988; Raphael, 2005).

The networks' investment in research reflected institutional priorities. Those such as Robert Heller (1947) saw that research as helping radio make "its richest contribution to the democratic life." Others saw it differently. According to Levy (1982, p. 30), the Lazarsfeld–Stanton Program Analyzer "symbolized the marriage of convenience between mass media administrators and the academic community." For academics such as Paul Lazarsfeld, it furthered a social science that later would be sharply criticized for serving commercial ends and for downplaying, if not grossly underestimating, the media's impact on society (Gitlin, 1978). For CBS's Frank Stanton, it was "a razzle-dazzle thing to give to Hollywood and the advertisers," as he said years later (Smith, 1990, p. 153). The Analyzer's discouragement of that which "confused or annoyed" listeners, including abrupt shifts in tone or place, worked against radio's most creative impulses (Hallonquist & Suchman, 1979, pp. 292–296; Lenthall, 2007). Similarly, Ernest Dichter had focused on individual listeners' psyches as opposed to wide-ranging social remedies, and he soon turned his attention to marketing consumer goods.

In addition, criticism could be aimed at *The Eagle's Brood* itself. Shayon acknowledged that the program's style was deliberately melodramatic and "flamboyant" (Skutch, 1998, p. 177). It did not match the artistry of docudramas such as Norman Corwin's *On a Note of Triumph*, which had aired upon the Nazi surrender in 1945 and which was later recalled as a "high-water mark" in radio (Barnouw, 1968, p. 213). As for *The Eagle's Brood*'s delinquency focus, Gilbert (1986) has argued that the postwar fears about delinquency reflected less an actual increase in juvenile crime than they did a concern that the war had undermined the family and public morality; they also were part of a longstanding cycle whereby officials and pundits have periodically deplored the impact of mass culture on American youth. Saul Alinsky's community-organizing response to social ills also would come under scrutiny. Just as *The Eagle's Brood* was criticized for not addressing the structural inequities in society, Alinsky was lambasted for not promoting a broader, more truly radical program (Horwitt, 1989, pp. 532–536).

Given all that, how might *The Eagle's Brood* still be seen as an "exercise in poetry and utopian politics" *à la* Carey (1987, p. 14)? The program captured the optimism that followed the end of a cataclysmic war. Shayon (2001, p. 91) noted that those today "who view the world with a more cynical realpolitik attitude" may find such an outlook naïve. Still, it was genuine: "idealism in the flush of military triumph over evil—amid the sense that a new world was about to be born. The mood swept the allied world and gripped many of us in radio." The response of Shayon and his fellow documentarians was not toward "a journalism of information, fact, objectivity, and publicity" (Carey, 1987, p. 14), nor was it aimed at "finding a way for experts to gain effective voices in their mass society" (Lenthall, 2007, p. 153). It was instead directed toward a subjective, emotional appeal that Americans from all walks of life accept their common responsibility to remake their country for the better and clean out "the stagnant pools of ignorance, indifference, [and] injustice," as *The Eagle's Brood* put it (Shayon, 1952, p. 402).

That appeal was frankly utopian in the tradition of the American "reformist Left" that Richard Rorty (1998, pp. 43, 106) said was active for much of the twentieth century and that encompassed "lots of people who called themselves 'communists' and 'socialists,' and lots of people who never dreamed of calling themselves either." What they shared were "utopian dreams—dreams of an ideally decent and civilized society." In his 1947 speech to the Progressive Citizens of America conference, Shayon expressed confidence that "the concept of an American democracy ever-expanding rather than contracting the flow of its benefits to all the people" would eventually triumph (Shayon Papers, box 18, folder 83).

Of course, that speech helped get Shayon blacklisted, and to extricate himself, in 1953 he reluctantly issued a public statement declaring that "unintentionally and unwittingly, I helped the Communists in their policy of creating and intensify[ing] conflicts and tensions in our society" and of promoting a phony "dream of a materialistic Utopia" (Shayon Papers, box 114, folder 6). Thus did Shayon (2001, pp. 140–145) eventually come to see himself as "neither victim nor hero" and as "trapped in the tangle of peculiar times."

It is precisely such "moral and political ambiguities of journalism" that Carey (1997b, p. 109) said press historians should seek to uncover in contrast to Whiggish histories of expanding press freedom and professionalism. Postwar radio documentaries were able to air because they temporarily served the interests of the broadcasting industry and its captains, and they aired at irregular and less than ideal times. *The Eagle's Brood* was actively discouraged from turning a critical eye on the media, and its embrace of neighborhood councils could be critiqued as a comparatively safe approach to juvenile delinquency, as shown by the way in which even conservative media outlets applauded Alinsky's methods. The program's very focus on delinquency could be seen as partly reflecting a moral panic over perceived threats to so-called family values. Once television and McCarthyism took hold, such programs went into eclipse altogether.

At the same time, Carey (1997b, p. 109) also warned against what he termed an "anti-Whig interpretation of the press" reflecting a "contemptuous view from the academy toward journalism." Ettema and Glasser (1994, p. 5) similarly have questioned those who assert "in a tone of ironic knowingness that the media are inevitably the means to hegemonic power rather than democratic empowerment." Contrary to such views and assertions, *The Eagle's Brood* still stands as an exemplar of a commercial broadcasting network—the very embodiment of the mainstream, corporate media—granting free airtime to the theme of democratic empowerment. Such programs were enabled by institutional self-interest; at the same time, they reflected the hopes and aspirations of not only their writers but also the moguls in charge of the networks that aired them. Shayon (2001, p. 147) observed that William Paley and NBC's David Sarnoff had both served in the war; for a brief time afterward, "the smell of wartime clung to the men in the grey flannel suits, and in their civvies, they continued to honor the national purpose."

Journalism studies should continue to be sensitive to just such historical moments when flux and ambiguity in the institutional and cultural environment make room for innovative, public-spirited work, including that produced by the major media, which are often seen as having been traditionally inhospitable to such work. Scholars ought to maintain a keen focus on the "exercise of power" during such moments, just as Nord (1988, p. 11) argued; at the same time, they should avoid the pitfalls of "anti-Whiggism" or what Schudson (1997, pp. 470–471) describes as "declinism": the notion that the press grows steadily worse over time.

In addition, scholars should examine journalistic forms beyond the routine daily newspaper report (Carey, 1997b, pp. 109–110). For example, audio documentary is a robust and growing field, taking advantage of relatively inexpensive recorders and desktop computer software. Prisoners, teenagers and others have begun producing their own stories that help bridge divisions of race, class and age. The Internet allows easy distribution of those stories and grants them a permanence that radio work has not enjoyed until recently (Ehrlich, 2003). Radio documentaries past and present thus have been said to have nudged broadcast journalism closer "to the utopian ideal that we use these airwaves to share our stories as we try to understand each other better, to not be afraid of each other, to come a little closer together" (Allison, 2001, p.16). In such examples across different media, genres and eras, one can find glimmers of "an ideally decent and civilized society" (Rorty, 1998, p. 106) and a poetic journalism rooted in hope.

## Historical Methods Exercises

1. Pick a journal article based on historical research. Look at all of the footnotes, endnotes and references and evaluate the types of evidence that were used. How does the author use primary and secondary source material? What concepts or theoretical framework does the author draw on to help frame her or his story?
2. Spend a day at a community archive and try to find as much research as possible on a local event that has been celebrated for at least twenty years.
3. Choose a topic that you are interested in studying. See what types of records are available online at the United States' National Archives or through another online archive.

## References

Alinsky, Saul D. (1946). *Reveille for radicals.* Chicago, IL: University of Chicago Press.
Allison, Jay. (2001). Radio storytelling builds community on-air and off. *Nieman Reports, 55* (3), 16–17.
Barnouw, Erik. (1968). *The golden web: A history of broadcasting in the United States, 1933–1953.* New York: Oxford University Press.
Berger, Arthur Asa. (2000). *Media and communication research methods: An introduction to qualitative and quantitative approaches.* Thousand Oaks, CA: Sage.
Billboard. (1949, July 9). Shayon, Roland among 175 out in 1½ million CBS slash. *Billboard,* p 6.
Bliss, Edward Jr. (1991). *Now the News.* New York: Columbia University Press.
Bluem, A. William. (1965). *Documentary in American television: Form, function, method.* New York: Hastings.

Brennen, Bonnie, & Hardt, Hanno (Eds.). (2011). *American journalism history reader: Critical and primary texts.* New York: Routledge.

Carey, James W. (1974). The problem of journalism history. *Journalism History, 1* (1), 3–5, 27.

Carey, James W. (1987, March/April). The press and the public discourse. *The Center Magazine,* pp. 4–16.

Carey, James W. (1997a). The problem of journalism history. In Eve Stryker Munson & Catherine A. Warren (Eds.), *James Carey: A critical reader* (pp. 86–94). Minneapolis: University of Minnesota Press.

Carey, James W. (1997b). "Putting the world at peril": A conversation with James W. Carey. In Eve Stryker Munson & Catherine A. Warren (Eds.), *James Carey: A critical reader* (pp. 95–116). Minneapolis: University of Minnesota Press.

Carr, David. (2012, March 20). Theater, disguised as real journalism. *New York Times.* Retrieved from http://www.nytimes.com/2012/03/19/business/media/theater-disguised-up-as-real-journalism.html?scp=1&sq=ira%20glass&st=cse.

Carson, Saul. (1949). Notes toward an examination of the radio documentary. *Hollywood Quarterly, 4* (1), 69–74.

Crosby, John. (1947, March 11). Radio in review: "The Eagle's Brood." *New York Herald-Tribune,* p. 25.

Curtin, Michael. (1995). *Redeeming the wasteland: Television documentary and Cold War politics.* New Brunswick, NJ: Rutgers University Press.

Darnton, Robert. (2009). From *The great cat massacre and other episodes in French cultural history.* In John Tosh (Ed.), *Historians on history* (2nd edn, pp. 324–330). Harlow, UK: Pearson Longman.

Donnelly, Mark, & Norton, Claire. (2011). *Doing history.* London: Routledge.

Douglas, Susan J. (1999). *Listening in: Radio and the American imagination.* New York: Times Books.

Ehrlich, Matthew. (2003). Poetry on the margins: *Ghetto Life 101, Remorse* and the new radio documentary. *Journalism: Theory, Practice and Criticism, 4* (4), 423–439.

Ehrlich, Matthew C. (2006). A pathfinding radio documentary series: Norman Corwin's One World flight. *American Journalism, 23* (4), 35–59.

Estrin, Daniel. (2012, March 20) Einstein papers to be posted online. *Milwaukee Journal Sentinel,* p. A4.

Ettema, James S., & Glasser, Theodore L. (1994). The irony in (and of) journalism: A case study in the moral language of democracy. *Journal of Communication, 44* (2), 5–28,

Frankel, Lou. (1947, March 15). In one ear. *The Nation,* p. 304.

Furman, Bess. (1943, December 2). Urges new agency on child welfare. *New York Times,* p. 24.

Furman, Bess. (1946, November 21). Agencies map fight on teen-age crime. *New York Times,* p. 36.

Gilbert, James. (1986). *A cycle of outrage.* New York: Oxford University Press.

Gitlin, Todd. (1978). Media sociology: The dominant paradigm. *Theory and Society, 6* (2), 205–253.

Gould, Jack. (1947a, September 19). Adoption of code in radio expected. *New York Times,* p. 46.

Gould, Jack. (1947b, March 2). Children's programs: Protests on crime shows raise subject anew. *New York Times,* p. 75.

Gould, Jack. (1947c, March 9). *The eagle's brood. New York Times,* p. 11.

Hall, Stuart. (1989). Cultural studies: Two paradigms. In Tony Bennett et al. (Eds.), *Culture, ideology and social process: A reader* (pp. 19–37). London: Batsford in association with the Open University Press.

Hallonquist, Tore, & Peatman, John Gray. (1947). Diagnosing your radio program. In O. Joe Olson (Ed.), *Education on the air: Seventeenth yearbook of the Institute for Education by Radio* (pp. 463–474). Columbus: Ohio State University.

Hallonquist, Tore, & Suchman, Edward. (1979). Listening to the listener. In Paul F. Lazarsfeld & Frank N. Stanton (Eds.), *Radio research 1942–1943* (pp. 265–334). New York: Arno.

Hardt, Hanno. (1989). The foreign-language press in American press history. *Journal of Communication, 39* (2), 114–131.

Heller, Robert P. (1947, October 26). Reporting by radio. *New York Times,* p. 11.

Heller, Robert P. (1952). The dynamic documentary. In Max Wylie (Ed.), *Radio and television writing* (pp. 382–386). New York: Rinehart.

Hilmes, Michele, & Loviglio, Jason (Eds.). (2002). *Radio reader: Essays in the cultural history of radio.* New York: Routledge.

Horwitt, Sanford D. (1989). *Let them call me rebel: Saul Alinsky: His life and legacy.* New York: Alfred A. Knopf.

Jameson, Fredric. (1971). *Marxism and form.* Princeton, NJ: Princeton University Press.

Katz, Oscar. (1944). The Program Analyzer as a tool. In Josephine H. MacLatchy (Ed.), *Education on the air: Fifteenth yearbook of the Institute for Education by Radio* (pp. 265–269). Columbus: Ohio State University.

Kellner, Hans. (1989). *Language and historical representation: Getting the story crooked.* Madison: University of Wisconsin Press.

Kercher, Leonard C. (1947). Social problems on the air: An audience study. *Public Opinion Quarterly, 11* (3), 402–411.

Klein, Judith. (1946, June 16). Entertainment-education plan urged for radio. *New York Herald-Tribune,* p. 5B.

Lenthall, Bruce. (2006). *Radio's America.* Chicago, IL: University of Chicago Press.

Levy, Mark R. (1982). The Lazarsfeld–Stanton Program Analyzer: An historical note. *Journal of Communication, 32* (4), pp. 30–38.

Lichty, Lawrence W. (2004). Documentary programs on U.S. radio. In Christopher H. Sterling (Ed.), *Museum of broadcast communications encyclopedia of radio* (vol. 1, pp. 474–477). New York: Fitzroy Dearborn.

Life. (1946, April 8). Juvenile delinquency: War's insecurity lifts youthful crime 100%. *Life,* pp. 83–93.

Lohman, Sidney. (1946, April 14). One thing and another. *New York Times,* p. 55.

McDowell, W.H. (2002). *Historical research: A guide.* London: Longman.

Meyer, Agnes. (1945, June 4). Orderly revolution: The Back of the Yards Neighborhood Council. *Washington Post,* p. 9.

Meyer, Richard J. (1962a). "The Blue Book." *Journal of Broadcasting, 6,* 197–207.

Meyer, Richard J. (1962b). Reaction to "The Blue Book." *Journal of Broadcasting, 6,* 295–312.

Nerone, John. (1993). Theory and history. *Communication Theory, 3* (2), 148–157.

Nevins, Alan. (1963). *Gateway to history.* Chicago, IL: Quadrangle.

New York Herald-Tribune. (1940, August 21). Democracy in the "Jungle." *New York Herald-Tribune,* p. 20.

New York Times. (1946a, April 14). Radio's influence on children. *New York Times,* p. 55.

New York Times. (1946b, May 12). Clark fears era of lawless youth. *New York Times,* p. 15.

Nord, David Paul. (1988). A plea for journalism history. *Journalism History, 15* (1), 8–15.

Nord, David Paul. (1989). The nature of historical research. In Guido H. Stempel III & Bruce H. Westley (Eds.), *Research methods in mass communication* (pp. 290–315). Englewood Cliffs, NJ: Prentice Hall.

Packard, Vance. (1957). *The hidden persuaders.* New York: David McKay.

Palmer, Gretta. (1946, March) Back of the Yards: Democracy with teeth. *Reader's Digest,* pp. 123–126.

Peck, Seymour. (1947, March). "The Eagle's Brood" gives new importance to radio. *PM,* p. 19.

Radio documentaries take listeners into dark corners. (2001). *Nieman Reports, 55* (3), 13–15.

Radio production section meeting. (1947). In O. Joe Olson (Ed.), *Education on the air: Seventeenth yearbook of the Institute for Education by Radio* (pp. 380–391). Columbus: Ohio State University.

Raphael, Chad. (2005). *Investigated reporting: Muckrakers, regulators, and the struggle over television documentary.* Urbana: University of Illinois Press.

Rorty, Richard. (1998). *Achieving our country: Leftist thought in twentieth-century America.* Cambridge, MA: Harvard University Press.

Rosen, George. (1946, October 24). Radio must reform—or else. *Variety,* p. 90.

Rosen, George. (1947, March 12). Juve problem (the nation's canker) unveiled by CBS in notable broadcast. *Variety,* p. 46.

Schudson, Michael. (1991). Media contexts: Historical approaches to communication studies. In Klaus Bruhn Jensen & Nicholas W. Jankowski (Eds.), *A handbook of qualitative methodologies for mass communication research* (pp. 175–189). London: Routledge.

Schudson, Michael. (1997). Toward a troubleshooting manual for journalism history. *Journalism and Mass Communication Quarterly, 74* (3), 463–476.

Shayon, Robert Lewis. (1947). *The eagle's brood* (radio program). Memphis, TN: Radio Program Archive, University of Memphis.

Shayon, Robert Lewis. (1952). "The eagle's brood." In Max Wylie (Ed.), *Radio and television writing* (pp. 386–406). New York: Rinehart.

Shayon, Robert Lewis. (2001). *Odyssey in prime time.* Philadelphia, PA: Waymark.

Siepmann, Charles A. (1946). *Radio's second chance.* Boston, MA: Little, Brown.

Siepmann, Charles A. (1947, December 27). Radio starts to grow up. *The Nation,* pp. 697–698.

Siepmann, Charles A., & Reisberg, Sidney. (1948–1949). "To secure these rights": Coverage of a radio documentary. *Public Opinion Quarterly, 12* (4), 649–658.

Sills, David L. (1996). Stanton, Lazarsfeld, and Merton: Pioneers in communication research. In Everette E. Dennis & Ellen Wartella (Eds.), *American communication research: The remembered history* (pp. 105–116). Mahwah, NJ: Lawrence Erlbaum.

Skutch, Ira (Ed.). (1998). *Five directors: The golden years of radio.* Lanham, MD: Scarecrow.

Smith, Helena Huntington. (1946, May). We did it ourselves. *Woman's Home Companion,* pp. 24, 78–79.

Smith, Maryann Yodelis. (1989). The method of history. In Guido H. Stempel III & Bruce H. Westley (Eds.), *Research methods in mass communication* (pp. 316–330). Englewood Cliffs, NJ: Prentice Hall.

Smith, Sally Bedell. (1990). *In all his glory: The life and times of William S. Paley.* New York: Simon & Schuster.

Socolow, Michael J. (2002). Questioning advertising's influence over American radio: The Blue Book controversy of 1945–1947. *Journal of Radio Studies, 9* (2), 282–302.

Sperber, A. M. (1986). *Murrow: His life and times.* New York: Freundlich.

Sterling, Christopher H.. & Keith, Michael C. (2006). Where have all the historians gone? A challenge to researchers. *Journal of Broadcasting and Electronic Media, 50* (2), 345–357.

Stern, Barbara B. (2004). The importance of being Ernest: Commemorating Dichter's contribution to advertising research. *Journal of Advertising Research, 44* (2), 165–169.

Taylor, Robert Lewis. (1947, January 18). Let's find out. *New Yorker,* pp. 32–42.

Time. (1947, March 17). Between the ears. *Time,* pp. 92–93.

Tosh, John. (2009). Introduction. In John Tosh (Ed.). *Historians on history* (2nd edn, pp. 1–16). Harlow, UK: Pearson Longman.

Variety. (1946, October 23). Paley's primer on programming. *Variety,* p. 90.

Variety. (1949, July 6). CBS streamlining axes Shayon, six asst. directors; Chester heads news. *Variety,* pp. 28, 36.

What should be the criteria for broadcasting in the public interest, convenience and necessity? (1947). In O. Joe Olson (Ed.), *Education on the air: Seventeenth yearbook of the Institute for Education by Radio* (pp. 67–85). Columbus: Ohio State University.

White, Hayden. (1978). *Tropics of discourse: Essays on cultural criticism.* Baltimore, MD: Johns Hopkins University Press.

Williams, Albert N. (1947, April). "Eagle's brood." *Saturday Review,* pp. 62–63.

Williams, Raymond. (1974). *Television: Technology and cultural form.* London: Fontana.

Williams, Raymond. (1989). *Resources of hope: Culture, democracy, socialism.* London: Verso.

Wilson, Elmo C. (1948). The effectiveness of documentary broadcasts. *Public Opinion Quarterly, 12* (1), 19–29.

Zelizer, Barbie. (2004). *Taking journalism seriously.* Thousand Oaks, CA: Sage.

# CHAPTER 6

# Oral History

*Who built Thebes of the seven gates? In the books you will find the name of kings. Did the kings haul up the lumps of rock? And Babylon, many times demolished. Who raised it up so many times? In what houses of gold-glittering Lima did the builders live? Where, the evening that the Wall of China was finished, did the masons go?*
— Bertolt Brecht, "Questions from a Worker Who Reads"

Until the twentieth century, the study of history focused primarily on the lives and the struggles of the powerful. Historians chronicled the experiences of religious, military, economic and political leaders while the lives of ordinary working people were rarely considered.

Even when historians tried to understand the point of view of workers, it was often difficult to access information about their lives. While all kinds of documentary evidence such as legal records, letters and diaries existed about the experiences of the wealthy and powerful, and were held in archives and libraries, most of the written records about everyday people were not saved. For example, the thousands of letters written by John and Abigail Adams have been carefully preserved as part of the Adams family papers and are housed in the Massachusetts Historical Society in Boston. David McCullough (2008) used these letters along with family papers and diaries for his recent *John Adams* biography and the subsequent HBO mini-series. In contrast, most of the correspondence of non-famous colonist families no longer exists because these documents were not saved, preserved and/or archived.

While historians may lack sufficient archival documentation about the experiences of everyday people, the method of oral history helps to recover important information about their lives. Through the use of open-ended depth interviews that are usually tape-recorded, oral historians collect "reminiscences, accounts and interpretations of events" (Hoffman, 1996, p. 88) that can go beyond official records to give us a more nuanced understanding of the past. In addition, during the interview process, oral historians often recover photographs, newspaper articles, letters and other documentary evidence that people have saved over the years. Because most of these materials have not been archived, they are often unknown to historians; yet, this documentary evidence can provide important research information as well as relevant context for the life stories of working people who lived at a specific place and time.

The method of oral history was initially used to augment existing archival research and to fill in the gaps in the life stories of elite members of society. However, during the 1960s social historians began to raise important questions about the role of history, and a populist vision of the past from the "bottom up" emerged. Oral history began to be used to preserve the life experiences of individuals who did not have the time or the ability to write their own stories, "to radically alter historical practice by bringing ordinary people into the study of history" (Grele, 1991, p. 243). Since the 1960s, oral history has been used to give voice to otherwise voiceless individuals and groups in society. According to Paul Thompson (1990), in his seminal book *The Voice of the Past*, oral history not only challenges the official version of history, but by emphasizing the stories of "the under-classes, the unprivileged, and the defeated" (p. 6) it may also create a richer, more diverse and more authentic construction of the past.

For most of the twentieth century, historical work in media studies primarily focused on institutional aspects of the field, chronicling the histories of major newspapers, magazines, broadcasting stations, advertising agencies and public relations firms. These studies were augmented with biographies of founders, owners and publishers of media properties. While these histories emphasized ownership and property, they did not tell us much about the writers, reporters, photographers, copywriters and others who worked for these media outlets (Hardt & Brennen, 1995). However, in recent years oral histories have been used to help us understand the working conditions, expectations and experiences of rank-and-file media workers and to provide us with a more complete understanding of the field. These days, while researchers still focus on its emancipatory potential, the method of oral history is also being used in popular culture to provide historical reference points for popular entertainment. For example, to commemorate a decade of memories and experiences crafting the eight Harry Potter films, *Entertainment Weekly* showcased an oral history project with the films' stars and directors the week prior to the opening of the final film of the franchise, *Harry Potter and the Deathly Hallows—Part 2* (Markovitz, 2011).

## Technique of Oral History

At the most basic level, oral historians ask people questions in order to learn about their lives. Oral historians must be excellent interviewers; they need to learn strategies to establish trust and to help interviewees understand that their experiences are worthwhile and should be saved for posterity. Oral history is a time-consuming method but if you are willing and able to put in the effort, oral histories may provide you with important insights about all types of individuals and groups who lived at a particular place and time in society.

If you are interested in using oral history interviews in a research project, as with other qualitative methods the first step is to frame a research question—what is it you would like to learn and how might oral history interviews help you to answer your question? Your research question might grow out of past research you have done or it may be based on some new topic or issue you are interested in understanding. For example, my oral history project *For the Record: An Oral History of Rochester, New York, Newsworkers* (Brennen, 2001) was based on an interest in learning more about the routines, expectations and working conditions of journalists who had worked in Rochester, New York. My curiosity helped me to frame the research question for the project: "What was it like to work for Gannett as a journalist in Rochester, New York, during the first half of the twentieth century?"

My past research in this area had revealed that there was limited published information chronicling the lives of rank-and-file reporters and I decided to use oral history interviews to help fill in the research gaps. I chose Rochester, New York, as the research site not only because at that time I lived close to Rochester but also because I thought it would be interesting to focus on a city with more than one newspaper owned by the same person, group or company. The project taught me a lot about the method of oral history, and throughout this chapter, where it is relevant I will draw on aspects of my Gannett research project to help illustrate key aspects of doing oral history.

Once you have crafted a research question, the next step is to begin your background research. The more background information you gather, the better understanding you will have of the issues and concerns related to your topic. For the Rochester oral history project I learned about the local media business and I gathered historical and contemporary information on the Gannett Company and the two daily newspapers it owned in Rochester, the *Times Union* and the *Democrat & Chronicle*. The research provided important context that was invaluable to me throughout the interviews as well as during the writing process. In addition, I read local histories of Rochester, New York, including one written by Henry Clune (1947), whom I later had the privilege of interviewing for the oral history project. I was also fortunate to meet with the public service director for the Gannett Rochester newspapers, Tom Flynn, who graciously provided me with a list of retired Gannett journalists.

After your background research is under way and you have a clear idea for an oral history project, you should start to identify potential interviewees (also known in oral history as narrators) whom you would like to interview for the study. You may come across the names of relevant people to interview in your background research, or you may only know about potential interviewees by their titles or job descriptions and will need to do some digging to find out their names. After you have an initial list of contacts, your first challenge will be to establish rapport with the potential narrators. I recommend sending each person a written letter introducing yourself, explaining your research project and asking him or her to participate. It is important to explain how each person can contribute to your study; potential interviewees may have doubts about their ability to contribute to the research project and it may take some time, and reassurance that you are really interested in their experiences. That initial letter should be followed up with an email and/or phone call during which you will attempt to set up a first meeting. Be sure to keep track of all of your contacts because it may take a while to connect with potential narrators in order to set up a first meeting.

The initial meeting is an opportunity for you to "sell" the research project to the prospective narrator and to get to know more about the person. This meeting may be held in person or over the phone. At this point it is important to begin to establish rapport between you and the interviewee. Shortly after I began my Rochester oral history project, I started to think about my perceptions of the elderly and I wondered how challenging it might be to establish trust with them. I soon realized that my own journalistic experience, coupled with my commitment to the project, was a great icebreaker that helped me to establish trust with each of the interviewees.

Assuming the first conversation goes smoothly, you will be able to arrange a time and place to conduct your oral history interview. It is important to schedule the interview in a place that is quiet and without interruptions; remember that a ringing telephone or a television set on in the room can be heard on tape and can potentially impede the interview process. Oral history interviews are lengthy, and it is helpful to allocate an entire day for each interview so that you will not need to leave midway through a session. However, sometimes an interviewee will tire, or have another appointment, and you may find that it is necessary to schedule a follow-up interview.

## Interview Strategies

To become a successful interviewer, a researcher needs to become a great listener and to have a strong understanding of human relationships. Unlike in other types of interviews, where an interviewer maintains control throughout the process, oral historians shift power to those they interview. It is the narrator's stories and not the interviewer's interests that are most important. Oral history interviewers should be flexible and they should allow the narrator to take the interview in the direction he or she wants to go. However, interviewers still remain active participants in the interview process. An interviewer needs to know when to be quiet and when to ask follow-up questions, when to probe more deeply and when to switch topics. While reporters and law enforcement officials sometimes use silence to force a non-compliant source to speak, the use of silence in oral history interviewing is mainly used to help give a person additional time to think.

It is important for an interviewer to ask brief and open-ended questions that encourage an interviewee to talk and to provide examples and stories to illustrate his or her experiences. After some small talk and a few general icebreaking questions, it is helpful to remind the narrator about the purpose of the project. The beginning of the taped interview should include your name, the narrator's name, the date and location of the interview and the purpose of the project. Ask for the narrator's oral consent to participate in the research and to record the interview.

I recommend starting with a broadly based general question which is followed by more focused questions. A general question such as "How did you get started in the news business?" or "Tell me what it was like to be a cub reporter on the *Democrat & Chronicle*" elicited far more information than when I asked a simple yes/no question like "Was your first job at the *Times Union*?" or "Did you enjoy working on the *Democrat & Chronicle* better than the *Times Union*?"

Once a narrator becomes comfortable talking about his or her career, it is useful to ask follow-up questions to clarify and expand on his or her experiences. Start with easy questions that are simply stated and do your best not to become confrontational. The questions you ask and your responses to the narrator's comments will help to build trust between you and the narrator. Valerie Raleigh Yow (2005) suggests that "positive appraisal of the narrator's work in the interview contributes to the narrator's motivation to continue and to cooperate in the endeavor" (p. 97). It is important to reassure each interviewee that he or she is providing you with useful information. It is also helpful for interviewers to jot down key concepts or ideas that come up during each conversation so that they can follow up with related questions later in the interview. Feel free to use photographs, news articles, commentary from other sources and other documents to spark an interviewer's memory and to help focus the interview on a particular issue or topic. Other interviewing strategies are discussed at length in Chapters 3 and 4.

While a narrator may be comfortable talking about most aspects of his or her life, there may be issues, concerns and/or topics that are difficult for a person to address. Remember that oral history is a collaborative process; if your background research indicates challenging areas, or if an initial question is met with resistance, tread lightly and come back to it later in the interview.

For example, during my background research for the Gannett oral history project I learned that there had been challenges over the years between the reporters and editors regarding the role of the Newspaper Guild at Gannett. While some reporters had been active in the Guild, others distanced themselves from any type of union activities because they felt that journalists were not the same as other workers and should not be part of a labor union. Although I wanted to know whether each person had been a member of the Guild, I was careful not to begin to explore the topic with that question. Instead, I asked general questions about relationships between reporters and editors, which often sparked a comment about the role of the Newspaper Guild. When a narrator mentioned the Guild, I would follow up on the comment and ask about his or her views of the Guild. If an interviewee did not bring up the Guild, I would later ask what he or she thought was the role of the Newspaper Guild at Gannett and follow up that question with more specific probing questions.

In crafting your questions, it is important to be aware of the words you use. Be careful to use neutral words and try not to ask leading questions. While we all know the problems associated with asking a leading question such as "Do you still beat your wife?" many interviewers still ask questions that encourage narrators to give them information they want, rather than offer information they would like to share. A cooperative narrator may give you the requested answer to a question like "Do you think all copy editors are just frustrated writers?" However, this type of leading question should be avoided because an interviewer does not really learn anything new from the strategy. In addition, asking leading questions can affect the power relations of the interview: it can take control of the interview away from the narrator and it may encourage a narrator to shut down or even end an uncomfortable interview.

Pulitzer Prize-winning author Studs Terkel was one of the preeminent interviewers of the twentieth century. His extended conversations with rank-and-file workers, politicians, labor organizers, artists and entertainers chronicled American life and provided important insights into significant challenges, events and changes people faced during the twentieth century. Terkel maintained that oral history interviews differed from traditional journalistic interviews in key ways. In his first collection of oral history interviews, *Division Street: America*, Terkel (1967, p. xxi) explained the differences:

> I realized quite early in this adventure that interviews, conventionally conducted, were meaningless. Conditioned clichés were certain to come. The question-and-answer technique may be of value in determining favored detergents, toothpaste, and deodorants, but not in the discovery of men and women. It was simply a case of making conversation. And listening.

## Learning to Listen

Terkel first learned the value of listening as a child when he lived in a men's hotel that his mother owned; throughout his career, he insisted that listening helps to bestow dignity on people. During your interviews, careful listening will help you to understand how people feel about their lives; it will also provide you with insight on potentially interesting new topics and issues.

Sometimes it is difficult for interviewers to actually sit still and listen. Anderson and Jack (1998) suggest three listening strategies to help researchers understand a person's story from his or her perspective: first, consider a person's moral language; second, listen for meta-statements; and third, follow the logic of the narrative. When we consider self-evaluative statements, through moral language we can examine relationships between individuals and accepted cultural norms—"between how we are told to act and how we feel about ourselves when we do or do not act in that way" (Anderson & Jack, 1998, p. 166). Similarly, meta-statements are evaluations or judgments made by the narrator during the interview that may indicate a discrepancy between what is said and what you might expect to hear. The third listening strategy, assessing a narrative's logic, refers to considering the consistency and/or contradictions in the interview as well as focusing on the way recurring themes brought up by the narrator may relate to each other.

While listening to an interviewee, it is important to also consider his or her non-verbal body language and other signals, as well as to be aware of your own non-verbal responses. A person who stretches or yawns may be tired and need a break. If your interviewee crosses his or her arms and legs and refuses eye contact, he or she may be uncomfortable with the interview or may feel hostile to you as the interviewer. Be aware of your own responses to each narrator's commentary. If you take issue with something that has been said, be careful not to show judgment because your responses can negatively impact the interview. Try not to interrupt the interviewee, but feel free to use non-verbal cues to encourage a narrator: smiling, nodding, shaking your head affirmatively and maintaining eye contact are supportive responses that can help to build trust between you and the narrator.

During one of my interviews for the Rochester oral history project, the narrator began to make racist comments. I was shocked by the intensity of his commentary but I knew that race was an important issue that was not covered by the newspapers until after the 1964 Rochester riots. I wanted to understand his beliefs and I felt that if I responded negatively to his comments, the interview would end abruptly. I literally bit my lip to keep my emotions and body language in check. After a few minutes the narrator said, "The blacks have taken over the city and destroyed it. Now everything I say from here on makes me a racist pig" (quoted in Brennen, 2001, p. 64). In this case the narrator's self-evaluative statement helped me to understand his frustration with changes in his community. My strategy of keeping quiet helped the narrator to feel comfortable enough to open up and share his views with me.

As you prepare for your oral history interviews, it is helpful to practice interviewing and to work on learning to listen. While interviewing and listening are important skills to acquire, Charles T. Morrissey (1998) reminds us not to let the tools and procedures of oral history overwhelm us because it is also important to rely on our own intuition during the interviews. Morrissey suggests that oral historians should remain flexible, understanding and open to the unexpected.

Given that human memory can be faulty and subjective, some researchers have questioned the reliability and validity of oral history interviews. As with other types of qualitative research, Terkel (1997) explains that the goal of oral history is not to uncover plain unvarnished facts but rather to try to understand the deeper meanings and feelings about those facts. While feelings are constructed by individuals at a particular time in history, within a particular cultural context, oral history not only focuses on individuals' recollections of events but also inquires into the collective memories of a society. The experiences that we share with others influence us to forget some things and to remember other experiences and to interpret those shared experiences in particular ways. Yow (2005) reminds oral historians to consider the relevant cultural context for the interviews as well as the potential influence of shared experiences and collective memories on each individual's interview.

There are also a variety of ways to verify the factual information obtained from oral history interviews. During each oral history interview it is possible to test the interviewee's memory by asking for specific names, dates and places. Be sure to ask the narrators for the correct spelling of their names as well as the spelling of the names of others they mention. Factual information can also be verified through other interviews that you complete and from other types of primary source material, archival evidence and historical records. Oral history interviewers should be skilled enough to be able to approach the same issue or topic from a variety of approaches or to ask similar questions in different ways to determine whether a narrator's answers are consistent.

## The Editing Process

All interviews should be audiotaped using a cassette tape or a digital voice recorder so that they can be transcribed. While some oral historians prefer to videotape their interviews, I would suggest that even when video is used, it is still important to run an audiotape to aid the transcription process. Each oral history interview should be transcribed in a timely manner. There are individuals and professional services that specialize in transcribing interviews; however, they are costly. Also, even if you are able to pay transcription costs, learning to transcribe an interview is a good skill to acquire, so I would encourage you to try it at least once. Some researchers maintain that oral historians should transcribe their own interviews because the transcription process allows them to become more familiar with the material.

Voice recognition software is now available to help transcribe interviews. Basic speech recognition programs come with Windows Vista and Microsoft Office for the Macintosh. Dragon NaturallySpeaking works with any Windows program and, with some training, it learns to correct mistakes and can approach 99 percent accuracy. Dragon Dictate for the Macintosh uses the same Dragon recognition technology and is considered fast and accurate. However, a major challenge with the current technology is that at this point none of the voice recognition software can recognize more than one voice. While most oral historians await the development of voice recognition software capable of recognizing multiple voices, Jennifer L. Matheson (2007) has developed a cost-effective voice transcription computer technique using a digital voice recorder and an MP3 player, along with voice recognition and transcription software. Although the process requires listening to an interview through headphones and speaking the words into a microphone, the technique is cost-effective and less time-consuming than other transcription techniques.

After an interview tape has been transcribed, the editing process begins. The interviewer should be the first person to edit the written transcript. If you listen to the tape-recorded interview while you read the transcript, you will often catch a variety of errors that have been made during the transcription process. False starts and duplications should also be removed during the editing process. Once transcripts have been edited, they should be sent to the interviewees for their corrections and feedback. At this point in the process, some interviewees may wish to change information in their interviews to clarify previous remarks. Reading the transcript can spark new memories, and narrators may provide you with additional stories and commentary. It is possible that some interviewees may become concerned when reading their remarks and they may ask you to edit portions of their transcripts. Remember that it is their stories that you want to tell, not yours, and it is important to respect their wishes.

During the *For the Record* editing process, one of the reporters I had interviewed became uncomfortable with his commentary after he read the transcript of his interview. He wrote to me that he felt his statements "rambled" and that some of the information he shared with me was "incoherent." Deciding that he was not a "good interviewee," he returned the transcript of his interview with several sections crossed out. His cover letter said he did not wish to embarrass his friends or former colleagues or to question the business that he had loved and respected many years ago, and he asked me if it was possible to "forget the whole thing." Out of respect for his feelings I decided to pull his interview from the project. While I was disappointed by his request, this experience actually helped me to understand more fully the goal of oral history.

Oral historians will use the final corrected transcripts for their research, and copies of final transcripts should also be sent to the interviewees for their files. After each oral history project is complete, it is appropriate to consider archiving the audiotapes and the final transcripts for future use.

## Ethical Considerations

Given the nature of oral history, it is imperative to receive informed consent from each interviewee. All narrators should understand the purpose of their interviews, the planned use of the transcripts and/or audiotapes and their right not to answer any questions they find objectionable. They should be reminded that they can withdraw from the project at any time. Narrators should also be informed that the purpose of the interviews is to elicit in-depth commentary about their experiences and that they should tell their stories in as much detail as they feel comfortable sharing. Because of the importance of identity and context in the construction of oral history, interviewees are usually identified by name in the interviews. However, if necessary it is possible for a narrator to choose to be anonymous, and that option should be discussed with all interviewees.

The "General Principles for Oral History" (2010) created by the Oral History Association remind interviewers to respect the interviewees' authority and their right to answer questions on their own terms and in their own style and language. Oral historians should also avoid misrepresentations or the use of stereotypes and should be careful not to manipulate narrators' words or take them out of context. Other specific guidelines regarding oral history principles, best practices for pre-interview preparation, professional and technical standards and the preservation of interviews are also available on the Oral History Association website: www.oralhistory.org.

## Research Using Oral History Transcripts

Researchers use oral history transcripts in a variety of ways. One strategy is to present the complete life histories of individuals without assessment; the interview transcripts are reprinted in full without additional editorial commentary or scholarly analysis. At most, an editor provides an introduction to the life story or reorganizes the interview transcript around topics and themes. A second strategy involves researchers choosing to group life history excerpts from a variety of interviews around common issues, themes and concerns. This approach usually provides a broader historical explanation and often integrates critical analysis and commentary into the research. A third approach used by researchers is to utilize information gathered from oral history interviews just like any other historical evidence. Researchers incorporate interview quotations with other evidence that is analyzed, critiqued and woven into a historical narrative. All three approaches are appropriate ways to use oral history transcripts and can help to tell important stories about the rank and file. But no matter how you plan to use your oral history interviews, it is important to make sure that any quotations used in the research are put in the proper context and that the quotations that are selected do not misrepresent a narrator's commentary.

The following excerpts from *For the Record* illustrate the second strategy outlined above as a way to use oral history transcripts in media studies research. In crafting the research project, I drew extensively on the oral history interviews I had completed with the Gannett journalists and combined lengthy quotations with critical analysis, relevant contextual information and commentary. For this project, I incorporated Raymond Williams' concept of structure of feeling, which describes the actively felt and lived meanings, experiences and values of a society. Williams (1977/ 1988) suggests that structure of feeling is often found in the documentary culture of a society, in its novels, music, films and newspaper stories, and in other elements of popular culture. My research used the oral history interviews from journalists to provide evidence of a specific structure of feeling that was illustrated on the Rochester, New York, *Times Union* and the *Democrat & Chronicle* during the first half of the twentieth century.

The research project began with a brief biography of Frank Gannett and provided information regarding the development of the Gannett media empire. This background provided important historical context in which to place the journalists' stories. While most of the information in the first excerpt came from traditional historical sources, information from my interview with Henry Clune also provided relevant historical context.

---

## From *For the Record: An Oral History of Rochester, New York, Newsworkers*, by Bonnie Brennen

Frank Gannett's introduction to the newspaper business began in 1885 when the 9-year-old began delivering copies of the Rochester *Democrat & Chronicle* to his neighbors in Blood's Depot, New York. Forty-three years later, the *Democrat & Chronicle* became the thirteenth in his newspaper group when Gannett purchased the paper for $3.5 million.

After graduating from Cornell University, where he had received a four-year scholarship, Gannett was hired as city editor at the *Ithaca Daily News*. In 1906, Gannett purchased a half interest in his first newspaper, the *Elmira Gazette*, for $20,000. The *Gazette* was an established daily newspaper with shopworn and outdated equipment located in an industrial railroad town of 30,000 people.

According to Frank Tripp, who was a *Gazette* reporter at the time and later became general manager and chairman of the board of Gannett Newspapers, in 1906 the *Gazette* plant was "rickety, dingy, poorly ventilated; it had creaking stairs, splintered floors, a tiny freight elevator which periodically dropped three floors, and pied type forms in the basement. The press was powered by a natural gas engine whose cough could be heard for blocks" (quoted in Merrill, 1954, p. 17).

After the purchase, Gannett immediately took editorial control over the *Gazette* while his co-owner, Erwin R. Davenport, focused on the business aspects of the newspaper.

From this modest beginning, Gannett began building his media empire. In 1918, Gannett and Davenport set their sights on the Rochester market. Rochester was a thriving city in upstate New York that was proud of its heritage as a "flour city" (Brandt, 1993, p. 33). Rochester was complete with mills powered by the Genesee River and supplied by locally grown wheat, and it was a city that at the beginning of the twentieth century was suspicious of outsiders. As the locally famous Rochester columnist Henry Clune (1994b, p. 8) recounts:

> There was a social hierarchy here, controlled by maybe a hundred people, just as there was in New York City, where Ward McCallister formed the Four Hundred. There was a woman here named Mrs. Warren Whitney, and she was the social leader of the town. There was a woman on the *Post Express* named Emily Mond, and she ran a social column. It was like a social registrar. If you didn't belong to the right clubs, she never mentioned you.

In 1918 there were five daily newspapers competing for readership in Rochester; three of them were staunchly Republican and two served Democrats' interests. The Republican *Democrat & Chronicle* and the Democratic *Herald* were published in the mornings, while the afternoon newspapers included two Republican newspapers, the *Post Express* and the *Times*. The head of the local Republican Party, "Boss" George W. Aldridge, was one of the owners of the *Times*. The Democrats' *Union & Advertiser*, also published in the afternoon, had begun on October 15, 1826 as the *Daily Advertiser*, and was the first daily newspaper published between the Hudson River and the Pacific Ocean. After a merger in 1856 it became the *Union & Advertiser*.

Interested in controlling the afternoon market in Rochester, Gannett and Davenport purchased the *Times* and the *Union & Advertiser* and promptly merged them into the *Times Union*. On March 9, 1918, the *Union & Advertiser* ran a prominent advertisement on page 7 which notified readers of the change in ownership:

> The oldest and the newest are now brought together, consolidated into one GREAT NEWSPAPER under new and progressive management and

united for A GREATER AND BETTER ROCHESTER. [Signed] Frank E. Gannett, president and editor; Woodford J. Copeland, vice president; E. R. Davenport, secretary-treasurer and manager. First issue out Tuesday. Order early.

(quoted in Brandt, 1993, pp. 36–37)

The *Times Union* initially fashioned itself as an independent alternative in a city of political party organs. Gannett opposed the strong-arm political tactics of men like Boss Aldridge and, together with George Eastman, the founder of Kodak, fought successfully to change Rochester's city government from strong-mayor form to a city manager form (Zeigler, 1983, p. 16). The *Times Union* quickly became Gannett's flagship newspaper, and Gannett's presence was regularly felt in his suggestions to the editorial staff regarding such things as the wording of headlines, or the way a specific news story should be played. The *Times Union* was the only Gannett newspaper that consistently carried Frank Gannett's editorials and that listed his name in the staff box as editor (p. 23). Six years after purchasing the *Times Union*, in 1924, Frank Gannett bought out his partners and, as controlling owner of six upstate New York newspapers, formed the Gannett Company. Over the next few years Gannett would double his holdings.

In 1928 Gannett purchased the *Democrat & Chronicle*, long considered the city's premier newspaper. The *Democrat & Chronicle* began in 1834 as the *Daily Democrat*, and after a merger with the *Daily Chronicle* in 1870 the *Democrat & Chronicle* was established. Frank Tripp, Gannett's general manager, initially opposed the purchase because he felt it would "weaken the influence of both papers and jeopardize the reputation of the publisher" (Zeigler, 1983, p. 22). Yet, Gannett had learned that William Randolph Hearst was interested in purchasing the *Democrat & Chronicle* and he feared Hearst's growing influence in the Rochester market. Hearst had purchased the *Post Express* in 1923 merely for its circulation list and subsequently had established his own *Sunday American* and the *Evening Journal* in Rochester.

When Hearst's empire began to falter in 1937, Gannett bailed Hearst out of his financial problems in Albany and in the process acquired the presses and equipment of Hearst's Rochester *Journal* and *American*. Gannett closed both of Hearst's newspapers and established a monopoly in Rochester through his ownership of the two remaining newspapers in town, the morning *Democrat & Chronicle* and the afternoon *Times Union*. Gannett exercised daily control over the newspapers as an active, hands-on manager/owner.

In the next excerpt, Mitch Kaidy's experience as a political reporter provides important context regarding the *Times Union*'s editorial policy.

Commentary from his oral history interview is quoted in full in the next part of the brief biography of Gannett.

---

Under Gannett's leadership, the *Times Union* began as an independent newspaper; however, over the years its editorial policy began to shift and the paper became staunchly Republican. The *Democrat & Chronicle* was always a Republican paper and under Gannett's control it soon became increasingly right-wing. As *Democratic & Chronicle* Political Reporter Mitch Kaidy explains:

> The Gannett newspapers were always right-wing. As a matter of fact, if you know anything about Frank Gannett, you know that he ran for president. He was one of the very early militant ideologues on the right; Gannett hated Franklin Roosevelt with a vengeance. I've read all this, that's how I know about it. He was certainly one of the first to organize the public to oppose a president's policies. He founded the Committee for Constitutional Government. I believe that was the earliest pacesetter for many other political action committees that would come along later. It was intended to mobilize public opinion against Roosevelt's policies, especially Roosevelt's attempts to pack the Supreme Court.
>
> Frank Gannett himself was far to the right of his editorial staff and far to the right of his editorial writing staff. The editorial writers and the editorial staff were separate. As a matter of fact, it's probably true, as a lot of people have observed, that young reporters generally are idealistic. Generally they tend to be on the left of the political spectrum. Not far on the left. They exaggerate about how leftist the young reporters are. They're reformers at heart; they're not radicals.
>
> However, in Frank Gannett's day he was very paternalistic. That word was made for Frank Gannett. He used to give out turkeys and have parties and picnics. His wife and he used to come and he treated us as his family. We didn't think in those days that he was looking down on us, or patronizing us. We accepted that in good faith and we cherished it. But paternalism is rejected out of hand these days. I don't think we rejected it in those days.
>
> (1994, p. 8)

Criticism regarding Gannett's newly fashioned media monopoly in Rochester was quick and sustained. Gannett vowed that the two newspapers would maintain separate staffs and would operate independently—a promise that he kept throughout his life. When Gannett purchased the *Democrat & Chronicle*, it was located on Main Street and the *Times Union* was housed in the current Gannett Rochester Building on Exchange Street. It was only years later, when Allen Neuharth ran Gannett, that the *Times Union* and the *Democrat & Chronicle* staffs and facilities were merged.

---

Landing my first interview with Henry Clune became a defining moment for this research project. Initially, most of the former Gannett journalists were resistant to participate in the oral history project. Some suggested they were too old, others felt that their experiences were ancient history and still others felt that they wouldn't be interesting subjects to interview because they had not become editors or publishers. Clune was the most senior Gannett journalist who was still alive and residing in the Rochester area in the 1990s; his experience spanned most of the twentieth century and it provided me with important context about how journalism was practiced in Rochester. The other Gannett reporters revered him, and once they heard he was part of my oral history project, several of them became willing (and even anxious) to participate. In addition, Clune provided me with the names of other former Gannett newsworkers, and a few of them eventually participated in the project.

I have always been interested in how people got interested in journalism, and during the Gannett oral history project I asked each narrator about how he or she got started in the field. As the following excerpt illustrates, I chose to focus on each narrator's first journalistic experiences as a strategy to transition from the Gannett historical context into the individual journalists' stories. This section also provided examples of relevant background information on the narrators whose stories were featured throughout the rest of the book project.

---

Several of the journalists interviewed suggested that during the 1950s and 1960s the *Times Union* and the *Democrat & Chronicle* were at the peak of their influence in Rochester. The *Times Union* was considered Gannett's flagship paper, and Paul Miller's influence as publisher and editor gave the newspaper strong leadership and increased its visibility. Allen Neuharth became general manager of both Rochester newspapers on February 1, 1963, and brought with him a philosophy of hands-on management as well as very specific views about the publishing of daily newspapers.

During this era, most newsworkers began their journalism careers at small newspapers or as copyboys or gofers on larger publications like the *Times Union* and the *Democrat & Chronicle*. Clune, who provided the earliest stories for this oral history project, began his sixty-year newspaper career in 1910 as an unpaid sub-reporter on the Rochester *Democrat & Chronicle*. As Clune explains:

> When I first started in the newspaper business, I worked for a city editor who was a man named Morris Adams. Mr. Adams was about the best newspaper executive I've ever known. He was an utterly dedicated man; he didn't get married until he was in his seventies and he was a wonderful person to start under. [While I was still a sub reporter] he told me that I wasn't suited for what I was trying to do and told me I'd ought to try something else. I'd been a kind of a failure as a youth and I wanted to succeed. I pleaded with him. I wasn't getting paid except with street car tokens so he let me stay on and finally—I think it was in April and I started there in June of 1910—in April of 1911 they started to pay me a little. That's the first time I really joined the staff. I started at eight dollars a week. I don't believe they would allow that today. The union wouldn't stand for keeping a man working there for eight months without any money, any pay.
>
> (1994a, pp. 4–5)

Clune's determination to succeed in the newspaper business is echoed by other Gannett newsworkers, particularly when they speak about how they got started in journalism. While their reasons for becoming interested in the newspaper business vary, as did their initial experiences, what remains consistent is the journalists' perseverance and genuine interest in writing. Their experiences getting started in the newspaper business certainly still provide guidance for aspiring journalists.

From the time he was 6 years old, Art Deutsch wanted to become a newspaper reporter:

> I used to drive my mother crazy because in those days I would spend a nickel on a day's circuit of newspapers and have them send me the papers so I could compare how they treated the story. I would get the *Pittsburgh Press*, and the *Post Gazette*, the *Philadelphia Inquirer*, and I'd get the *New York Post* and the *New York Herald Journal*, and the *Cleveland Plain Dealer* when it was a national story, just to see how they did it.
>
> (1994, p. 8)

Deutsch, who worked as an investigative reporter for the *Democrat & Chronicle* from 1956 through 1964, began his journalism career while he was still in high school as a copyboy for the *Philadelphia Inquirer*. Each day he would take the number 37 trolley into Philadelphia from Chester. Deutsch remembers:

> The great managing editor of those days was there, the original front-pager, Eli Z. Dimitman. Oh boy! He was a terror. Dressed like a father and was as earthy a man as you could find. And he had rules. The copy boy had to put out one dozen number two pencils, all drilled to a point. And copy paper, this and that, a carafe of ice water. One day there was a big fire in the Frankfurt section, the industrial section of Philadelphia, and all the reporters were sent out. It was pretty late. And he said, "Hey, come here kid, go down there and grab a hold of the nearest phone and don't leave it. Don't let anybody else use it, except our guys." I got a hundred nickels from the grocer, and I went down there and I kept the phones open for our people.
>
> In those days they had the *Evening Record*, the *Afternoon Record*, they had the *Courier*, the *Daily News*, the *Bulletin* morning, the *Bulletin* evening. God, there must have been eight newspapers. Finally, I'm calling in and a guy on the phone in rewrites said, "Dimitman says to come back in." I got on the trolley and went back. Dimitman said, "Hey kid, grab a phone. You told me once you wanted to write, so write whatever they call in." I said, "I have to tell my mother I'm going to be late." I told my mother about working late because of the big fire. Then I took the story from the phone and checked whatever I could.
>
> When it was all done, time to go, it was about six in the morning. We were exhausted. We all smelled the smoke and it was fun. It was very heady stuff for a kid. Dimitman said, "I suppose you think you're a newspaperman." I didn't say anything. He said, "You won't make a patch on a newspaper man's butt." And I felt dreadful. Friday was payday, you got paid in cash, in little envelopes. I went down there and the cashier said, "Sorry to tell you this, you're through." My face must have fallen down to my ankles. She then said, "No, no, you got a five dollar raise."
>
> (1994, pp. 8–9)

As a junior at the Rochester Institute of Technology, Floyd King became disillusioned with engineering and decided to quit school. King, who remained an active journalist for more than sixty-five years, explains how he decided to embark upon a journalism career shortly before the Great Depression began:

> I was walking down the street in Rochester thinking, "What in the world am I going to do with my life? I don't know what I want to do, I haven't

the slightest idea." And then just like it came out of the blue, just as if it was from heaven, I remembered what a fifth-grade teacher said to me. She said, "Floyd, I don't know what you're going to make of your life, but I think you ought to make writing a part of it. I think you have a gift for it." It was as if everything opened up immediately. That was the answer. Rochester had three newspapers at the time.

Now, keep in mind that I'd never written a news story in my life. I didn't even know how to start it. I applied at the three newspapers for a job. I guess two of them offered me jobs, the *Times Union* and the Hearst paper, the *Journal*. They both offered me jobs, and the Gannett *Democrat* said, "We just haven't anything now, but keep us in mind. You seem to have a talent." I took the job at the Hearst paper. How did I get it? I don't know but it just seemed that I could do it.

I was a reporter when the financial editor walked out of the financial room and he said, "The stock market has just crashed in New York City. People are jumping off the skyscrapers, going right down." I thought to myself, "What the hell, that doesn't mean anything to me. I haven't any money to speak of in the stock market." I went back to typing and everybody else went back to typing. Within two weeks we were all out of a job. The Hearst paper couldn't get any advertising.

I went over to the *Times Union* where the managing editor had been very good to me. I told him what happened, and he said, "Floyd, we just haven't got a thing in Rochester. Maybe you would like to go down to the Elmira paper [also owned by Gannett]. They need somebody for the summer, and you never know what could happen if you go down there and get a start." I thought, "Geez, I can't lose. I don't have a job anyway." I went to Elmira and got a job as a reporter for the *Star Gazette*. I suppose that I was lucky because I didn't know anything about reporting, but on a small-town paper like that I could pick it up kind of fast, and I did.

One day I was working late and we got word a big freight crashed just outside of Elmira and at least four men were dead. The boss said to me, "Get going and cover the story." I got going and it was just towards night, not quite yet, but there was a great big full moon up there. Steam engines puff when they're standing still. This engine had a dead man at the throttle and a dead man at the break. Both of their hands were still on it and the engine was going "sho, sho, sho." The engine was buried in the caboose. There was a train that hadn't gotten far enough off the track and had killed two men in the caboose also.

The damn story just had everything. I mean, that beautiful full moon, and there were very few people there. I had it all to myself. I went back to the paper and wrote the story. Now it was just one of those lucky things that has happened to me all my life. While I was doing this, L. R. Blanchard, who was then the supervising editor of all the Gannett newspapers, happened to be visiting down there. He never said one damn word about my story. I knew it was a good story and it hurt my feelings. He didn't say one single word. Next week I got a letter from Blanchard in Rochester inviting me to join the *Democrat & Chronicle* as a reporter. I did and I've been there ever since.

(1994, pp. 1–3)

As a senior at St. Andrew's Seminary, Tom Flynn decided that he wanted to become a newspaper reporter. Flynn, who has spent his entire career with Gannett, explains how his persistence eventually landed him his first job as a copyboy for the *Times Union*:

I remember the first Monday I walked in; I had sort of carefully hatched this plan—naïvely, as it turned out, even in 1957—that I would walk in, fill out the job application and as soon as I was available, they would hire me. I showed up in my black seminary suit and white shirt and my black briefcase, and filled out the job application. I was told there were no openings but that they would keep me in mind. Of course, I was still in school, so it was okay because I figured that in June this would be a fait accompli. Someone had told me that that it was important for people to remember who you are, so I came down every week and became a kind of fixture/pest. In any event, that process went along and I was told the same thing each week, that there was still no opening.

In June, when school concluded and I waved good-bye to St. Andrew's Seminary, I was then working part time, as I had for a couple of years, for Schmitt's Meat Market on Joseph Avenue, picking up sides of beef. There was no job at the newspaper in the summer of 1957. But in August of 1957, I got a call that if I was interested, I could start in September at one dollar an hour as a copyboy, and of course I was.

I walked into this building on September 9, 1957, and except for having worked at the original *Democrat & Chronicle* building on Main Street, I've never left. I dutifully enrolled at the University of Rochester and tortured my way through approximately six and a half years to get my BA degree in English. I have no affection for the University of Rochester. It's not their fault. But when you're running in and out of a school at nine o'clock at night and are taking classes under those conditions, it isn't like going to college. It was kind of like going to the dentist.

One dollar an hour, forty dollars a week, thirty-two dollars and eight cents after tax. It seemed like a lot of money, but of course it wasn't. As an editorial clerk, or copyboy, in those days there were no computers, of course, and we would get a lot of information, routine information like birth lists and statistical data, because the *Times Union* has always been the paper of record of sorts in this community. We who were clerks would go to the county clerk's office, or the real estate offices, and gather up [the information], or sometimes essentially take the information down. There was a responsibility there to get it right, and that was good training.

We ran stories on deadline from the newsroom to the composing room, which was, depending on various changes in the building, either on the third floor or the fourth floor—we were always a floor off. A lot of running page proofs to the editors because a lot of things had to be done quickly and things checked. There was some routine typing and some input.

There was pasting-up stocks; the stock quotations would come in every afternoon by a ticker-tape process from New York when the market closed. The *Times Union* had the complete closing stock list in its "Blue Streak" edition, which was a very popular final edition because we had a much larger street sale. Because factory gates were traditional, crowds would pour out of there at four o'clock. There was an urgency to get the stocks listings, which then were pasted up on streets in the exact order as they came in. And you dared not mess it up. Then they were literally typeset in a very short time in the composing room by a number of compositors who were waiting to do this. The new pages were matted, the lead plates cast, and on to the press, and the *Times Union* "Blue Streak" was onto the street no later than 4:00 P.M. It was eagerly grabbed up by downtown commuters, and bus traffic was much heavier, a much greater downtown presence than today. There was a substantial sale of that edition and that was one of the clerical things that we would do.

Sometimes you would go out on deadline to the home of a family who just lost somebody in an accident to negotiate the picture, which was an interesting early experience in diplomacy because most of the time you were in an ugly situation. I found then, and later as a police reporter, that the family members generally were the least of the problem. They were eager, in a semi-shocked state, to talk to you and to provide information. It was the well-meaning neighbor or the nosy brother-in-law who wanted to beat your brains out for stepping into their tragedy. Like all things, I had heard stories about reporters snatching photos when the family wasn't watching. I never did that. I did have to sweet-talk a number of people and in fact, occasionally personally drive back with the photo because it would have been awful if something had happened to it. They accepted the word that the newspaper wanted to present a photo and took us in good faith. I think that's a major part of our responsibility.

I know I got a very good early opportunity at these newspapers because even in 1957 it was not normal that someone who had not had some experience or college education would be allowed to start reporting. I was working for the *Times Union* in a daytime situation as a copyboy or a wire photo operator and [undertaking] various clerical newsroom duties, and I would practice writing news briefs on Saturday afternoons when the *Times Union* still published a Saturday afternoon paper. It was a thrill to see some of those published, of course anonymously, as a clerk.

About eighteen months into that experience, the job in the night library, or news morgue as it was called, became available. It meant more money and it meant more flexibility for school hours. I applied and got it, and worked in the news library for about nine months. I had, by dint of that, become friends with the *Democrat & Chronicle* crowd, which, of course, was mostly a nighttime workforce, and which had recently moved into this building which had expanded to bring them from the Main Street facility. I had made my ambitions known to a number of those people.

(1994, pp. 1–3, 8–10)

As you can see from the previous excerpt, which describes how four of the Gannett reporters got started in journalism, the oral history interviews included considerable information about the craft of journalism. The interviews also produced helpful background information and interesting stories about media practices in the early twentieth century, as well as providing important context for the rest of the book. The following chapter summary connects Gannett's institutional history with information on newsroom routines and the training of journalists. These themes were explored more fully throughout the rest of the book.

Flynn's experiences both as a *Times Union* copyboy and as a clerk in the Gannett morgue not only illustrate the extensive job training that many Gannett journalists received, but also reveal the level of determination that newsworkers maintained throughout their apprenticeships. Although copyboys and cub reporters alike often endured routine, repetitive tasks like clipping and filing articles, and even filling paste-pots, their desire to prove themselves and succeed in the business carried them through the most boring of tasks.

Before the 1960s, educational requirements for journalists were minimal and some Gannett newsworkers began their journalism careers while still in high school. During the first half of the twentieth century a college degree was not required for men aspiring to a career in journalism; however, women, who had always had a difficult time gaining access to the newsroom, generally found that earning a college degree was a valuable asset. Rather than pursuing a formal education, young people who wanted to become journalists needed to possess a flair for writing, a sense of adventure and a willingness to work extremely long hours for little or even no pay. Most reporters worked their way up in the field, beginning as correspondents or cub reporters for smaller papers and then moving on to larger daily newspapers like the *Times Union* or the *Democrat & Chronicle*. A newsworker who was able to land his or her first job on a metropolitan daily newspaper usually began as a copyboy, or in Clune's case as a "sub" reporter.

Fred Fedler suggests that during the late nineteenth and the early twentieth centuries, rather than seeking out formal education, journalists often taught themselves by reading, comparing, and analyzing articles published in the major US newspapers (2000, p. 19). Several Gannett journalists spoke of rewriting newspaper articles to teach themselves how to write. Like Deutsch, who felt the pull to journalism from the age of six, these aspiring newsworkers frequently compared the coverage of national stories in a variety of urban daily newspapers.

Frank Gannett's own rise to power from delivery boy to media mogul also reflects this spirit of self-reliance, as well as his particular determination to produce newspapers suitable for all members of his community. When Gannett's ownership of the *Times Union* and the *Democrat & Chronicle* created a monopoly situation in Rochester, Gannett vowed to keep each newspaper independent and competitive—a promise that he kept throughout his life. The competition between newspapers was lively, heated and sometimes hostile, and not only encouraged excellence but also helped to keep the citizenry informed. The newsworkers interviewed for this project frequently bemoaned the company's decision to combine the editorial staffs of the two newspapers, and several accurately predicted the subsequent demise of the *Times Union*.

---

The background research that I completed for the Gannett oral history project indicated that during the first half of the twentieth century, women reporters faced a variety of gender-based challenges in the news industry.

During each interview I asked specific questions about the role of women in the newsroom and followed up each answer with more probing questions on the topic. Not surprisingly, the female journalists never waited for me to ask gender-related questions and volunteered commentary on specific challenges that they faced in a male-oriented work environment. The next excerpt focuses on the views of male journalists who worked for Gannett. While it offers specific information about working conditions for women reporters, it also provides insight into the prevailing early twentieth-century (male) philosophy about the role of women in the newsroom.

---

While women worked on both the *Democrat & Chronicle* and the *Times Union* throughout the twentieth century, many of the reporters interviewed suggested that until at least the mid-1960s, women were treated differently than their male counterparts. Pulitzer Prize-winning reporter Kaidy, who covered labor and politics for the *Democrat & Chronicle* for fifteen years, echoes the sentiments of several male reporters when he observes:

> In the 1950s and 1960s we had on the editorial staff a strict quota for women. There's no question that women played a back seat in those days, that they had some kind of a written or unwritten quota. They had good female reporters, no question about it. But it was sort of a given that journalism was a male occupation.
>
> (1994, p. 21)

Women were often seen as a necessary obligation rather than as equal members of the editorial staff. Some reporters, like Robert Beck, suggest that one reason there were few women journalists on the newspaper staff at that time is that they were not as "sophisticated" as their male counterparts:

> During the war, because of the absence of men, they had to hire a few. You had old-time Hearst people like Ruth Chamberlain, who was a fashion and society editor. She made all the others look like carhops. A real tough broad. A nice girl. One of the reasons they didn't have many women at newspapers in those days is that women were not as sophisticated as they are today. They had no concept of the double entendre, for example. We had a reporter named Elizabeth Keiper and she wrote a garden column. A lovely person, about seventy years old. I remember hearing the expression, "Stop the presses!" and it had to do with one of her stories. It was a picture of a garden with a rooster on a

fence behind it, crowing at the dawn. Three columns wide with the headline: "The Big Red Cock Greeted the Morning Dawn."

(1994, pp. 10–11)

Other Gannett newspapermen described the few women who worked news-side as hard-bitten, cigarette-smoking old maids. The one woman who worked in a Rochester newsroom during the 1920s was in charge of society news. According to Clune:

She was a kind of a fussy old woman, but she had a good following and, being the only woman in there, she was subjected to certain jokes and things, but she was all right. Augie Anderson was her name, Augusta Anderson. She was a general reporter, but the clergy were fond of her and the woman's clubs, and she was a favorite of the people that ran the amateur theatricals. There were a lot of people who thought a good deal of Augusta Anderson.

She was a fine woman, a little absent-minded. I saw her go out one February night; of course she worked like the rest of us until midnight or after. It was below zero and she went down to get the streetcar without her coat.

Later there were girls who first came in to work for the women's department, for society. They finally got a society editor, a women's editor. That began to open the door for them and the woman society editor always had an assistant who was always a woman, although I was the assistant society editor for a brief period in the 1920s.

(1994a, pp. 13–14)

She wasn't identified, we had no bylines in those days. There were no bylines.

(1994b, 2)

By the 1950s, more women began working in the *Times Union* and the *Democrat & Chronicle* newsrooms. Other male reporters echo Luckett's perception that female reporters were pleased with their treatment at Gannett:

Sally Ann Watts [Sarah Watts] and Margaret Goetz were very attractive female reporters. Elizabeth Keiper, who was a copy editor, was in a sense a prototypical old maid. She was a spinster lady. Her father had been a well-known patent attorney in Rochester. Betty Keiper was very deaf, had two hearing aids, and all the reporters lived in fear of having her stalk over to your desk with a piece of copy and a question about something, because you were pretty sure you weren't going to be able to answer whatever the question was, and if you could, you probably couldn't make Betty hear what your answer was.

Ruth Chamberlain was the society editor and Peg Doyle was her assistant. And that was really it. There were a handful of women. I think that there was a young woman who was a sort of secretary for the city desk, sort of a gofer-type person. There were some copygirls carrying copy around. I don't think that there was any discrimination. Who knows? I'm a male, but it may have been perceived by the women certainly, in terms of the assignments they got from the city desk. I don't really remember a lot of griping from Sally or from Marge. They may have been seething internally; I'm not sure.

(Luckett, 1994, pp. 10–11)

During the course of his interview, Art Deutsch described a few women on the *Democrat & Chronicle* during the 1950s and 1960s who challenged prevailing notions regarding women in the newsroom:

One woman that we worked with, Gail Sheehy, covered women's stuff. Against the wall were the women's desks. Gail sat there. I used to listen to her talk. Her first husband at that time was going to medical school here and she turned phrases neatly; I noticed that. I said to Red Vagg one day when we were having lunch, I said, "Geez, why don't you put Gail on city side? She can write." "Ah, of course, she's a goddamn woman. You know they're nothing but a pain." After Gail made it pretty big one day [Sheehy is the best-selling author of *Passages*], I bought a paperback and I sent it to Red Vagg. I said, "This is from me and relates to the girl who didn't know what to do in the city room." He called me up and said, "Deutsch, you're a son of a bitch!" I said, "I know it." He said, "But you were right."

We had others who were good. We had a gal named Connie Gunthers who came from San Francisco. She led a charmed life. She had never been to New York, to the United Nations, so she decided to take a day off and go through it. That's the day that Stevenson and Khrushchev met. She writes a first-person story. She was there. Another time she's coming home from San Francisco, the plane lands in Chicago, O'Hare. Plane collapses, burns, four people dead, one from Rochester, and she files a first-person story. I said, "Jesus Christ, how does that happen? It never happened to me."

We had some pretty good female writers over the years. Jean Walrath, who is dead now, wrote everything in the paper. She did theater, she did women's garbage, society stuff, which she hated, but she also was a good hard news reporter. And I loved that. Jean retired long ago. I covered stuff with her, the opening of the Seaway, that kind of thing. Hard-nosed, [would] take no guff from any one reporter. To me, it doesn't matter if you're a homosexual, a lesbian, or a male or female, what difference does it make? Can you do the job? I see this all the time. People say, "Oh, she can't do that," or "he can't do that," or "he is a pussy cat, I wouldn't send him out now," except that he can write rings around you.

(1994, p. 21)

According to Fradenburgh, there were always women working in the *Times Union* newsroom. What Fradenburgh found difficult to accept, however, was Gannett's decision in the 1960s to put women on the police beat:

I think one of the major changes that happened was we made the decision to let women cover the police beat. A lot of thought went into that because you're going into some areas that you might consider dangerous and there was a lot of soul searching. Now, of course, it's commonplace. One of the most difficult things for me was when the dress code began changing and the women and girls began to come in with jeans on instead of skirts. This is horrible when you've been brought up to see women dress up. This is old school, isn't it? I questioned women going out to meet the public like that. I remember going into my managing editor, John Dougherty, and telling him my concerns. He just said, "Forget it." So I forgot it.

(1994, p. 16)

Flynn also remembers women working in the newsroom throughout his career:

I've worked with women all my life here. I remember strong women that I observed when I was a copyboy on the *Times Union*; they were the society editor, the women's columnist kind. A couple of them were on the copy desk. At the risk of sounding crude, they seemed like hard-bitten, cigarette-smoking old ladies, old maids, who probably had spent their entire life working in an environment that was not feminine or female, certainly. But they held their own and were sort of one of the boys. That was kind of the image.

Rose Sold is an interesting person. I would guess Rose is probably in her eighties. She covered a variety of news, general assignment kinds of things. Her husband, Earl Hoch, for many, many years covered courts.

They were married when I came here in 1957. Rose always struck me as very feminine, very small, diminutive kind of person. Kind of a pretty, attractive person, as opposed to Betty Keiper with the heavy rouge, and Ruth Chamberlain with the gravely voice and the cigarette hanging out of her mouth who wrote all that drivel about society. Ruth did it with great style, and was beloved in the high society halls of Rochester; she knew everybody, and nobody moved without checking with Ruth. But she was like the iron-fisted bitch who just looked like something that came out of a movie. Those were the women.

Some reporters were beginning to show up and one of them, Sally Miles Watts [Sarah Watts], was a young female reporter in the early 1960s on the *Times Union*. She was very attractive, perhaps also by contrast to those crones who were around her—and I say that sort of with affection. Of course, I'm looking at all this through seventeen- or eighteen-year-old eyes. It struck me that Sally was quite flirtatious. Not with me, because she was five or six years older, but with several of the males, some of whom she wound up going out with. You could see all this sort of playing out. Ultimately she married one of them. I would say, though, that the women I've worked with for the most part just have been just outstanding people. I don't think that we who were here made a big deal out of that. Women here have pretty well held their own.

We have many more women who have come into the work environment in the news area in the last twenty-five years than perhaps the first ten or so that I was there. There were relatively few. But it has clearly swung the other way. With few exceptions, they're all as good as anybody I know and worked with, and have enjoyed working with. With one exception. I can think of some men I've worked with whom I consider to be complete fools, just people that drive you nuts. I can only think of one woman that even I would grudgingly call a real bitch, who was just a nasty person. But people are people, so it doesn't make any difference, does it? I think women have enjoyed good working conditions here—Gannett has always been a leader in that. I think we practice what we preach around here.

(1994)

---

Upon reflection, I felt that my strategy of contrasting the views of male and female Gannett journalists was successful in that it brought issues to light and also illustrated two very different worldviews. During the interviews I sometimes found it challenging not to show emotion or to argue with the men who insisted that women loved working for Gannett. Of course, it was important that all of the journalists I interviewed felt comfortable to tell their own stories, so I learned not to argue with them. The following commentary suggests a very different story regarding the experiences of women journalists who worked for the Rochester, New York, *Democrat & Chronicle* and the *Times Union*. As you can see, this perspective differs significantly from most of the information provided by the male reporters.

---

Most of the men interviewed said that they thought the female newsworkers were happy working for the *Rochester Times Union* and the *Democrat & Chronicle*. Although a few men, like Flynn, suggest that Gannett had always been a leader in the hiring and treatment of female reporters, the women interviewed for this oral history project had somewhat different perceptions regarding their value to Gannett. Each woman mentions sometimes being given marginal assignments and occasionally being treated in a patronizing manner. *Times Union* feature writer Margaret Beck eventually became dismayed by the cynicism of both her editors and her male colleagues, and left journalism for a career in advertising. When she started work at the *Times Union* in 1952, Beck was the only reporter with an electric typewriter, which she thought might give her somewhat of an advantage. Unfortunately, her typewriter didn't seem to matter much to her male editors:

> I think there was quite a bit of chauvinism, quite a bit. Kermit Hill, who had been the political reporter, dreamed up this story he wanted me to do. At Ontario Beach Park they still rented bathing suits; you could go and rent black wool tank suits. Somehow the idea came up that they should update their image, and he arranged an interview. I worked pretty hard on the story and one of the reporters came up to me and said, "It was a good story, who wrote the lead for you?" So there was that kind of attitude.
>
> (1994, pp. 2–3)

Feature writer Sarah Watts, who later became editor of the *Times Union* weekend entertainment supplement, is described in these interviews by her male colleagues as attractive and flirtatious. Watts says that although some editors treated female reporters fairly, in general during the 1950s and 1960s women at Gannett were "second-class citizens":

> Among the things that happened to me was great liberty under Howard Hosmer, and I was riding high on that for several years. And then the

editors changed. He became managing editor, which was wonderful for him, but not for me because the new editor, John Dougherty, was a tough guy. I don't think he really liked women in the newsroom. I wanted to take classes offered to all reporters in speed writing that were being given at a public high school, tuition free. I asked if I could do that. He said, "No, because you're no doubt going to get married and have babies and leave us, and it won't be worth the one hundred dollar investment"—which I thought was terrible.

I looked around for things to do at the paper and I talked to a woman named Ruth B. Chamberlain. Why do we always remember their middle initials? Because the bylines were there every day. A wonderful woman who was a maiden lady, and a lady she was, who cared for her invalid sister, and ran the society page in the days when society pages were that. She had a little three-by-five [inch] file card index about everybody in Rochester, and whom they'd married, and so forth and so on. She was also a true trade unionist.

I asked her, "What are my chances around here?" She said, "If you're lucky and if I die, you could become society editor." The only other woman of any stature on the paper was Rose Sold, who had been there forever and had the church beat, hardly one I was coveting. There was a future for me opening up through a man named John C. Hadley who came into Rochester and was editing special sections, which included a weekly tabloid and then specials on fashion, on cars, even on the hot dog. I became his sole staff person, and it was an interesting job.

(1995, p. 6)

One other thing happened which again shows the status of women on that newspaper. When raises were handed out, I was offered a raise, but only got a modest, the lowest of the low, a five-dollar-a-week raise—two hundred and fifty dollars for the whole year. Because I had a husband who was working, he was supposed to provide for me. That's what I was told by the managing editor, a man named Vernon Croop.

(1995, p. 8)

The attitude toward women was just horrible and best explained, I think, by Gannett's treatment of a young woman named Pat Lemm who came to the paper when I was first there. A lovely woman, but without a lot of education and without much newspaper experience. Her father was the president of Edwards Department Store, the fourth largest department store in downtown Rochester, and she was given this job. But she was never trained. Nor was I trained. There was a lousy system. There was never any mentor for you. Bill Ringle kind of took me under his wing, and he was wonderful. I remember his helping me on a story about covering a gypsy funeral for one thing. But no one was there. There was no kind of training going on as there has been subsequently since those days in the fifties and sixties.

(1995, p. 20)

When I first arrived in 1956 at the *Times Union*, I went into what I thought was the rest room. I saw people coming and going. There were lockers there, but I never needed it because it was summer and I kept my purse in my desk. I just went in to use the bathroom. It was not until I was there several weeks and I heard this titter, did I realize that it was the men's room, and they were just trying to catch me there in the act. That was their idea of having fun with the women. I thought it was pretty childish but let them have their fun.

(1995, p. 22)

Jean Giambrone's experiences with Gannett were perhaps most telling regarding the role of women at Gannett during this era. Initially employed as a freelancer to write a women's athletics column while she was a student at the University of Rochester, Giambrone was hired on a full-time basis after her college graduation. For four years during World War II, Giambrone covered local news for the *Times Union*. After the war, Giambrone married and went back to writing a sports column on a part-time basis. She covered both women's and men's golf, bowling, soccer and other sports, and often wrote a variety of stories for the newspaper each day:

Eventually, I covered everything that you can shake a fist at. I never covered a football game but I interviewed football players. You know what I'm saying? If they were stuck at the office, they'd say, "will you?" I'd go cover a basketball game or I'd go cover a soccer game—boy's, girls, high school, college, whatever. For my love of sports and my knowledge, etc. I would go cover those things. In my lifetime I've interviewed many athletes.

(1994, p. 5)

Giambrone recounts with pride becoming the first women allowed into the interview room of the Master's golf tournament:

The first year I went, they wouldn't let me in. When I finally got in— some people talk about male chauvinism and all that stuff, they can talk all they want—I had nothing but thanks to the guys because they were the ones who got me in. The second year I went, they said, "What are you doing here?" I was the only woman; there were all men covering it, two to three hundred men at the Master's golf tournament.

I looked at Will Grimsley, who in my book is one of the all-time great sportswriters. He was with AP [Associated Press] and I said, "I'll tell you what, I'm not here to write about Mrs. Arnold Palmer's clothes or something; I'm here to do what you do. I have a bigger assignment this year. I don't do this just for my paper—I'm doing it for the whole Gannett news service and I can't get in there to do interviews and I can't use the typewriters and I can't get at the Western Union machines at those times, and so I've got a problem." He said, "That's not fair; let me see what I can do about it."

He spoke to a colleague and they went to a man who was retired and was a liaison between the press and the powers that be that run the tournament. At that time it was Clifford Roberts, and before that, Bobby Jones. They said to Clifford Roberts's secretary, "Give her press credentials; she needs to do what we do." She said, "Oh no, not until you speak to Mr. Roberts." They looked at me and said, "Come back in an hour," the guys did. I said, "Baloney, I've got to figure out a way to do this without having access to all this stuff." But, when I went back in an hour, the secretary was typing up my Class A press credentials.

(1994, p. 5)

I couldn't get into the men's locker rooms from where they were getting great stories. I'd be the only woman there, and once or twice I had the men come out and say, "Want to listen to my tape?" But, for the most part I did my own work. I had terrific cooperation from the athletes themselves because once or twice I'd stop them short of the locker room and they understood my predicament, so they'd talk to me. There was one incident with Ken Venturi when a whole big mess of guys were standing around listening to the interview and they started interjecting their own questions. All of a sudden he looked up and said, "She can't go in the locker room; you can. Let her talk."

(1994, p. 11)

When the US Open was here, I think it was 1988, I just wanted to go back and visit. Because of the number of events I had covered for the US Golf Association I got a permanent pass; it's a pin with my name engraved on it and I can go into any of the things. I went and I said, "I don't want to run around the golf course, I want to go in the press room and see the people." I was amazed at the number of women in there. In the old days I was the only woman.

(1994, p. 6)

Giambrone considered herself lucky that she was at the right place at the right time to become the first woman to cover sports for Gannett in Rochester. However, after World War II, although she often worked more than forty hours a week for the remaining thirty-five years of her career with Gannett, she was considered a freelancer and she worked without employee benefits or retirement pay.

---

My strategy of letting each person tell his or her own story and comparing and contrasting individual perceptions during the writing process worked better than when I initially attempted to question male journalists' views on women reporters during the interview process. When I tried to use Jean Giambrone's experiences to illustrate challenges women faced in the Gannett newsrooms, the men I was interviewing began to shut down. They either became quiet, changed the topic or they suggested that Giambrone was not a "real" journalist but merely a "freelancer" or a part-time worker. As my goal for the oral history project was to gather the newsworkers' experiences, for them to tell their own stories, I knew that I had to earn and maintain their trust throughout the entire interview process. I felt it was important to tread lightly in controversial areas and therefore my strategy was to bring up sensitive topics, casually and matter-of-factly, when the narrators were discussing related issues. In presenting a variety of experiences and opinions, a larger structure of feeling about working as a journalist for Gannett began to emerge from the interviews. The book project showcased the experiences of rank-and-file reporters who worked in Rochester, New York. Over the years, the feedback I have received from the men and women who were involved in the research project has been inspirational. Some of the narrators shared the book with family members and they found that it helped them to talk more openly about their journalistic careers.

---

## Oral History Exercises

1. Conduct an open-ended oral history interview with an individual about his or her career. Plan for an hour-long in-person interview and be sure to tape it. Before the interview, obtain some background about the person you plan to interview. To prepare for the interview, think about topic areas that you wish to explore but only craft one opening question. Remember, it is important to listen to the person speak and to ask additional questions based on the person's commentary.
2. Following the open-ended interview, transcribe the complete interview. After the transcription process is complete, go back and edit the interview.
3. Following the open-ended interview, complete an analysis of the interview process. Consider the behavior of the interviewee as well as your own behavior. What was your comfort level during the interview? How did non-verbal communication impact the interview process? How valuable was the information you obtained? It is helpful to compare your experiences during this interview with other, more structured interviews you have previously completed.

## References

Anderson, Kathryn, & Jack, Dana C. (1998). Learning to listen: Interview techniques and analyses. In Robert Perks & Alistair Thomson (Eds.), *The Oral History Reader* (pp. 157–171). London: Routledge, 1998.

Beck, Margaret. (1994, August 5). Interview by Bonnie Brennen. Oral History of Gannett Newsworkers project.

Beck, Robert. (1994, August 5). Interview by Bonnie Brennen. Oral History of Gannett Newsworkers project.

Brandt, J. Donald. (1993). *A history of Gannett, 1960–1993*. Arlington, VA: Gannett.

Brennen, Bonnie. (2001). *For the record: An oral history of Rochester, New York, Newsworkers*. Bronx, NY: Fordham University Press.

Clune, Henry. (1947). *Main Street beat*. New York: W. W. Norton.

Clune, Henry. (1994a, May 4). Interview by Bonnie Brennen. Oral History of Gannett Newsworkers project.

Clune, Henry. (1994b, June 6). Interview by Bonnie Brennen. Oral History of Gannett Newsworkers project.

Deutsch, Art. (1994, June 13). Interview by Bonnie Brennen. Oral History of Gannett Newsworkers project 13.

Fedler, Fred. (2000). *Lessons from the past: Journalists' lives and work, 1850–1950*. Prospect Heights, IL: Waveland, 2000.

Flynn, Thomas. (1994, November 4). Interview by Bonnie Brennen. Oral History of Gannett Newsworkers project.

Fradenburgh, Don. (1994, July 7). Interview by Bonnie Brennen. Oral History of Gannett Newsworkers project.

General principles for oral history. (2010). Oral History Association. Retrieved from http://www. oralhistory.org.

Giambrone, Jean. (1994, July 6). Interview by Bonnie Brennen. Oral History of Gannett Newsworkers project.

Grele, Ronald J. (1991). *Envelopes of sound: The art of oral history* (2nd edn). New York: Praeger.

Hardt, Hanno, & Brennen, Bonnie. (Eds.). (1995). *Newsworkers: Toward a history of the rank and file.* Minneapolis: University of Minnesota Press.

Hoffman, Alice. (1996). Reliability and validity in oral history. In David K. Dunaway & Willa K. Baum (Eds.), *Oral history: An interdisciplinary anthology* (pp. 87–93), Walnut Creek, CA: Sage.

Kaidy, Mitch. (1994, July 5). Interview by Bonnie Brennen. Oral History of Gannett Newsworkers project.

King, Floyd. (1994, June 23). Interview by Bonnie Brennen. Oral History of Gannett Newsworkers project.

Luckett, Charles. (1994, September 7). Interview by Bonnie Brennen. Oral History of Gannett Newsworkers project.

Markovitz, Adam. (2011, July 8/15). Casting the spell: An oral history. *Entertainment Weekly,* pp. 36–47.

Matheson, Jennifer L. (2007). The voice transcription technique: Use of voice recognition software to transcribe digital interview data in qualitative research. *Qualitative Report, 12* (4), 547–560.

McCullough, David. (2008). *John Adams.* New York: Simon & Schuster.

Merrill, Arch. (1954). *Mr. and Mrs. Ezra R. Andrews: Our master builders.* Rochester, NY: Rochester Institute of Technology.

Morrissey, Charles T. (1998). On oral history interviewing. In Robert Perks & Alistair Thompson (Eds.), *The Oral History Reader* (pp. 107–113). London: Routledge.

Terkel, Studs. (1967). *Division Street: America.* New York: Pantheon.

Terkel, Studs. (1997). *My American century.* New York: The New Press.

Thompson, Paul. (1990). *The voice of the past: Oral history* (2nd edn). Oxford: Oxford University Press.

Watts, Sarah. (1995, November 21). Interview by Bonnie Brennen. Oral History of Gannett Newsworkers project.

Williams, Raymond. (1977/1988). *Marxism and literature.* Oxford: Oxford University Press.

Yow, Valerie Raleigh. (2005). *Recording oral history: A guide for the humanities and social sciences* (2nd edn). Walnut Creek, CA: AltaMira Press.

Zeigler, Michael. (1983, January 2). Frank E. Gannett. *Upstate Magazine,* pp. 14–26.

# CHAPTER 7

# Ethnography and Participant Observation

*Any gaze is always filtered through the lenses of language, gender, social class, race and ethnicity. There are no objective observations, only observations socially situated in the worlds of the observer and the observed.*
— Norman Denzin and Yvonna Lincoln (1998, p. 24)

Ethnography focuses on understanding what people believe and think, and how they live their daily lives. It is used to answer questions about people's beliefs, rituals, attitudes, actions, stories and behaviors, emphasizing what people actually do rather than what they say they do. Grounded in the concept of culture, ethnography was first associated with anthropology and involved long-term field research observing activities and behaviors and interacting with people from different cultures. Researchers originally lived and worked consistently with members of other cultures for many months or years.

More recently, ethnography has become a popular qualitative approach used by researchers in a variety of disciplines, including sociology, education, public policy, media studies and marketing, to understand people's interests, practices and experiences. In the twenty-first century the realm of ethnography has expanded to consider many types of foreign and domestic cultures and interest groups, including organizational and online communities. Journalists and writers use ethnographic approaches to add greater depth of interpretation to their storytelling, and ethnography is currently used in business and industry as a strategy to assess consumers' actions, going beyond their self-reported activities and opinions.

Researchers suggest that the recent popularity of ethnography may be due to fundamental changes occurring in Western societies. Gobo (2011) sees Western cultures as being fixated on observation, and maintains that being observed and observing others are central aspects of our contemporary lives. For example, surveillance cameras document our public actions, we film our social interactions and activities on video cameras and cell phones, and we routinely post images and videos on YouTube, Google+ and Facebook. It is currently estimated that sixty hours of video are uploaded to YouTube each minute and that YouTube content is viewed 1 trillion times each year (Grossman, 2012). In an era in which the public and private realms have become blurred, it makes sense that ethnography, with its emphasis on observing people's actions and behaviors, has become a widely used methodology.

As the field of ethnography has evolved, researchers have drawn on a variety of strategies, philosophies and theoretical positions, which have influenced the types of ethnographic research that have been produced. Some ethnographers continue to favor systematic observations in an attempt to uncover structures, patterns and relationships. Other researchers, particularly postmodern ethnographers, maintain that it is impossible to discover a final, fixed or authoritative meaning of people's actions, and in their work they stress the open-endedness and incompleteness of their observations, as well as their own role in the ethnographic process (Denzin & Lincoln, 1998). These days, even the term ethnography has become some-what contentious: it has been called a synonym for all qualitative research, or described as a philosophical orientation, a methodology or a research tool. Some researchers insist that ethnography means the on-site study of foreign cultures over an extended period of time, while others suggest that ethnography may be done locally, within a researcher's culture, and that it need not take years to complete, as long as it helps us to understand a specific group, community or culture. In this chapter I use the term ethnography to describe the qualitative method of observing, talking to and interacting with people in their natural environments; that is, where they live, play and/or work. While researchers' definitions of ethnography may vary, observation is central to all understandings of this method.

## Thick Description

Ethnography emphasizes listening, watching and interacting with people as they go about their lives. Researchers work to establish rapport and select informants so that they can observe, interview and participate in activities with members of a group, culture or organization in order to learn about the explicit and tacit realms of their experiences, routines and practices. The explicit aspects of culture are those that individuals are able to address and discuss with a researcher, while the tacit parts of a culture are those things that are outside people's consciousness or awareness (DeWalt & DeWalt, 2011). Establishing the relevant context for a researcher's observations is an integral aspect of ethnography. The contextual background may focus on key historical, political, economic or social aspects of the group or culture being observed, providing key information to give a researcher the relevant frames of reference for her or his observations.

Cultural anthropologist Clifford Geertz (1973) sees ethnography as a blending of observation and interpretation, which together provide the "thick description" of a culture or group. Within the interpretation process, researchers consider the relevant social context, which helps them to understand that their observations are representations of a group's cultural reality. Geertz uses an example of the differences between a twitch and a wink to illustrate the importance of context in creating thick description. At first glance, a twitch and a wink may look exactly the same to an observer. However, a twitch is usually an involuntary action while a wink is considered a deliberate act of communication. A person who winks is drawing on a specific social code to attempt to communicate something in particular to someone else, on the sly. It is up to a researcher to understand the appropriate context and intention of the action in order to determine whether the facial movement is a twitch or a wink. As Geertz (1973) explains, the information that researchers collect is not objective data but is "really our own constructions of other people's constructions of what they and their compatriots are up to" (p. 9). Most of the information that a researcher collects about a group of people, or an event, activity or custom requires additional contextual information before it can be fully comprehended.

## Ethnography in Media Studies

The development of cultural studies, particularly its emphasis on the reception and consumption of texts, inspired the use of ethnography in communication and media studies. Researchers began to draw on ethnographic methods in an attempt to draw out broader contexts surrounding media usage, as well as to understand how people actually engaged with media. Researchers focused on the contexts for media consumption, the process of reception as well as the many experiences and practices of people as they used media (Morley & Silverstone, 1991). Drawing on Hall's (1980) model of encoding and decoding—which is discussed more fully in Chapter 8— researchers observed the routine usage of technologies and texts by audience members. In their audience-centered studies they focused on the role readers and viewers played in the production of meanings. These days, researchers often refer to the time when media studies began to emphasize the role of the audience as "the ethnographic turn" (Machin, 2002, p. 74).

Contemporary ethnographic research projects in media studies often focus on work practices in communication industries and audience reception to popular cultural texts. The fieldwork is usually completed in a few months rather than over several years. Instead of living within a specific community, communication and media researchers often observe the work process at media outlets such as researching online investigative news agencies, broadcast news stations, newspapers, advertising agencies and public relations firms. For example, the ethnographic research project "The Culture of a Women-Led Newspaper: An Ethnographic Study of the *Sarasota Herald-Tribune*," reprinted and discussed at the end of this chapter, studied newsroom culture through participant observation and depth interviews. The researcher spent three weeks observing all aspects of the newsroom in one-week increments during a nineteen-month period and interviewed twenty-six reporters, editors, photographers and designers about newsroom policies and practices.

Communication and media studies researchers also use new media to conduct ethnography online with special interest groups, professional organizations and virtual communities, a process sometimes referred to as "netnography" (DeWalt & DeWalt, 2011, p. 173). People with similar interests, values and beliefs create virtual communities in an effort to identify and bring together like-minded people to hang out, discuss issues and topics, and coordinate activities. Often these online communities are based on popular culture interests, such as a favorite actor, musician or television show. However, people with particular political identifications, health problems, specific social values or similar religious beliefs often come together on the Web. Researchers study the conversations, stories, practices and rituals of these groups to understand how people communicate in virtual communities. One benefit of web ethnography is that email messages, blog postings, online chats and other virtual communication can be stored, archived and searched by the researcher. Since media studies ethnographers working online are unable to observe the non-verbal social cues of their research participants, they focus on the context for the users' commentary as well as their writing style, use of acronyms such as LOL (laugh out loud), and how participants use emoticons such as ☺ to indicate their attitudes or emotions (Lindlof & Shatzer, 1998).

In contemporary media studies, some researchers use the terms ethnography and participant observation interchangeably. Others define participant observation as fieldwork through which a researcher observes and interacts with others, or as ethnography done in one's own culture rather than in a foreign country (Machin, 2002). Media studies researchers doing ethnography suggest that because they often study aspects of their own culture, it is often challenging for them to obtain enough critical distance from their projects in order to make ordinary and everyday situations seem "strange" (Stokes, 2003, p. 139).

## Participant Observation

Participant observation is integral to ethnography, often being referred to as its primary methodological tool. Researchers use participant observation to understand the language, practices and activities of a specific group, culture or institution. In participant observation, researchers go into the field to gain knowledge about activities, beliefs, values, relationships and interests so that they may learn more about how others make sense of their everyday lives. Participant observation is an open-ended and flexible research process that may be carried out by one researcher or by a research team.

Hoping to develop rapport with those being studied, researchers often live in the community, watching and participating in daily activities, rituals and ceremonies and observing, describing and documenting their actions and experiences. Participant observers learn and use the local language, listen to conversations, ask questions, watch what happens and learn the basic rules and procedures so that they can provide detailed descriptions of life at a particular time and place. Often, the closer the relationships that participant observers develop, the greater access they have to the social experiences of those being studied. Atkinson and Hammersley (1994) suggest that all social research should be seen as a type of participant observation because it is not possible to study aspects of our social world without actively engaging in it. From this perspective, participant observation is seen not as a specific research technique but instead as "a mode of being-in-the-world characteristic of researchers" (p. 249).

One of the most challenging aspects of participant observation is gaining access to a group, culture or organization. Some researchers use their personal and work contacts to begin the process, while others opt for topics of study that they already have personal access to or knowledge about. It is helpful for participant observers to be outgoing, enthusiastic and friendly, and for them to enjoy interacting with others. Gaining access for participant observations of businesses and institutions often begins with researchers determining the organizational hierarchy and getting the approval of those in charge.

Of course, gaining access also requires members of the group being studied to communicate openly with researchers. It is important for participant observers to develop rapport with members of the group or organization so that the members will open up and speak freely with them. Building rapport takes time and requires researchers to have good communication skills and to be open and truthful about their intentions. In order to build rapport with group members, sometimes it is necessary for researchers to illustrate their interest in, respect for and commitment to the community (DeWalt & DeWalt, 2011). When researchers and participants share the same goals for a research project, it is clear that rapport has been established.

Once researchers gain access and develop rapport, other challenges that they face in participant observation include deciding on a focus for their observations, learning how to document what they hear and see without overtly impacting group dynamics, separating researchers' descriptions from their interpretations and negotiating the involvement required to build rapport but without abandoning their role as a researcher (Berger, 1998). Researchers draw on their theoretical frameworks to help them craft their research questions and focus their observations.

It is helpful for researchers to be flexible, adaptable, resourceful and curious. While participant observers know that their background, sex, race or ethnicity may affect the way they are perceived, they must also understand that their clothing, hairstyles, speech habits and/or facial gestures may also influence people's response to them. Participant observers should be careful to avoid preconceived notions about a culture or group and they should remain open to learning new observation strategies. Community members may be less likely to talk with researchers who appear rigid and inflexible about their research goals or who portray themselves as knowing too much about a group or organization.

The realm of participant observation is generally grouped into four major categories: complete observer, observer as participant, participant as observer, and complete participant. The complete observer, sometimes referred to as a non-participant observer, is someone who observes from a distance and has no interaction with the people, group or community that is being observed. At first glance, it may be difficult to envision a researcher on-site who does not interact with participants in any way, because the presence of a researcher generally has an influence on a group of people and their environment. However, some researchers have done observations through one-way glass mirrors or by using binoculars to observe others at a distance. More recently, some researchers choose to record activities and events on video cameras that are strategically placed around the site. These non-participant observers watch and analyze the recordings off-site at a later date.

The description observer as participant applies to researchers who are on-site but who distance themselves from those being observed. Such researchers may talk with and interview people in an organization or community but they do not actively participate in activities, rituals or events. Their field notes and observations emphasize what they have seen rather than what they have experienced, and they usually do not stay with members of the community because they find that their research role limits their interaction with those being studied.

The participant as observer, by contrast, is fully integrated into the culture being studied. This type of researcher lives in the community, participates in activities, and adopts specific interests, practices, rituals and procedures while taking extensive field notes about his or her observations and experiences. Considering full participation integral to the research process, the participant as observer strives to understand the meanings of actions within the community from an insider's position.

The complete participant has fully bonded with the organization, group or culture, adopting its members' values and beliefs, and has abandoned his or her research role in a process often known as "going native." The complete participant no longer takes field notes or observes activities; instead, the researcher adopts the cultural values, interests and concerns of the group. Once researchers have gone native, they usually reject their analytical role as a researcher and abandon the ethnographic project. While most researchers warn against going native, Jorgensen (1989) suggests that if researchers can return to their research projects after going native, they may get much richer information as a result of their direct access to and experience with the groups, organizations or cultures.

## Going Native in *Avatar*

In this section I draw on the 2009 film *Avatar* to provide clear examples that illustrate the four different types of participant observation. This science fiction film, written and directed by James Cameron, is at the time of writing the highest-grossing North American film ever made. *Avatar* takes place during the mid-twenty-second century on Pandora, a moon in the Alpha Centauri star system. The 10-foot tall, blue-skinned Na'vi are the indigenous people of Pandora; they are a wise and insightful humanoid culture who live in harmony with nature. Pandora is more than four light years from Earth and its atmosphere is uninhabitable by humans, yet the RDA Corporation is on Pandora mining the precious mineral unobtanium because it is the most efficient superconductor in existence. Although the corporation's mining threatens the Na'vi culture, RDA can sell each kilo of unobtanium that it takes for $20 million. In an effort to learn more about the Na'vi culture, researchers created remotely controlled avatars, which are genetically engineered hybrid bodies that mix human and Na'vi DNA.

Jake Sully (played by Sam Worthington) is a paraplegic former Marine who is chosen by RDA management for a mission on Pandora. Sully's initial goal is to use his avatar to interact with the Na'vi, gathering information about them from the inside to help researchers find a diplomatic solution to the unobtanium problem. Once on Pandora, Sully's avatar is attacked, and a beautiful young warrior, the daughter of the Na'vi tribe leader Neytiri (Zoe Saldana), rescues him. Although Neytiri considers Sully stupid, she is directed to teach him about the Na'vi culture.

Now that I have provided some contextual material about the film *Avatar*, we can see that Sully's role on Pandora may initially be seen as that of a participant as observer. Through his avatar he learns about Na'vi customs, beliefs and behaviors. Neytiri teaches him their language and Sully actively participates in Na'vi rituals and activities. Yet, he learns about the Na'vi in an effort to gain useful information about them that may later be used by others to control them. Sully documents everything he sees, feels and learns in daily video logs that are shared with the researchers, RDA management and members of the security team in the human compound.

Sigourney Weaver plays Grace Augustine, who is an exobiologist and the head of the avatar program on Pandora. Grace mentors Sully and serves in the roll of an observer as participant. Through her avatar she observes the Na'vi, studying them and learning about their culture mostly from a distance. While she speaks their language, her interactions with the indigenous people of Pandora are strictly professional. As a researcher she is interested in understanding the Na'vi culture but does not wish to participate in their rituals and/or activities or become a part of their culture.

Colonel Miles Quaritch (Stephen Lang) is the head of RDA's private security force, and we can see him as illustrating the role of a complete observer. He has no interaction with the Na'vi (apart from killing them) but often observes them on the video feeds provided by the surveillance cameras. Because the Na'vi have no knowledge that they are being watched, it is unlikely that their actions are influenced by his observations.

As Sully learns the ways of the Na'vi, he begins to become a member of the tribe. His military background helps the Na'vi warriors relate to him. Sully comments during one of his final video logs that everything has become backwards, that his time interacting with the Na'vi through his avatar is now his real life and that his time in the compound has become a dream. After Sully participates in a final ceremony to become a Na'vi man, he picks Neytiri as his mate and his allegiance shifts to the Na'vi tribe. He has gone native and may be seen to illustrate the complete participant role. Sully leads a successful Na'vi battle against the RDA, and all humans are deported from Pandora. At the end of the film, Sully abandons his human body for his avatar form and chooses a full-time existence as a Na'vi warrior.

Thus, the *Avatar* example illustrates the four main ways in which participant observers interact with members of a culture, and details a process of learning about a group of people in an effort to understand their lives.

## Field Notes

While many qualitative researchers consider the participant as observer the most effective category of participant observation, it is important to remember that the mere presence of a researcher changes the group dynamics and impacts the way people will react. At best, the inclusion of a participant observer will be comfortable to the group and his or her presence will become natural and normal. However, even when an ethnographer is fully integrated into a community, the researcher is unable to know what community members are really thinking or how they will react when he or she is not there.

Systematic and purposeful observation helps researchers to understand the relationships, customs, rituals and the sense-making practices within a community or group. Researchers observe as much as they can in order to gather impressions and information about the group being studied. However, it is important for these observations to be documented so that they can be analyzed and interpreted.

While it is helpful for participant observers to have excellent short-term memories, most researchers also keep detailed field notes throughout the observation process. Researchers include information regarding the locations of their observations, the dates and times that the observations take place and a description of the physical space where the observations are held in their field notes. They record information about the people they observe, including their ages, backgrounds, races and ethnicities, as well as commentary on their physical characteristics, style of dress and use of language. In their field notes, researchers describe the activities and rituals they observe and participate in, the rules and standards for activities and events, and patterns of behavior between individuals in the group. They document the types of interactions between men and women, young and old, and people of different classes, races and ethnicities. They also record the verbal comments that they hear, the relevant non-verbal communication they observe and their reactions to their own participation in events and activities, as well as their observations and reflections on the research process.

You may wonder whether it is necessary for researchers to write down everything that they see and hear. Participant observers usually keep a written record of all of their initial observations. As their observations progress, ethnographers' theoretical frameworks and research questions help them to shape their topics and interests, and to put their observations into the relevant context. While it may seem impossible for researchers to document all of their observations, as they gain access to a group or community and become more comfortable with the observation process they begin to focus on activities, events and conversations that are new or different than their initial observations. They also become more at ease with the group, and community members become more comfortable with them.

Some participant observers jot down key words and phrases during their observations and later craft more detailed notes and descriptions. Others use audio and video recording devices during interviews and events to augment their field notes. Researchers also keep calendars and logs of events and activities they observe, as well as the names of people they speak with. It is important for ethnographers to be comfortable interviewing others as they will need to augment their observations by asking formal and informal questions about what they see and hear. Some ethnographers ask casual questions during their observations, while other researchers conduct formal interviews with group members. Additional detailed information about interviewing is provided in Chapters 3 and 6.

Throughout their fieldwork, researchers also make mental notes about their observations that they find are particularly relevant to their research questions, a process known as inscription. While people tend to see things that they are trained to recognize as interesting or important to their culture, the inscription process encourages researchers to get outside of their comfort zone to observe things that are important to others (LeCompte & Schensul, 1999). Researchers' mental notes on their observations are later written down as field notes. Throughout the ethnographic process, researchers consult their field notes, rereading them, annotating them, reflecting on their observations, adding additional commentary and using them to provide preliminary analysis and interpretations.

It is important for new media researchers who do ethnography in virtual settings and online observing of social media, chat rooms, blogs and websites to keep field notes too. While many of these online interactions are recorded and archived electronically, field notes help media researchers to capture their own descriptions and perceptions of the interactions, and they also reinforce the research function for participant observers.

## Reflexivity

Contemporary ethnographers think critically about their role in the research process, a concept known as reflexivity. Denzin and Lincoln (1998) find that at one level, reflexivity "is associated with self-critique and personal quest, playing on the subjective, the experiential, and the idea of empathy" (p. 395). However, reflexivity may also help researchers to consider the difficulty of understanding those being observed, particularly when their values, rituals and experiences are different than those of the researcher. An emphasis on reflexivity also challenges ethnographers to explain their theoretical positions and remind them of the possibility that there may be alternative interpretations for their observations.

Reflexivity may also be used to showcase the collaborative nature of ethnography and to help researchers understand that, as outsiders, they may have only limited access to the lives of those being studied, which may impact the richness of their analysis and understanding. Researchers also use their field notes to think critically about their interpretations of their observations. In their field notes, ethnographers consider their role in the research process and their intentions for the research. Critically thinking about "the place from which they observe" (DeWalt & DeWalt, 2011, p. 93), researchers try to understand the relationships between themselves, those they observe and the stories they choose to tell about these interactions.

## Analyzing and Interpreting Ethnographic Material

Ethnographers observe groups of people engaged in everyday activities. They record their interpretations of what they see and hear, and analyze the documents and artifacts relevant to the group, culture or organization. For Geertz (1973), cultural interpretation is not a scientific method but, instead, a fluid process, with researchers "guessing at meanings, assessing the guesses, and drawing explanatory conclusions from the better guesses" (p. 20).

Through the analysis of their fieldwork, ethnographers use specific conceptual frameworks to uncover patterns, themes and experiences that they compare with other patterns, themes and experiences. Researchers analyze similarities and differences within events, rituals and interactions; they assess the omissions, gaps and/or absences in their observations, identify sequences and frequencies of commentary, activities and rituals. They discuss key observations, select relevant examples for further commentary and provide likely explanations for their observations. Some ethnographers use strategies from textual analysis to evaluate contextual information and transcriptions of their interviews, often comparing them with other documentary evidence that they obtain. Textual analysis is more fully discussed in Chapter 8.

Ethnographers' interpretations are based on understanding the relevant social context for the activities, rituals and events they observe, as well as the tacit and explicit information they collect. They may revisit their research questions, discuss their observations with other researchers and reconsider key concepts and relevant theories to help them interpret their information. Through their interpretations, researchers create meanings from the materials they collect. After they have gathered their evidence and interpreted their findings, ethnographers create a written account of their interpretations to share with others. These stories are theoretically informed interpretations of the culture of a group, organization or community being studied. Ultimately, in ethnography it is important to remember that research is "always a matter of interpreting, indeed constructing, reality from a particular position" (Morley & Silverstone, 1991, p. 161).

## Ethical Considerations

Informed consent is integral to all ethnographic research. As with other qualitative methodologies, it is crucial that no participant be harmed during the research process. Because participant observers usually spend considerable time watching and interacting with group members, it is easy for those being observed to forget that they are being watched and studied. Researchers should be up front about their intentions and should remind those being studied of their research goals. Because they spend a lot of time with members of a group or community, researchers often learn personal information about the lives of the people whom they observe. Some of this information is private and it could do potential harm to those involved if the information was disclosed. Therefore, it is imperative that all participants are able to willingly choose to participate in any ethnographic research projects, and they must be given the right to privacy throughout the research process.

The amount and type of interaction that researchers have with a group, organization or culture is a major ethical concern within ethnography. By definition, participant observation generally implies that researchers will become immersed in the culture and emotionally involved with those they observe. And yet, for participant observers to become successful researchers they must be able to step away from the community in order to craft field notes and think critically about what they have seen and heard. While ethnographers who develop relationships with group members have better access to the community, it is imperative that researchers be honest about their intentions.

In the field of media studies, ethnographic research is regularly done with online special interest groups and organizations. Given the ease of joining such groups, you may wonder whether it is acceptable to join a group and do research without getting explicit permission. It is important to remember that with qualitative research it is never acceptable for a researcher to deceive an individual or a group about her or his research intentions. Infiltrating any group, whether it is online or in person, without the members' specific permission is ethically wrong. It is deception if a researcher does not disclose, to any people who might be involved, her or his intentions about a research project. Researchers who join groups without disclosing their research intentions are using others and lying to them about their role in the group or organization. While it may seem expedient at the time, I would strongly urge all researchers not to do it.

An additional ethical issue postmodern ethnographers have recently raised regarding traditional ethnographic research is the role that the researcher plays in the observation process. Concerned that a participant observer may privilege the gaze of the researcher over that of those being observed, or may use the fieldwork merely to enhance his or her career, postmodern ethnographers attempt to dismantle the distinction between the observer and the observed in favor of a model of cooperative dialogue (Atkinson & Hammersley, 1994). Postmodern researchers maintain that when it is used ethically, ethnography may create opportunities that will enhance the quality of life for the people in the group, culture or organization.

## Research Using Ethnography

Geertz (1973) suggests that researchers should consider ethnographic reports to be fictional interpretations, not because they are false or inaccurate but because they are interpretations made by a researcher. While Geertz raises an important point, other ethnographers maintain that it is not enough for researchers to consider ethnographic writings interpretive accounts; it is also important for them to address the theoretical perspectives framing the research as well as the literary devices and narrative conventions researchers use in constructing their reports.

The following research example, "The Culture of a Women-Led Newspaper: An Ethnographic Study of the *Sarasota Herald-Tribune*," by Tracy Everbach, used participant observation and interviews to understand how an all-female management team shaped the newsroom culture at the *Sarasota Herald-Tribune*. In her introduction and literature review, Everbach discusses changes in newsroom culture as more women began to work in journalism. and addresses the patriarchal structure of news that emphasizes male issues and concerns.

---

## "The Culture of a Women-Led Newspaper: An Ethnographic Study of the *Sarasota Herald-Tribune*," by Tracy Everbach

From *Journalism and Mass Communication Quarterly, 86* (3), 2006, 477–493.

The mainstream media in the United States emphasize male viewpoints, occasionally focusing news coverage on women and their concerns. The frequent absence from and trivialization of women in mass media have been labeled "symbolic annihilation,"[1] describing a public agenda that reports mainly men's activities, interests, and experiences.[2] While women have composed a majority of journalism students for three decades, their work in newsrooms has not significantly changed dominant news values in the United States. Few women serve in the highest ranks of news organizations, where decision-making power lies.[3] In 2006, 18 percent of newspaper publishers were women, the highest percentage ever, but far from an equitable distribution with men.[4]

Mass media scholars suggest that female journalists view news differently from male journalists.[5] Since women increased their newsroom presence, starting in the 1970s, they have changed some definitions of news, Kay Mills notes.[6] Women's greater numbers in newsrooms coincided with an increase in stories addressing social problems, personalities and human interest.[7] Still, changing newsroom culture, meaning overall shared values, beliefs and expectations, has been a slow struggle.[8] Male interests continue to define dominant news values and shape workplace culture.

This research examines the only large American newspaper with an all-women management team at the turn of the twenty-first century. A female publisher, executive editor, managing editor and two assistant managing editors led the *Sarasota* (Florida) *Herald-Tribune* from 1999 to 2003, creating an unusual opportunity for a case study. This research examines the female managers' influences on the newspaper's culture, using theoretical bases in feminism and management. The central research question is: Did the all-women management team at the *Sarasota Herald-Tribune* shape newsroom culture in a gendered way?

## Literature Review

Journalism's routines and practices force reporters and editors to focus news coverage on government and corporations, and on sources who have authority and power, as Gans and Tuchman showed in seminal ethnographic studies of news organizations.[9] Those who hold "the reins of legitimized power" have greater access to mass media than other groups and therefore are more likely to be quoted.[10] In a patriarchal society such as the United States, that powerful group has become institutionalized as white, middle-aged males.[11] Topics deemed "female" take secondary status in news.[12] By reinforcing legitimized values and power structures while repressing and eliminating elements that contradict norms, the news is socially constructed to emphasize male concerns.[13]

Before the 1970s, societal and labor market discrimination kept all but a few women from progressing to the upper ranks in journalism.[14] The second wave of the women's movement helped change women's roles in newsrooms, offering them new career opportunities.[15] Starting in the 1970s, newspapers pledged to diversify their staffs and create newsrooms more reflective of their readers.[16] The results for women thirty years later were disappointing: By 2006, women composed nearly 38 percent of newspaper employees in the United States, a percentage that had increased only slightly since the early 1980s.[17] In comparison, by the early twentieth century, women represented 46 percent of the total US workforce.[18] The American Journalist Survey reported that "compared to the U.S. civilian work force in 2000, women journalists are considerably less prevalent than women in other professions. Women journalists also are less likely to be managers than women in other areas of the professional work force."[19]

Women have not received opportunities equal to men's in the working world, including opportunities in education, training, hiring, promotion, contacts, and networking. They have faced barriers in part because of perceptions that their role in society should be that of family caretaker.[20] Structural barriers, discrimination, gender stereotyping and gender differences have precluded many women from advancing to management positions in US corporations and businesses.[21]

In mass media organizations, culture is "largely defined in male terms," according to Carter and her coauthors.[22] In 2001, women made up only 13 percent of top executives in media, telecom and high-tech firms, and only 9 percent of seats on corporate boards of these companies.[23] Women composed 26 percent of newspaper executives in 2002, and most of the high-ranking women held personnel, community affairs and legal positions, "areas not historically on the right track for moving into the highest positions."[24] In 2003, Al Neuharth, former chairman and CEO of Gannett Co. Inc., one of the largest American newspaper companies, criticized the newspaper business for continued lack of diversity. "Too many middle-aged white men still make the decisions" in newsrooms and journalism classrooms, Neuharth said.[25] Management and staff homogeneity contribute to decreases in newspaper circulation and drive away potential audiences, including young people, women and people of color.[26]

During the three decades during which newspapers have attempted to diversify their staffs, circulation has dropped. Women are more likely than men to give up reading newspapers.[27] In 2003, men comprised 55 percent of newspaper readers and women comprised 45 percent.[28] Some reasons for the smaller proportion of female readers include women's lack of representation in content and a dearth of articles that appeal to their interests.[29] In readership studies, women report that they want stories that are relevant to their lives.[30] They are

> interested in topics such as their children's education and how they learn (not the politics of the school board); time and money and how to save both; safety and health issues; women in the workplace; social concerns, such as homelessness; and family and personal relationships.[31]

Women also are interested in stories that have depth and sensitivity, rather than the detachment and factual superficiality attributed to stereotypical masculine news values.[32] In addition, women are interested in different types of news from men, demonstrated by a survey in which women said their top reading choices were community news, advice columns and international news, while men preferred professional sports, international news and local school sports.[33] Many women stop reading newspapers because they say the content is not relevant to them.[34]

Therefore, newspapers might attract more female readers if they published content that appealed to women's interests and portrayed women in positions of authority and power. Some journalists and scholars maintain that a newspaper headed by women would appeal to female readers.[35] Because "women are responsible for 81% of consumer buying" in the United States, newspapers, which depend on advertising, could improve business by reaching out to women, according to Miller.[36]

However, including more female decision makers does not necessarily change news content. A 1994 study of women's magazines from the 1960s through the 1980s found that female editors did not substantially alter negative and stereotypical portrayals of women in magazine content.[37] The authors concluded that the female editors adopted the same stereotypes male editors had used in the past, and speculated that changing magazine content would require more than female leadership; it would demand "changes in the dominant culture."[38] A 2005 study by Lavie and Lehman-Wilzig noted that both men and women internalize news traditions that focus on male hegemonic values, which makes change difficult no matter the leaders' gender.[39]

A companion study to the present ethnography found that the content of the *Sarasota Herald-Tribune* under the all-women management team did not differ from that of other mainstream US newspapers.[40] The content analysis revealed that the *Herald-Tribune*'s front page, local news, business, sports and lifestyle sections represented few women, so the female management team clearly did not change news values regarding content selection. For example, only 25 percent of sources quoted on the *Herald-Tribune*'s front page were female, consistent with what is reported in studies of male-managed newspapers.[41]

Although female management did not change newspaper content, female managers might influence workplace culture. Some management studies show that people's perceptions of "good managers" favor a "masculine" style.[42] For many years, stereotypical male behavior has been considered the norm for powerful positions.[43] So-called masculine leadership traits emphasize control, strategy, lack of emotion, and analysis, while so-called feminine traits include flexibility, empathy, collaboration and performance.[44] However, some studies show that men and women are similar in their overall effectiveness as leaders.[45] In one study, researchers considered defining management styles as "masculine" and "feminine" stereotyping and noted that empirical studies have found no significant gender differences in managerial behavior, personality or effectiveness.[46] Other research notes that societal socialization forces female managers into classifications based on stereotypes.[47] Aggressive women are characterized as "bitches" or "pushy" when displaying the same traits as are considered desirable in men.[48] Women also are accused of exploiting their sexuality to advance.[49]

Recent literature hypothesizes that women perceive power differently than men. While *Fortune* magazine in 2003 published its sixth annual list of the fifty most powerful women in the US workforce, it also published an article maintaining that women "see it [power] in terms of influence, not rank."[50] In an October 2003 *New York Times Magazine* cover story, Lisa Belkin postulated that women are retooling the male definition of work, which has long been about money and power.[51] Belkin wrote that women's work definition also is liberating for men: "Because women are willing to leave, men are more willing to leave, too—the number of married men who are full-time caregivers to their children has increased 18%."[52] The non-profit research firm Catalyst, which tracks trends and numbers of women in business, reported in its study "Women in U.S. Corporate Leadership: 2003" that 26 percent of women who have not yet reached the most senior posts say they do not want those jobs. Therefore, achieving hierarchical positions might not define success for women.

---

Using feminist standpoint theory to guide her observations, analysis and interpretation, the researcher looked at ways gender may have influenced newsroom practices and procedures.

---

## Theoretical Basis

When female journalists enter male-dominated newsrooms, they become indoctrinated to accept "masculine" news values as professional standards.[53] Women have not achieved sufficient autonomy or authority to change dominant newsroom culture; therefore, male and female journalists conduct their jobs in similar ways, with an emphasis on news that can be termed masculine.[54] Certain norms, values, styles and practices in journalism are perceived as masculine or feminine, Van Zoonen has observed. The so-called masculine topics include politics, crime and finance, reported with overwhelmingly male sources. Feminine topics include consumer news, human interest stories, culture and social policy, with mainly female sources.[55]

News judgment and news values in mainstream news media are based on what white men consider news, according to Gist.[56] Female journalists are socialized to view these standards as journalistic objectivity, allowing the news to become "masculinized" even when reported by women.[57]

While men lead a majority of newsrooms, some scholars and journalists contend that female management would foster its own form of newsroom culture. Cultural feminism views women with their own values, practices and "standpoint."[58] Using feminist-standpoint theory, this research seeks to analyze ways the *Sarasota Herald-Tribune*'s management team's gender shaped newsroom culture.

Previous research that included the *Sarasota Herald-Tribune* is relevant to this examination. *Impact*, a study of 100 American daily newspapers, found that the *Herald-Tribune*'s culture differed from that of 80 percent of other study subjects. The study classified the newspaper's culture as "constructive," defined as "encouraging members to work to their full potential, resulting in high levels of motivation, satisfaction, teamwork, service quality and sales growth." Cooperation, teamwork, communication, and higher profitability and readership also are associated with constructive cultures.[59]

In contrast, a majority of US newspapers had "aggressive defensive" cultures, defined as workplaces where change occurs slowly, hard work and devotion to the job are valued, and "people are expected to approach tasks in forceful ways to protect their status and security."[60] These findings mirror management research that identifies stereotypical masculine and feminine management styles.[61] Masculine management is characterized as less interpersonal and more auto-cratic, and feminine management is called more interpersonal and democratic.[62] Management and communication research shows that women and men learn to interpret power differently, with men generally regarding power as status and women interpreting it in terms of connections.[63] Women generally place impor-tance on community and connections while men tend to be concerned with competition and status.[64] The attributes associated with female leadership, including communication, collaboration and innovation, are more consistent with a constructive culture than with a defensive one.[65]

Because the newspaper industry, facing waning readership and circulation, is being forced to adapt technologically and economically, a constructive culture that encourages innovation and change could provide a successful business model for newspapers' future.[66]

This study recognizes constructive culture as reflective of a feminine man-agement style marked by openness, concern for family issues, collaboration, teamwork, and acknowledgement of workers' viewpoints and perspectives. This is not to say that women are the only managers capable of employing a feminine management style; men also can display these traits.

---

This ethnographic study focused on issues of gender within newsroom culture. In the next section, Everbach discusses the ethnographic pro-cess used for her research. Observations at the *Sarasota Herald-Tribune* newsroom were held for three one-week sessions and were combined with depth interviews with twenty-six employees regarding the workplace environment and management practices. Everbach, in email correspon-dence with the author (February 14, 2012), found the participant obser-vations "particularly effective" in understanding the newsroom culture. She was given a desk in the newsroom where she was able to observe the work process. Her newsroom access, as well as the support of her research project by newsroom managers, helped her to establish trust and build rapport with the employees. Ultimately she noted that the employees eventually came to accept her as a co-worker.

## Method

This ethnographic case study examined the *Sarasota Herald-Tribune*'s newsroom culture for three weeks during a nineteen-month period in 2002 and 2003. The researcher employed observation and in-depth interviews to study the workplace.

The researcher observed daily work routines inside the newsroom and conducted in-depth interviews with managers and employees to gather evidence on practices, policies and routines.[67] Depth interviews consisted of questioning newsroom workers to gather information on their perspectives and beliefs and to create rapport that allowed her to understand and interpret behavior.[68]

Fieldwork took place during one-week periods in June 2002, September 2003 and December 2003. These weeks were chosen after negotiation with the newsroom managers. The researcher observed newsroom operations, including editors' budget meetings, conferences among employees and managers, story assignments, story proposals, editing sessions, reporter interviews with sources, general discussions among employees, decisions on news coverage, and other newsroom routines and practices.

Interviews took place in the newsroom and outside of work to provide discussion freedom. The researcher conducted open-ended, in-depth interviews with twenty-six female and male reporters, photographers, page designers and editors about the workplace and their impressions and feelings about management practices and policies. All employees were promised anonymity except the top editors and the publisher, who agreed to be identified by name in the study. The interviewees answered a standardized list of open-ended questions developed by the researcher with provisions for follow-up, specific questions, and comments.

After the interviews and observation, the researcher coded all interview and observation subjects, then organized data into categories pointing to key concepts that revealed the nature and culture of the newspaper. For example, the researcher considered issues, symbols and rituals involved in the news process; news conventions, indoctrination and training; and employees' and managers' interpretations of their newsroom roles.

The researcher examined the data for influences the management team had on the newsroom culture, including interactions and communication between and among managers and employees, policies and practices, and general workplace atmosphere. She paid particular attention to women's standpoint as that of a marginalized or oppressed class and the reversal of this standpoint at the *Herald-Tribune* because the top managers were women. Also taken into account was management and journalism literature that noted women tend to bring emotion, cooperation, intimacy and a "holistic" approach of blending personal and professional lives to the workplace.[69]

The *Herald-Tribune*, owned by the New York Times Company, had a daily circulation of 106,000 in 2004, making it one of the 100 largest newspapers in the United States. The newspaper is located along Florida's west coast in Sarasota County, which has a population of about 335,000. Before the women assumed control of the newspaper in 1999, the daily circulation was about 110,000. However, it would not be fair to attribute a drop in circulation directly to the female management. Almost all American newspapers saw circulation decreases during this time.[70]

The *Herald-Tribune* distributes five zoned editions, four beyond the boundaries of Sarasota County, in Manatee County, population 275,000; and in Charlotte County, population 147,000.[71] The total audience comprises a population of about 757,000 in three counties. The news organization operates bureaus that produce zoned editions in Venice, Bradenton, Charlotte, and Englewood. The *Herald-Tribune* newspaper was created in 1938, when the *Sarasota Herald* bought the *Sarasota Daily Tribune*.[72] The New York Times Company bought the paper in 1982.

*Herald-Tribune* Publisher Diane McFarlin, Executive Editor Janet Weaver and Managing Editor Rosemary Armao said that when they formed their management team in 1999 their goal was to "put out a hard charging, high quality newspaper in a more effective newsroom—one that is fun, family friendly and diverse."[73] The employees called the newsroom "Amazonia" because of the all-women management team. The managers noted that filling the top jobs with women was not intentional.[74] As of September 2003, the paper employed 155 newsroom workers, 41 percent of whom were women, a higher percentage than the 37 percent national newsroom average for female employees that year.[75]

In the next section, note how the researcher coded all interview and observation information into key concepts related to the news process. In Everbach's analysis she discussed overarching themes related to newsroom culture that emerged in the research. Ultimately, her interpretations of the analysis of her research once again drew on elements of feminist-standpoint theory to help contextualize her research findings.

## Results

In interviews, *Herald-Tribune* managers said they believed their gender influenced the newspaper's culture in positive ways. Noted Publisher Diane McFarlin:

> This organization probably has more "feminine" traits than other newspapers. We tend to be more communicative. There is more of a sense of

> well-being of employees, more of a nurturing environment, and this is
> true of our male employees, too.[76]

The consistent themes that arose among employees and managers regarding the workplace culture were the newspaper's family-friendly policies, an atmosphere of openness and transparency in decision making, a consensus-building managerial style, and clear communication between management and employees.

The concept of balancing work and personal life is a relatively new US workplace phenomenon, coinciding with women's entry into management positions after the feminist movement of the 1970s.

In interviews, *Herald-Tribune* managers said they made particular efforts to accommodate families and employees' family issues. This contradicts a phenomenon many women with children have reported in the corporate world, known as the "mommy track." In the 1970s through 1990s, female managers who left corporations temporarily to raise children found that when they returned, they did not attain the same status they had had when they left.[77] The "mommy track" concept not only caused women to lose managerial ground but also ignored the needs of men interested in assuming greater roles in raising children.[78]

In fact, a male *Herald-Tribune* reporter,[79] considered one of the top reporters at the *Herald-Tribune*, said that the paper's female leadership allowed him a family life he did not have in previous journalism jobs. Over more than a decade as a single father, he had not found a job that allowed him to spend time with his son.[80] When he interviewed at the *Herald-Tribune*, Publisher McFarlin asked him what made him happiest. "I know my answer should have been 'Having a page one story on Sunday,' but I said, 'My son,'" the reporter recalled. "I was mortified, but she looked at me and said, 'Good answer.'"[81]

The managers value family life, a philosophy that fosters employee loyalty, according to the male reporter and other employees interviewed. "I worked eight straight days after 9/11 and I had no problem with it," said Reporter No. 1.[82]

Several veteran employees reported that before the female management team assumed power, the newspaper's culture dictated that they separate work and personal lives. Managing Editor Diane Tennant said that mandate has changed: "It's different now. We make accommodations for people."[83] Publisher McFarlin said she recognized that "when employees get to interact with their kids, they are happier. We're going to feel more success if employees are happier."[84]

The female editors said they considered themselves role models for family-friendly policies. Executive Editor Janet Weaver gave birth to a daughter and took three months' maternity leave while serving as the newspaper's managing editor. Her husband, Mark Weaver, stayed home with their children.

The family-focused environment helps retain employees, the managers said. "Some of the ways to keep people from going to bigger newspapers is [for them] to see how inflexible they [other newspapers] are."[85]

Still, the policies are not perfect. One day in the newsroom, a female editor[86] with a 3-month-old baby talked with a colleague about the difficulty of seeing her husband, also an editor at the paper. She said they were working different shifts to share childcare duties, and she often was asleep when he arrived home from work.[87]

Weaver said the newspaper's family accommodations were attributable in part to female leadership, but also to a "generational" phenomenon.[88] "You have people in there [the newsroom] that don't want to live that kind of life— outdrink 'em, work a billion hours, outcuss 'em," she said, referring to the stereotypical journalists' lifestyle. "Younger people are coming in and saying they don't want to live in newsrooms. People are saying they don't want to work 80 hours a week."[89]

As Tannen has noted, a male communication style tends to emphasize hierarchy, status and competition.[90] In contrast, the female leaders at the *Herald-Tribune* made a point of welcoming employee input, offering open-door conversation policies and coming out of their offices to communicate with the staff. McFarlin noted of the newsroom, "There are more conversations here. Meetings are not directive. They're very open."[91] Tennant added, "We want people to question and debate."[92]

Employee input became important in an extraordinary way in December 2003, when the paper hired a new executive editor to replace Weaver, who left for another job. Employees met with candidates applying for the management position, a non-hierarchical method. When McFarlin announced she had decided to hire a male executive editor, therefore breaking up the all-female team, she gathered the staff in the newsroom and told them in person, rather than issuing a memorandum.[93] "You made a great choice," she said. She also told the staff that the new male editor, Mike Connolly, was the best candidate, no matter his gender. Allowing the staff to participate in the decision to hire an upper-level manager by offering their feedback to the publisher, meeting the job candidate in person and asking him questions, and announcing the decision in an open forum are actions contradictory to the hierarchical, rational, bureaucratic structures of most newsrooms.[94]

Another theme that emerged was the *Herald-Tribune*'s consensus-building management approach. Managing Editor Tennant said team participation is a style superior to strict hierarchical formulas. "I still think that the best solutions come from a team—not from a managing editor or some other editor."[95]

As part of the managers' team approach, *Herald-Tribune* employees were encouraged to express their opinions about the newspaper in an intranet site called the "Hot Spot." The site encouraged employees to get to know each other and included an employee face book. On an inter-office message board, employees openly teased managers. On the inter-office message board, after an announcement about the Poynter Institute's National Writers Workshop featuring an all-male list of speakers, a male columnist[96] posted a tongue-in-cheek reply: "Sounds like that all-male journalism group we've been planning." A male employee answered him: "Thank God! We finally get a voice. Power, brothers."[97] This facetiousness showed that male employees did not feel their female bosses stifled their words.

The managers' openness extended to newspaper readers. They allowed and even welcomed input from the public and from employees. McFarlin instituted the Reader Advocate, a telephone hotline that readers could call with concerns and complaints, and invited members of the community to sit in on planning meetings, an unusually open policy for a newspaper.[98] Open connections with the community continued in other sections of the newspaper. Executive Editor Weaver said she encouraged reader and source input, noting that she often "disarmed" people by giving them her home and cell phone numbers and asking them to call her.[99]

Several employees said they welcomed the workplace environment created by the female management team. The female managers made the newsroom more "interesting and creative" than previous regimes, said a longtime male editor.[100] A male reporter who has worked at the paper since 1974 said the female team created a more comfortable work environment: "Women editors definitely make a difference."[101] Male Reporter No. 2 said a friend who had worked for a large California newspaper was visiting him in the newsroom when McFarlin stopped by his desk to say hello. The friend was incredulous. "He said, 'You know the *publisher*!'" The publisher at his newspaper never came into the newsroom or talked to newsroom employees.[102]

Longtime employees said the *Herald-Tribune*'s female managers abolished past sex discrimination. A male reporter who worked at the paper for two decades said a past male editor instituted a policy that women could not cover the police beat. "The bureau chief felt they [women] were endangered," covering crime, the reporter said.[103] Some female employees said they felt more comfortable working for female managers than for men. A female photographer said she felt she could show emotion in the *Herald-Tribune* newsroom: "I've cried in the newsroom. I've broken the cardinal rule."[104] She noted that in three previous, male-dominated large newsrooms where she had worked, managers frowned upon crying, but tolerated "men showing anger." A female reporter who began working at the paper in 1986 said that when the women took over, the newspaper addressed some social issues it had ignored in the past, including homelessness and affordable housing.[105]

One employee offered a throwback to the practice of men hiring other men, known as the old boys' network: she said she landed her job as a page designer through connections in the "old girls' network."[106]

Despite positive responses to the female management, some employees said they saw downsides to working for female bosses. One female employee admitted she could not use her sexual wiles to charm her female managers as she had male bosses in the past.[107] Another female reporter acknowledged that the newsroom had more of a family structure than other newsrooms where she had worked, but "I do feel more cattiness."[108] She reported that gossip served as a staple of interactions between her supervisor and her employees. "Not that men can't gossip, but there is more of a blur here between work and personal life." Tennant noted that some women prefer working for men because they consider female management a "coffee klatch thing."[109]

On the other hand, former Managing Editor Rosemary Armao, known as an advocate for hard, investigative news, said the female-led newsroom discouraged traditional, tough male journalists from applying for jobs. She said she saw two types of people come in for job interviews: "Strong, intelligent, powerful women, and men who are not assertive."[110] Armao asked, "Where are all the big men of journalism, the Jimmy Breslins? We're not seeing it anymore."

The *Herald-Tribune* employed a slightly higher percentage of women, 41 percent, than the national average of 37 percent female newsroom employees. The perception by many outside the newsroom was that the *Herald-Tribune*'s diversity problem was men—"that was the running joke," McFarlin said.[111] When McFarlin hired a man for the executive editor position, she joked that she was implementing a diversity program. She said she enjoyed the distinction of being the only large, female-led newspaper in the United States, but "it was not a mantle we were required to wear forever."[112]

Although the newsroom displayed gender diversity, the staff suffered from a lack of racial and ethnic diversity. Before the female management team took over the newspaper, the *Herald-Tribune* reported that 11 percent of its newsroom employees were from racial and ethnic minorities. By 2003 the percentage had dropped to 8 percent.[113] In the meantime, the community had become more diverse, about 11 percent non-white.[114] Turnover among younger reporters, minority and white, was common, and many left the *Herald-Tribune* after two or three years for larger newspapers. The managers conceded that they had trouble retaining minority employees, in part because some could get better-paying jobs elsewhere. Managing Editor Armao explained:

> We're a 100,000-circulation newspaper in an area that has lots of bigger, better-paying papers (for example, the 233,000-circulation *Tampa Tribune* and 344,000-circulafion *St. Petersburg Times*[115]). The

population is old and white. Getting young people is hard, period. It's particularly hard to get young minorities.[116]

Weaver said that other newspapers "offer more money and prestige" to minorities. She also confirmed that the paper's minority recruiting efforts had been "unfocused."[117]

---

In her conclusion, notice how the researcher revisits the influence of gender in a female-led newsroom culture. Ultimately she suggests that while the *Sarasota Herald-Tribune* leadership may be seen as nurturing a constructive culture, its news content continues to embrace male-oriented standards for what constitutes news.

---

## Conclusion

Under the female leadership team at the *Sarasota Herald-Tribune*, teamwork, collaboration and the balancing of family and professional lives were primary goals. Several employees said they were satisfied with their jobs and motivated to work because of the supportive, egalitarian environment.

The managers brought their experiences as women to the newsroom culture. They forged their own approach to the workplace, different from the traditional hierarchical male approach of most newsrooms. In fact, the *Impact* study confirmed this by characterizing the *Herald-Tribune* as part of the 20 percent of US newspapers with "constructive" cultures.

Manifestations of the culture included an open newsroom, exemplified by top editors' willingness to keep office doors open most of the time. Employees understood they could approach managers about problems and concerns without having to go through hierarchical levels. Problem solving was often done by consensus and teamwork rather than by unilateral decisions. These are characteristics of a feminine management style rather than a masculine, or hierarchical and bureaucratic, one.[118]

As Tannen noted, most women deal with problems and decisions in terms of connection and community rather than in terms of hierarchy.[119] Many of the *Herald-Tribune*'s major decisions involved teamwork and consensus, such as choosing a new executive editor. Employees could voice their opinions on the newsroom's intranet bulletin board. Even readers had a say in what the paper published, through the Reader Advocate telephone line.

The managers' family-friendly policies also reflected the newsroom culture. Employees said if they needed time off to take care of family members, children, the ill or elderly, they would be able to take it without reprisal. The managers set the stage for these policies by observing them as well.

However, it should be noted that while the *Herald-Tribune*'s culture can be characterized as "feminine," such a culture is not exclusive to women. As Executive Editor Weaver noted, the *Herald-Tribune*'s family-friendly policies cater to a generation of journalists, male and female, who put more emphasis on family and personal time than past generations. One of the employees who benefited most from these policies was a single father. It also is important to point out that other newsrooms identified in the *Impact* study as having "constructive" cultures must have been led by male managers, since the *Herald-Tribune* was the *only* female-managed US newspaper during this time.

The *Herald-Tribune* did not exclude or marginalize female perspectives in the workplace, as many male-dominated newspapers do. When *Herald-Tribune* employees became indoctrinated to the organization's expectations, they did not see women as being held back from advancement. Neither men nor women interviewed for this study viewed gender as an obstacle to advancement within the organization. In fact, many employees reported a sense of well-being and comfort in their positions. Employees reported that the organization considered men and women to be on an equal playing field. However, employees did acknowledge that while gender was not an issue affecting hiring, promotion, salary and rank, the newspaper staff lacked racial and ethnic diversity. Minorities did not hold any of the top positions at the *Sarasota Herald-Tribune*. Also, the feminine culture had no effect on the newspaper's content, which favored a male perspective.

Overall, employees were generally positive about the organization, particularly its acceptance of family concerns, its gender fairness, the openness of management, and the feeling that the newspaper staff worked as a team rather than a hierarchy. This standpoint reflects women's roles as communicators who flourish in networks of connections and relationships, including family and work colleagues.[120]

It should be pointed out that this research provides a window into the management, operation and content of the newspaper; a study in which a researcher spent considerably more time in the newsroom might have produced different results.

The *Herald-Tribune*'s culture may serve as a model for other newspapers to retain employees, particularly those with families, and improve employee morale by valuing employees' input and opinions. Both female and male employees can benefit from working in an open and encouraging environment. Since constructive cultures foster innovation and change, the *Herald-Tribune*'s cultural model also could serve as a means to revitalize the sagging newspaper industry.

**Participant Observation Exercises**

1. Pick a research topic that you are interested in exploring. Explain how participation observation might be used to study this topic. Discuss the advantages and disadvantages of using participant observation as your research method.
2. With a partner, observe an event for one hour. Both of you should write down everything that you see and hear. Then compare your observations with those of your partner. How similar were each of your observations? Where did they differ? Did each of you see the same things? If you saw different things, why do you think your observations differed?
3. Observe an event or an activity for at least one hour. Try to blend in and do not interact with others or take any notes. Following your observation, write down what you think you observed. Then try to critique your observations and attempt to understand why you think you saw what you saw.

## Notes

1 Gaye Tuchman, Arlene Kaplan Daniels, & James Benet (Eds.), *Hearth and home: Images of women in the mass media* (New York: Oxford University Press, 1978), 3–38.
2 Kay Mills, "What difference do women journalists make?" In Pippa Norris (Ed.), *Women, media, and politics* (New York: Oxford University Press, 1997), 43.
3 Maurine H. Beasley, "Is there a new majority defining the news?" In Pamela Creedon (Ed.), *Women in mass communication*, 2nd edn (Newbury Park, CA: Sage, 1993), 130–131. See also Maurine H. Beasley & Sheila J. Gibbons, *Taking their place: A documentary history of women and journalism* (Washington, DC: American University Press, 1993), 26.
4 Mary Arnold & Mary Nesbitt, *Women in media 2006: Finding the leader in you* (Evanston, IL: Media Management Center at Northwestern University, 2006), 13.
5 Mills, "What difference do women journalists make?" 41–42.
6 Mills, "What difference do women journalists make?" 39.
7 David Weaver, "Women as journalists." In Norris (Ed.), *Women, media, and politics*, 38–39.
8 Arnold & Nesbitt, *Women in media 2006*, 18; Weaver, "Women as journalists," 39.
9 Gaye Tuchman, *Making news: A study in the construction of reality* (New York: The Free Press, 1978). See also Herbert Gans, *Deciding what's news: A study of* CBS Evening News, NBC Nightly News, Newsweek *and* Time (New York: Pantheon Books, 1979). Both Tuchman and Gans spent months observing routines and practices in newsrooms, interviewing and following journalists. Their groundbreaking ethnographic studies focused on the notion that the news is a social construction rather than a reflection of events that happen each day in the world.

10  Tuchman, *Making news*, 133.

11  Tuchman, *Making news*, 152.

12  Tuchman, *Making news*, 138.

13  Tuchman, *Making news*, 292–299.

14  Mary Arnold Hemlinger & Cynthia C. Linton, *Women in newspapers 2002: Still fighting an uphill battle* (Evanston, IL: Media Management Center at Northwestern University, 2002), 19.

15  David H. Weaver & G. Cleveland Wilhoit, *The American journalist: A portrait of U.S. news people and their work* (Bloomington: Indiana University Press, 1991), 181.

16  AJR staff, "Diversity delayed," *American Journalism Review, 20* (1998): 9. See also American Society of Newspaper Editors, 2002 Newsroom Census. Retrieved from http://asne.org/Article_View/ArticleId/936/Newsroom-employment-drops-sharply-diversity-increases.aspx (accessed June 18, 2012).

17  American Society of Newspaper Editors 2006 census. Retrieved from http://asne.org/Article_View/ArticleId/871/ASNE-census-shows-newsroom-diversity-grows-slightly.aspx (accessed June 18, 2012); Indiana University School of Journalism American Journalist Survey, "Women journalists aren't increasing overall." Poynter Online, http://www.poynter.org (accessed July 28, 2003). These figures are part of data collected by David H. Weaver & G. Cleveland Wilhoit for an update to their book *The American Journalist* (personal correspondence, March 22, 2004).

18  U.S. Department of Labor statistics. Retrieved from http://www.dol.gov/dol/topic/statistics/employment.htm (accessed June 18, 2012).

19  Indiana University School of Journalism American Journalist Survey.

20  Sue A. Lafky, "The progress of women and people of color in the U.S. journalistic workforce: A long, slow journey," in Creedon (ed.), *Women in mass communication*, 100–110.

21  Claartje J. Vinkenburg, Paul J. W. Jansen, & Paul L. Koopman, "Feminine leadership: A review of gender differences in managerial behaviour and effectiveness," in Marilyn J. Davidson & Ronald J. Burke (Eds.), *Women in management: Current research issues*, vol. 11 (London: Sage, 2000), 120–137.

22  Cynthia Carter, Gill Branston, & Stuart Allan, *News, gender and power* (London: Routledge, 1998), 2.

23  Carrie Johnson, "Women at the top? 'We're still talking token numbers,'" *Austin American-Statesman,* April 1, 2001, J10.

24  Hemlinger & Linton, *Women in newspapers 2002*, 15.

25  Matthew Daneman, "Former Gannett CEO Neuharth crusades for media diversity," *Democrat and Chronicle* (Rochester, NY), February 21, 2003. Retrieved from http://www.democratandchronicle.com/news/0221story19_news.shtml.

26  Daneman, "Former Gannett CEO Neuharth crusades for media diversity."

27  *Editor and Publisher*, "Newspapers post strong 3Q profits," October 17, 1998, 16.

28  Newspaper Association of America booklet *Facts about newspapers: A statistical summary of the newspaper industry*, 2003.

29  Debra Gersh Hernandez, "Good and the bad about women's news in newspapers," *Editor and Publisher*, May 21, 1994, 17. See also Karen Schmidt & Colleen Collins, "Showdown at Gender Gap," *American Journalism Review, 15* (6), 1993, 39–42.

30  Hernandez, "Good and the bad about women's news in newspapers"; Schmidt & Collins, "Showdown at Gender Gap."

31  Hernandez, "Good and the bad about women's news in newspapers"; Schmidt & Collins, "Showdown at Gender Gap."

32  Liesbet van Zoonen, "One of the girls? The changing gender of journalism," in Carter et al. (Eds.), *News, gender and power,* 36.

33  Susan Miller, "Opportunity squandered—Newspapers and women's news," *Media Studies Journal, 7* (1–2), Winter/Spring 1993: 16.
34  Kim Walsh-Childers, Jean Chance, & Kristin Herzog, "Women journalists report discrimination in newsrooms," *Newspaper Research Journal, 17* (3–4), 1996: 86–87.
35  Hernandez, "Good and the bad about women's news in newspapers," 17.
36  Miller, "Opportunity squandered—Newspapers and women's news," 167.
37  Lee Jolliffe & Terri Caflett, "Women editors at the 'Seven Sisters' magazines, 1965–1985: Did they make a difference?" *Journalism Quarterly, 71,* Winter 1994: 800–808.
38  Jolliffe & Caflett, "Women editors at the 'Seven Sisters' magazines, 1965–1985," 806–807.
39  Aliza Lavie & Sam Lehman-Wilzig, "The method is the message: Explaining inconsistent findings in gender and news production research," *Journalism, 6* (1), 2005: 67–69.
40  Tracy Everbach, "The 'masculine' content of a female-managed newspaper," *Media Report to Women, 33,* Fall 2005: 14–22.
41  Everbach, "The 'masculine' content of a female-managed newspaper," 20–21.
42  Gary N. Powell, *Women and men in management* (Newbury Park, CA: Sage, 1993), 153–169.
43  Ann Harriman, *Women/men/management,* 2nd edn (Westport, CT: Praeger, 1996), 2–4.
44  Linda L. Lindsey, *Gender roles: A sociological perspective*, 3rd edn (Upper Saddle River, NJ: Prentice Hall, 1997), 262–264.
45  Powell, *Women and men in management,* 167.
46  Vinkenburg et al., "Feminine leadership," 123–124, 130.
47  Lindsey, *Gender roles,* 53–59.
48  Angel Kwolek-Folland, *Incorporating women: A history of women and business in the United States* (New York: Palgrave, 1998, 2002), 168–169, 201.
49  Kwolek-Folland, *Incorporating women,* 202.
50  Patricia Sellers, "Power: Do women really want it?" *Fortune,* October 13, 2003.
51  Lisa Belkin, "The opt-out revolution," *New York Times Magazine,* October 26, 2003, 45.
52  Belkin, "The opt-out revolution," 86.
53  Van Zoonen, "One of the girls?" 33–46.
54  Van Zoonen, "One of the girls?" 34.
55  Van Zoonen, "One of the girls?" 35–36.
56  Marilyn E. Gist, "Through the looking glass: Diversity and reflected appraisals of the self in mass media," in Creedon (Ed.), *Women in mass communication,* 109–110.
57  Stuart Allan, "(en)gendering the truth politics of news discourse," in Carter et al. (Eds.), *News, gender and power,* 126, 133; Gist, "Through the looking glass," 108–109.
58  Josephine Donovan, *Feminist theory: The intellectual traditions of American feminism* (New York: Continuum, 1992), 199.
59  Arnold & Nesbitt, *Women in Media 2006,* 19; Readership Institute, Media Management Center, *Impact study* (Evanston, IL: Northwestern University, January 2000).
60  Readership Institute, *Impact study.*
61  Harriman, *Women/men/management*; Powell, *women and men in management.*
62  Harriman, *Women/men/management*; Powell, *Women and men in management.*
63  American Press Institute, *Women, men and newsroom leadership* (DVD), 2003.

64 Deborah Tannen, *You just don't understand: Women and men in conversation* (New York: Ballantine Books, 1990), 24–25.

65 Arnold & Nesbitt, *Women in media 2006*, 52.

66 Arnold & Nesbitt, *Women in media 2006*, 16–17.

67 Norman K. Denzin & Yvonna S. Lincoln (Eds.), *The landscape of qualitative research: Theories and issues* (Thousand Oaks, CA: Sage, 1998), 134–136.

68 Thomas R. Lindlof, *Qualitative communication research methods* (Thousand Oaks, CA: Sage, 1995), 5.

69 Linda McGee Calvert & V. Jean Ramsey, "Bringing women's voice to research on women in management: A feminist perspective," *Journal of Management Inquiry, 1*, March 1992: 79–88; Harriman, *Women/men/management*; Liesbet van Zoonen, *Feminist media studies* (London: Sage, 1994), 56–64.

70 Newspaper Association of America, "Facts about newspapers: A statistical summary of the newspaper industry." Retrieved from http://www.naa.org (accessed August 17, 2004).

71 US Census Bureau, http://quickfacts.census.gov/qfd/states (accessed September 15, 2003).

72 Sarasota County records.

73 Sherry Ricchiardi, "Where women rule," *American Journalism Review, 23* (1), 2001: 52.

74 ASNE 2003 annual census; Ricchiardi, "Where women rule," 52.

75 Ricchiardi, "Where women rule," 52.

76 Interview with *Sarasota Herald-Tribune* Publisher Diane McFarlin in her office, September 11, 2003.

77 Kwolek-Folland, *Incorporating women*, 203–205.

78 Kwolek-Folland, *Incorporating women*, 203–205.

79 Male Reporter No. 1, interview with author, September 11, 2003. Note: Employees interviewed for this study are not identified by name as per agreement with the author, the *Sarasota Herald-Tribune* managers, and the University of Missouri's Institutional Review Board. The decision to keep employees anonymous was intended to allow them to speak freely without fear of retribution.

80 Interview with Male Reporter No. 1 in *Sarasota-Herald Tribune* newsroom conference room, September 11, 2003.

81 Male Reporter No. 1, interview.

82 Male Reporter No. 1, interview.

83 Interview with *Sarasota Herald-Tribune* Managing Editor Diane Tennant at a Sarasota restaurant, September 10, 2003. Tennant replaced Rosemary Armao as managing editor after Armao resigned in June 2002 over an ethics dispute with Executive Editor Janet Weaver.

84 McFarlin, interview.

85 Janet Weaver, interview with author, September 12, 2003.

86 Female Editor No. 1.

87 Newsroom observation of Female Editor No. l's conversation with another employee, December 17, 2003.

88 Weaver, interview.

89 Weaver, interview.

90 Tannen, *You just don't understand*, 38.

91 McFarlin, interview.

92 Tennant, interview.

93 McFarlin, interview.

190 • Ethnography and Participant Observation

190 • Ethnography and Participant Observation

94  Newsroom observation, December 19, 2003.
95  Linda Steiner, "Newsroom accounts of power at work," in Carter et al. (Eds.), *News, gender and power*, 146.
96  Tennant, interview.
97  Male Reporter No. 6, posting May 16, 2002.
98  Intranet posting, May 23, 2002.
99  Observation of news budget meeting, June 6, 2002.
100  Observation of editors' meeting, September 10, 2003.
101  Interview with Male Editor No. 1 in the newsroom, June 6, 2002.
102  Interview with Male Reporter No. 2 in the newsroom, December 15, 2003.
103  Male Reporter No. 2, interview.
104  Interview with Male Reporter No. 3 in news bureau office, December 16, 2003.
105  Interview with Female Photographer No. 1 in the newsroom, June 5, 2002.
106  Interview with Female Reporter No. 2 in the newsroom, June 5, 2002.
107  Interview with Female Page Designer No. 1 in the newsroom, June 5, 2002.
108  Interview with Female Reporter No. 4 at a restaurant, December 16, 2003.
109  Interview with Female Reporter No. 3 at a restaurant, December 16, 2003.
110  Tennant, interview.
111  Interview with Rosemary Armao in newsroom conference room, June 2, 2002.
112  McFarlin, interview.
113  Lisa Rab, "H-T publisher names new top editor," *Sarasota Herald-Tribune*, December 20, 2003: 12A.
114  Bill Dedman & Stephen K. Doig, report compiled for Knight Foundation, May 2004. Retrieved from http://powerreporting.com/knight/fl_sarasota_herald-tribune.html (accessed August 17, 2004).
115  McFarlin, interview.
116  *St. Petersburg Times*, "Circulation of Florida's largest newspapers." Retrieved from http://www.sptimes.com/Marketbook/circulation.html (accessed January 15, 2004).
117  Armao, interview.
118  Weaver, interview.
119  Steiner, "Newsroom accounts of power at work," 146.
120  Tannen, *You just don't understand*, 25.

# References

Atkinson, Paul, & Hammersley, Martyn. (1994). Ethnography and participant observation. In Norman K. Denzin & Yvonna S. Lincoln (Eds.), *Handbook of qualitative research* (pp. 248–261). London: Sage.

Berger, Arthur Asa. (1998). *Media research techniques* (2nd edn). Thousand Oaks, CA: Sage.

Denzin, Norman K., & Lincoln, Yvonna S. (1998). Introduction: Entering the field of qualitative research. In Norman K. Denzin & Yvonna S. Lincoln (Eds.), *The landscape of qualitative research: Theories and issues* (pp. 1–34). Thousand Oaks, CA: Sage.

DeWalt, Kathleen M., & DeWalt, Billie R. (2011). *Participant observation: A guide for fieldworkers* (2nd edn). Lanham, MD: AltaMira Press.

Geertz, Clifford. (1973). *The interpretation of cultures: Selected essays*. New York: Basic Books.

Gobo, Giampietro. (2011). "Ethnography." In David Silverman (Ed.), *Qualitative research: Issues of theory, method and practice* (3rd edn, pp. 15–34). Los Angeles: Sage.

Grossman, Lev. (2012, January 30). The beast with a billion eyes. *Time*, pp. 38–43.

Hall, Stuart. (1980). Encoding/decoding. In Stuart Hall, Dorothy Hobson, Andrew Lowe, & Paul Willis (Eds.), *Culture, media, language: Working papers in cultural studies, 1972–79* (pp. 128–138). London: Hutchinson.

Jorgensen, Danny L. (1989). *Participant observation: A methodology for human studies*. Newbury Park, CA: Sage.

LeCompte, Margaret D., & Schensul, Jean J. (1999). *Analyzing and interpreting ethnographic data.* Walnut Creek, CA: AltaMira Press.

Lindlof, Thomas R., & Shatzer, Milton J. (1998). Media ethnography in virtual space: Strategies, limits, and possibilities. *Journal of Broadcasting and Electronic Media, 42* (2), 170–189.

Machin, David. (2002). *Ethnographic research for media studies.* London: Arnold.

Morley, David, & Silverstone, Roger. (1991). Media audiences: Communication and context: Ethnographic perspectives on the media audience. In Klaus Bruhn Jensen & Nicholas W. Jankowski (Eds.), *A handbook of qualitative methodologies for mass communication research* (pp. 149–162). London: Routledge.

Stokes, Jane. (2003). *How to do media and cultural studies.* London: Sage.

# CHAPTER 8

# Textual Analysis

*Humanity is a mess and it takes the immensity of a coiled and supple language to do it justice.*

— Pat Conroy (2010, pp. 87–88)

Textual analysis is all about language, what it represents and how we use it to make sense of our lives. Language is a basic element of our human interactions, and it is through language that the meanings of our social realities are constructed. As cultural theorist Raymond Williams, who was one of the founders of British Cultural Studies, explains:

No expression, that is to say—no account, description, depiction, portrait—is "natural" or "straightforward." These are at most socially relative terms. Language is not a pure medium through which the reality of a life or the reality of an event or an experience or the reality of a society can "flow." It is a socially shared and reciprocal activity, already embedded in active relationships, within which every move is an activation of what is already shared and reciprocal or may become so.

(1977, p. 166)

For Williams, language does much more than describe our lives: it actually helps us to create our social realities. I recently came across a short film that nicely illustrates Williams' understanding of language as a shared and active experience. The film, *The Power of Words*, has gone viral and has been watched more than 11 million times on YouTube and Facebook. Created by online content specialists Purplefeather, the film opens with a blind man sitting on a piece of cardboard in a public area; he has an empty can and a handwritten sign that reads, "I'm blind please help." People are enjoying the sunny day and as they walk by him, a few toss the man a coin or two. A young woman walks past the man and his sign but quickly returns to him. As he feels her trendy leather shoes, she grabs his sign, writes something on it and leaves. Many people now throw the man coins and his can quickly fills up. After a while, the woman returns and the man asks her, "What did you do to my sign?" She replies, "I wrote the same but different words." A little overwhelmed, he thanks the young woman and we finally see what she wrote on his sign: "It's a beautiful day and I can't see it." The film ends with the words "Change your words, change the world."

## What Is a Text?

Understanding the concept of a "text" is a key aspect of the method of textual analysis. In qualitative research we use the term text to describe more than a printed document, textbook or a written cell phone message. In textual analysis we see texts as cultural artifacts, material documentary evidence that is used to make sense out of our lives. Cultural theorist Stuart Hall (1975) defines texts as "literary and visual constructs, employing symbolic means, shaped by rules, conventions and traditions intrinsic to the use of language in its widest sense" (p. 17). In other words, texts are things that we use to make meaning from. Books, films, newspapers, magazines, websites, games, television programs, radio broadcasts, advertisements, fashions and popular music are all examples of the types of texts that qualitative researchers interpret in an effort to understand some of the many relationships between media, culture and society. From this perspective, texts are thought to provide traces of a socially constructed reality, which may be understood by considering the words, concepts, ideas, themes and issues that reside in texts as they are considered within a particular cultural context (Atkinson & Coffey, 2011).

When we do textual analysis, we evaluate the many meanings found in texts and we try to understand how written, visual and spoken language helps us to create our social realities. Rather than only judging the strengths, weaknesses, accuracy or inaccuracy of texts, qualitative researchers look at the social practices, representations, assumptions and stories about our lives that are revealed in texts. Qualitative researchers do not study texts to predict or control how individuals will react to messages but instead to understand how people use texts to make sense of their lives. Researchers consider texts rich with interpretation and meaning that may be assessed through many different types of qualitative analysis. For example, contemporary studies of *Star Trek* illustrate how texts may be used to help people understand major changes in their lives. Researchers have completed several different types of textual analyses based on this television show and they suggest that the socially progressive role of technology depicted over the years on *Star Trek* has provided Americans with a conceptual framework that has helped them to understand NASA's space exploration program (McKee, 2003).

## The Development of Textual Analysis

In media studies the development of textual analysis is linked to the publication of "The Challenge of Qualitative Content Analysis" by German sociologist and critical theorist Siegfried Kracauer. Kracauer (1952–1953) questioned the use of quantitative content analysis in communication research disputing the reliability and objectivity of a method that broke things down into separate pieces and parts and then counted them. For Kracauer, quantitative content analysis focused entirely on describing the surface content of texts, a strategy that resulted in incomplete and often "inaccurate analysis" (p. 632). Content analysis considered repetition an important measure of value, insisting that the more times a word, concept or idea was coded in a document, the greater significance there was to the evidence. In contrast, for Kracauer, repetition was less important than a consideration of texts in their entirety as a complete entity. He explained that analysis was an act of interpretation that considered both the surface meanings and the underlying intentions of a text. Kracauer maintained that the goal of textual analysis (which he initially called qualitative content analysis) was to bring out the entire range of potential meanings in texts.

One way in which the differences between qualitative textual analysis and quantitative content analysis may be illustrated is for us to consider how each method might address a specific research project. As I write this chapter, it is Black Friday (in the United States, the day following Thanksgiving Day, and a busy shopping day), and so I thought that as an example we might consider the coverage of Black Friday that has been published in daily urban newspapers throughout the United States.

If we were to use a quantitative content analysis, we could sample urban newspapers and count the number of articles appearing in the newspapers that focused on Black Friday. We could count the number of references to Black Friday in each of the articles that ran in the newspapers. Apparently, my local newspaper, the *Milwaukee Journal Sentinel*, actually did such a study and found that in 2010 there were 350 references to Black Friday in the twenty daily newspapers with large circulations that its investigators studied (Romell, 2011, p. 7A). For a content analysis we could count how many times a particular word or phrase was used, count the number of images that accompanied the news articles or even count the number of sources used in each article. We could measure the length of the articles, measure the size of the images or even measure the size of the headlines accompanying the news articles. Another strategy might be to code each article as being a positive, negative or neutral story about Black Friday. We could even code each image accompanying the articles as illustrating a positive, negative or neutral depiction of Black Friday.

In contrast, if we were to use a qualitative textual analysis for our research on Black Friday we could look at the historical context for the development of the holiday, or we might consider whether Black Friday is merely a marketing or media slogan or if it has become a significant aspect of American culture. We could look at the themes that emerge in the newspaper articles on Black Friday, the content and structure of the articles; or we might consider the language used to describe Black Friday. We could consider the relationship between the images and the articles, the placement of the stories, and how sources are used in the articles. We could also consider the absences in each of the articles and how they might help to frame the stories in a particular way.

As you can see from my Black Friday example, qualitative textual analysis would look at the news coverage in its entirety and would attempt to make connections between Black Friday and larger issues in contemporary American society. In contrast, quantitative content analysis would focus on counting or measuring specific parts of the coverage, which would require us to break each newspaper article into a series of ratings, categories and components that we would have previously determined. For Kracauer, these categories, components and ratings are actually qualitative considerations that researchers make to simplify their work. Yet, Kracauer maintains that breaking a text into pieces and parts, rather than considering it as a whole, results in research of lower quality because there is less depth to the analysis.

## The Influence of Semiotics

The first qualitative textual analyses were often based on literary analysis. Researchers rejected the idea of sampling a limited number of materials and chose to immerse themselves in all of the available texts. After a "preliminary long soak" (Hall, 1975, p. 15) in all of the materials, during which they began to identify categories and select examples for more thorough analysis, qualitative researchers then used a deep reading or exegesis to interpret the range of meanings within the texts. In the early textual analyses, specific patterns, themes and categories of analysis were not predetermined but emerged from the researchers' immersion in the material and deep reading of the texts. During the 1960s, textual analysis became influenced by semiotics and the concept of exegesis began to give way to a more systematic approach, one that emphasized "fundamental narrative structures" (Larsen, 1991, p. 127).

Semiotics is the study of signs that exist in our social lives. Signs are drawings, photographs, paintings, words, acts, sounds, objects and gestures; that is, a sign is anything that represents or stands in for something else. While semiotics is a general term that includes a variety of different methodological tools and theoretical perspectives, it provides insights for analyzing texts within culturally specific social practices. According to the creator of the field of linguistics, Ferdinand de Saussure, each sign is made up of two elements: a signifier and a signified. A signifier portrays the physical letters, shapes or sounds, or other physical aspects of something.

For example, the letters R, O, S, E represent the signifier for the word *rose*. The signified is the idea characterized by the word, shape or sound. In the case of a rose, the signified could be described as a fragrant flower with thorns. The relationship between the signifier and the signified creates a sign, which is evaluated from conventions or codes that have been previously agreed upon in a culture. The understanding of codes is based on factual information as well as the contextual knowledge of living in a particular culture at a specific place and time.

In semiotics, the associations between the signifier and the signified are considered arbitrary; that is, there is no definitive reason why the letters that constitute a word must refer to that specific word. For example, there is no specific or natural reason why the concept of a rose should be represented by a particular word or sound made up of the letters R, O, S, E. However, it is through the codes, ideas and conventions of a culture that the specific meanings of a signifier and a signified become systematized and fixed (Strinati, 1995).

Researchers who draw on semiotics not only study the definitional meaning or the denotation of signs but also consider the representative or connotative meanings.

> Semiotics invites us to examine texts not just for their obvious content, for what they have to say. It also gets us to think about representation; that is, about how texts show us events, objects, people, ideas, emotions and everything else that can be signified.
>
> (Gripsrud, 2006, pp. 39–40)

Overall, semiotics may be seen as a type of textual analysis that helps us to interpret codes and signs in order to understand how aspects of a text work with our own cultural knowledge to make meaning in our lives.

Currently, there are many different types of textual analyses being done by researchers in communication and media studies. For many qualitative researchers, textual analysis is the preferred term to describe the broader category of qualitative content analysis. However, some communication researchers prefer the term discourse analysis because of its emphasis on words in texts and talk (Peräkylä, 2008). The use of the term discourse analysis reminds researchers that it is through our use of language that our reality is socially constructed. Some contemporary researchers continue to follow Kracauer and prefer to immerse themselves in the texts and let the themes of analysis slowly emerge. The research example "From Religiosity to Consumerism: Press Coverage of Thanksgiving, 1905–2005," found at the end of this chapter, is an example of this type of textual analysis. Other researchers prefer to use specific procedures and predetermined categories of analysis, such as ideological analysis, genre analysis, semiotics or rhetorical analysis.

## Theory and Interpretation

As I have previously discussed, a researcher's philosophical orientation and choice of theoretical framework is an integral part of all qualitative research. No matter what type of textual analysis they might undertake, most qualitative researchers also focus on the theoretical underpinnings of the text, because they see theory as central to the process of interpretation (Denzin & Lincoln, 1998). In textual analysis, researchers' theoretical perspectives can inform the type of textual analysis they use, as well as the types of questions that they ask. Using Lady Gaga's music video *Telephone*, featuring Beyoncé, as an example, we can consider how the choice of a theoretical framework influences the types of questions that we ask and how we might focus our textual analysis of the music video.

A good place to begin is with some contextual information about *Telephone*. This Quentin Tarantino-influenced music video, co-written by Lady Gaga and Jonas Åkerlund, was directed by Åkerlund. Released on

March 11, 2010, the nine-and-a-half-minute short film was watched by millions on television and viewed online more than 17 million times in the first four days of release (McCormick, 2010). Depicting prison violence, sexuality, consumer culture and mass murder, the explicit music video, as well as sanitized excerpts, continue to be easily assessed online. *Telephone* draws on comic strip superheroes Captain America and Wonder Woman, references pop culture icons Madonna and Michael Jackson, and is inspired by several Hollywood films, including *Thelma and Louise, Pulp Fiction* and *Natural Born Killers.* Tarantino's Pussy Wagon from the film *Kill Bill* serves as Beyoncé and Gaga's getaway vehicle, while Gaga's poison syrup recipe references the Star Wars movies, the science fiction novel *Dune* and the video game series Command and Conquer. Product placements for Diet Coke, Wonder Bread and Miracle Whip compete for attention with goods and services including Virgin Mobile cell phones, Polaroid and the dating website PlentyofFish.com.

The short film begins with Gaga in the county jail being led to her cell by two female guards. While in prison she is strip-searched, makes a fashion statement wearing yellow police tape, chains and sunglasses made of cigarettes, kisses another inmate and is bailed out by Beyoncé in the Pussy Wagon. They travel to a diner, kill several people inside with poisoned syrup and evade capture disguised as harem girls, driving the Pussy Wagon into the unknown while vowing never to return. Gaga starts singing the song "Telephone" nearly three minutes into the video, and the storyline is inter-woven with pop culture references and dance numbers both in jail and at the diner. Shortly after the release of the music video, Lady Gaga explained to *E! News* that all of her music videos contain hidden messages. Her intention with *Telephone* was to take a pop song with a surface meaning and use different popular culture forms and conventions to create a music video that offers viewers a critique of contemporary US society.

Now if we were to use political economy as a theoretical framework for our textual analysis of *Telephone,* we would want to focus on the economic aspects of the music industry as well as issues of ownership and control as they relate to the production of the music video. We could consider the commercial success of the video, the money made from *Telephone,* including product placements, the promotion of the song and of the pop star Lady Gaga herself, as well as increased earnings as a result of the music video. We could explore the production of the video, ownership issues in the popular music industry, the exclusion of recording artists who may lack broad-based appeal, and pressures that may be placed on Gaga to remain commercially successful.

British cultural studies would guide us to not only consider the social, political and economic context for the music video but also to address Gaga and Åkerlund's authority and intention in creating *Telephone*, as well as the way audience members interpret or decode the text. Because British cultural studies rejects the notion of a passive audience that uniformly accepts the intended meaning of a text, as researchers we might consider the many ways audience members make meaning from the music video. We could address the way dominant ideas of American culture (also known as the ideology) are showcased in the video. An emphasis on the stereotypes, visual imagery, use of language and popular culture references in the music video might also help us to understand specific cultural relationships in contemporary society.

If we were to use social feminism as our theoretical framework, we might look for examples of the oppression of women in the music video. We could consider whether the gender relations depicted in the short film perpetuate sexist stereotypes or whether they are used to empower women. We might address the economics of using female sexuality to enhance commercial success. Of particular interest to us might be to evaluate the depictions of women in stereotypical male roles. We might consider how these roles may help women to resist the power of men to dominate and oppress them—a concept known as patriarchy. An emphasis on Lady Gaga's role in the creation of the song and music video *Telephone* as well as her participation with Beyoncé in the short film could also be a primary focus of a feminist reading.

As you can see from this example, differing theoretical perspectives provide researchers with guidance, offering a conceptual framework to help guide their textual analyses. Theoretical frameworks do not actually analyze texts; they are used to suggest key issues and questions for researchers to address in their research.

## Encoding and Decoding

Researchers using textual analysis often focus on the production of texts. They consider the author's intention as well as his or her specific rationale for the creation of a text. Understanding the importance of context to the interpretation process, researchers seek out insights regarding the historical, cultural and economic relationships that exist between a text and a specific society at a particular place in time. When we research the relevant context for a textual analysis, it is important to consider the concept of inter-textuality, which is the way one text actually refers to other texts. It is actually possible for us to analyze a text in terms of the relationships it has with other texts, and therefore it is important for researchers to consider how the elements of a text may refer to other texts. For example, if we go back to the

*Telephone* example, let us suppose that we wanted to do a textual analysis of Lady Gaga's music video. In that case, we would also want to consider the reviews of *Telephone*, the news and entertainment coverage of the short film, as well as blog posts, relevant tweets, fan sites and other, related music videos. By looking at these other texts we would gain greater insight into the meanings of the music video.

Qualitative researchers also go beyond the production of texts to consider how meaning moves from the author or creator of a text to the readers and audience members who encounter the text. While all texts are produced for particular reasons at a specific place and time, a text's meaning may change once others evaluate it. Before Stuart Hall developed his encoding/decoding model of communication, researchers emphasized a sender/message/receiver approach to the communication process. The sender/message/receiver model focused on the construction of messages, maintaining that once a message was sent, then as long as there was no interference on the line, all people would understand the message as intended.

However, Hall (1980) explains that when a text is created, its author/ producer constructs or encodes a specific intended meaning into each text. This intended or dominant meaning is what the text's creator hopes we will all understand and take away from the text. Yet, Hall maintains that people actually interpret or decode texts in a variety of different ways. Some people will decode a text as the author intended, understanding the dominant code reproduced by the author. Others will take a negotiated position, understanding the intended meaning but also considering their own experiences and decoding the text while taking both views into consideration. Still others will take an oppositional view, rejecting the intended meaning and constructing a completely different interpretation of the message.

Political commercials on television that support a specific presidential candidate provide a good example to illustrate the ways viewers decode messages. The dominant encoded meaning that is constructed in the commercials urges viewers to support the featured candidate. Some viewers will see the commercials and agree with the positions outlined in the ads, and they may even vote for that presidential candidate. Other viewers will understand the intention of the commercials and they may add their own experiences or knowledge about the candidate to the television advertisements. They may or may not agree with the intended meaning of the commercials but they may consider the political commercials before making their voting decisions. However, other viewers will take the information in the commercials and turn it around, as evidence to support another candidate. These viewers will completely reject the intended meaning of the advertisements, refusing to accept the dominant position, and will instead construct an oppositional reading of the political commercials. Given that texts may be decoded in a variety of different ways, Hall suggests that it is important for researchers to go beyond the intended meaning that is produced in texts to explore the ways texts are understood by readers and audience members.

## Ideological Analysis

Ideology has been a central concept in textual analysis throughout the development of the methodology. Ideology may be understood as the dominant ideas of an individual, group, class or society, the way meanings are socially produced, or even as the false ideas upon which a social, political or economic system is based. Kracauer (1952–1953) maintained that texts represented dominant ideological positions within a culture at a specific historical place and time. He suggested that many of these dominant ideologies appeared to us as common sense—things that we logically did, rationally decided and morally believed were right. Our beliefs as well as our resulting actions were considered to be based on ideas that were used to create and maintain a particular worldview that was culturally specific and quite changeable. As Graeme Turner (1997), a key researcher in Australian cultural and media studies explains, from this perspective all societies are based on "sets of unspoken, unwritten assumptions about the way the world works." There is no need for these ideological values and/or assumptions to be written down in one place "because they are inscribed into virtually every aspect of one's life in that culture" (p. 327).

The common American tradition of giving one's fiancée a diamond engagement ring provides us with an example of how ideology works. I would suggest that many people consider giving a diamond engagement ring a romantic gesture and an appropriate custom. I would guess that most people assume that diamond engagement rings have a long and interesting history. Given that about 80 percent of American brides actually receive diamond engagement rings (O'Rourke, 2007), we can consider the custom part of the dominant American ideology. While the history of betrothal rings dates back to the thirteenth century, it might surprise you to learn that the popularity of diamond engagement rings actually began in the 1930s, when De Beers started a public advertising campaign to combat its declining sales of diamonds. In 1947, female copywriter Frances Gerety came up with the tagline "A Diamond Is Forever," which De Beers combined with an image of young, attractive honeymooning newlyweds in a new advertising campaign (O'Rourke, 2007). The advertising campaign was a hit, and diamond engagement ring sales rose dramatically. The custom of giving a diamond engagement ring quickly became part of the dominant ideology. In this case, external advertising forces subtly reshaped the American consciousness as it related to engagement customs, probably without people realizing it. The De Beers advertising campaign is an example of how economic relations can shape the cultural realm of a society, which in turn begins to influence people's consciousness and ideological beliefs (Berger, 2000).

The initial textual analyses were based on the view that a singular dominant ideology existed, through which a group maintained its power and legitimacy, and that it was a researcher's goal to uncover that ideology. As the field developed, some qualitative researchers, particularly those from a constructivist philosophical orientation, began to insist that while texts "function ideologically" (Larsen, 1991, p. 129) because they illustrate societal principles and values, they do not provide a single ideological vision but instead offer multiple versions of our socially constructed reality.

In contemporary media research, while some qualitative researchers identify multiple ideological positions in texts, others focus on understanding how dominant ideological power relations within race, class, age, gender and ethnicity are encoded in texts. Maintaining that texts help to construct our knowledge, values and beliefs, and reinforce our common-sense understandings, these researchers examine the political, economic and/or ideological perspectives that shape texts. The research example at the end of this chapter is an example of this type of research. In other words, these researchers understand that power can operate within the realm of ideas, and so they see texts as sources of power (Gillespie & Toynbee, 2006).

Clearly, ideology is a complex concept: it stabilizes and supports the status quo, reinforces the dominant beliefs of those with power in society, produces our socially constructed meanings and acts as "social cement and social control" (Cormack, 1995, p. 20). Researchers who focus on dominant ideological power relations analyze texts to understand how ideology works within a society's culture. Initially, researchers who undertook ideological analysis drew on literary methods of analysis, immersing themselves in the material and intuitively analyzing the texts.

Currently, most researchers doing ideological analyses draw on specific categories and guidelines to help frame their work. In his book *Ideology*, Mike Cormack (1995) outlines a specific method of analysis for an ideological critique, based on a British cultural studies framework, which assesses five main areas of emphasis: content, structure, absence, style and mode of address. Cormack suggests that assessing the content of a text, including the opinions, beliefs, values and other judgments, the vocabulary used, the stereotypes and characterizations of people, and the conflicts, resolutions and other actions within the text, help us to understand how a specific social reality is constructed. The structure, in particular the opening and closing aspects of a text, are also important to assess. The opening of a text not only sets an agenda but also frames how the issues, concerns and information will be handled. The closing often attempts to answer questions and solve any problems addressed in the text. Cormack explains that a text's structure and its emphasis on binary oppositions, such as good and evil, may guide readers or audience members toward a specific ideological view by limiting the ways a text may be interpreted.

For Cormack (1995), an emphasis on absence, the "elements which might have been expected to be in the text but which are missing from it" (p. 31), is crucial to understanding how ideology influences a text. You may wonder how it is possible to assess something that is not there. While at first glance this may seem to be a difficult undertaking, we actually expect to see certain things, an expectation based on customs, conventions and experiences. For example, if you watched a CBS broadcast news story about a major snowstorm, you would expect to see images of the storm: pictures of people digging out, playing in the snow, building snowmen, or even images of road closings, accidents, salt piles or plow trucks. If the broadcast included no images of the storm, you would be surprised and might wonder what had happened. Therefore, considering those aspects that are absent, unsaid, missing or avoided allows us to consider how a specific ideological argument may have been constructed.

A focus on style assesses aspects of the text apart from the actual language, including the use of color, design, fashion or genre, while, for Cormack, the mode of address considers the way each text talks to us. Does it speak to the audience directly or does the text use a strategy of indirect address? When taken together, the five areas of analysis outlined by Cormack may help us to understand the role of ideology in constructing a specific view of reality in a text that readers and viewers are encouraged to share.

## Genre Analysis

Earlier in this chapter I mentioned how one text often refers to other texts, which is a process known as intertextuality. In media studies we often try to make sense of one text by considering it in relation to other, similar kinds of texts. We call these different types of texts genres. News, documentary, sports, romantic comedies, drama, reality television, science fiction and cartoons are all different types of genres that help audience members, media producers and critics to communicate with each other. Genres also help us to distinguish, evaluate and make sense of various types of media.

Within each genre there are narrative and aesthetic conventions that reproduce and reinforce a system of beliefs about our social reality. The rules and conventions of different genres also help researchers to assess how audience members may evaluate any given text. For example, when we think about gangster films we expect to see movies that take place in a gritty urban environment, with Italian-American restaurants, violence, betrayals, police stakeouts and chase scenes. People like to go to genre films to watch the types of films that they know they like and to see how each element that is central to the genre has been reinvented or reinterpreted by the filmmaker (Stokes, 2003). Genres help us to categorize cultural texts by types and conventions, yet genre products should not be dismissed as merely standardized commodities. While genre texts include the repetition of central elements, they also include speculation and uncertainty. Genres work because we enjoy the predictability of the genre, and we also take pleasure from the differences, enjoying the surprises and trying to guess what might come next. As Alan McKee (2003) explains in his book *Textual Analysis: A Beginner's Guide*, "[W]hy would someone go down into a cellar by themselves in a horror film? Because it's a horror film" (p. 97). We all have certain expectations when we read the newspaper, watch a new science fiction television show or take in the latest action film at our neighborhood movie theater.

For instance, viewers familiar with the animated television show *South Park* did not worry that one of the characters, Kenny, was killed almost every week during the first five seasons of the program. They were familiar with the rules and conventions of cartoons, and understood that Kenny's death was a running gag, allowing another character to remark each time, "Oh, my God—they killed Kenny!" Viewers felt assured that Kenny would return alive during the next episode of *South Park*. However, when Charlie Harper died on the situation comedy *Two and a Half Men*, viewers realized that his death was authentic and that the character would not return to the show. Characters rarely die in situation comedies, but when they do, it is for real. In addition, the actor Charlie Sheen had been fired from his role as Charlie Harper following public disagreements with management and after a series of derogatory comments that Sheen had made about the series' creator. This context helped viewers to make sense of Charlie Harper's death on a metro platform in Paris.

In genre analysis, researchers consider other texts in the same genre, the wider social context for the text along with how the text may speak to other similar texts. Stories, issues and concerns raised by the text are explored. Researchers who study genre focus on broad patterns within specific texts. They are particularly interested in changes that occur in different genres and they assess what those changes may say about social and political issues in society. "Popular genres can be seen as revealing underlying preoccupations and conflicts in a social order. Studying genre may reveal how the media offer mythical solutions to these preoccupations" (Branston, 2006, p. 45).

Some genres, such as news and documentary, are considered to have a high modality because they are thought to be strongly connected to reality. These genres are expected to provide accurate information that we may draw on for guidance about our lives. In contrast, other genres, such as cartoons and science fiction, have low modalities, and the expectations that these genres will provide us with usable information are lower.

## Rhetorical Analysis

As I have mentioned throughout this chapter, there are many different types and techniques of textual analysis that we can use to analyze media texts. The use of a rhetorical analysis looks at how speakers and writers use words to influence readers and audience members. The use of rhetorical analysis is particularly appropriate when one is assessing aspects of advertising and public relations, or when persuasion is an integral part of a media text. Aristotle's three modes of persuasion—ethos, pathos and logos—are considered central to a rhetorical analysis. Ethos is concerned with the character, credibility and confidence of a writer or speaker; pathos involves rousing readers' and audience members' emotions through the use of description and word usage; and logos focuses on appeals to the reasoning skills of audience members and readers, specifically considering how arguments are framed in the text through the use of statistics and facts (Berger, 2000).

Researchers using a rhetorical analysis consider the relationships between a text, its author or producer, the intended audience for the text and the relevant context for the production and reception of a text. In their work, researchers use a variety of rhetorical devices to understand the persuasive aspects of texts. As with semiotics, they consider the metaphoric language used to reinforce an argument, comparing elements using analogy and association. They assess verbal appeals, including the use of sarcasm and irony, the offering of expert advice, problem solving and playing on people's anxieties and fears. For example, advertising campaigns for deodorants often target individuals' fear of rejection, loneliness and their desire for approval to persuade them to buy their products.

Rhetorical analysis also considers catchy slogans, melodies and jingles that can get caught in our heads and are nearly impossible to forget. McDonald's "You deserve a break today" and "I wish I was an Oscar Meyer Wiener," and Coca-Cola's "It's the Real Thing" are three of AdAge.com's top ten advertising jingles of the twentieth century. Advertising jingles are hard to forget; just writing about the Oscar Meyer Wiener made me start humming the jingle. Researchers using rhetorical analysis as a method may also focus on images and other visual aspects of a text, assessing how colors, typefaces and other typographical elements help sell a product or service to the public. For example, a researcher using a rhetorical analysis to analyze an advertising campaign could consider the people used in the advertisements, specifically assessing the age, gender, ethnicity, physical characteristics and expressions of the models. They could also assess the models' hairstyles, fashions, expressions and interactions within the ads (Berger, 1998). As in the use of semiotics, and other types of textual analysis, researchers find that assessing rhetorical concepts and appeals provides them with a variety of ways to understand how texts create meaning and help to shape individuals' socially constructed realities.

In this chapter I have described several different types of textual analyses, including semiotics, rhetorical analysis, genre analysis and ideological analysis. They are only a few of the many different types of textual analysis that qualitative researchers use. However, it is important to remember that as researchers work to understand the full range of meanings that exist within texts, textual analysis continues to evolve as a qualitative methodology. For me, the choice to use a specific type of textual analysis, with predetermined categories of analysis, or to instead allow categories to emerge after immersing myself in the material, is less important than making sure to go beyond surface representations to focus on the deeper meanings of the texts.

## Ethical Considerations

Given that there is no one correct way to analyze a text and that researchers bring their own interpretive strategies to their work, you may be wondering about the value of textual analysis as a qualitative methodology. Textual analysis, like other qualitative methodologies, does not provide researchers with knowledge that can be replicated or generalized within a wider population. Instead, researchers use textual analysis to try to understand how people use texts to make sense of their lives. While no two textual analyses produce the same interpretation, researchers draw on the relevant social, historical, political and/or economic context as well as their own knowledge of the text's place within the broader culture in order to understand the most likely sense-making strategies. While there is not one "true" interpretation of a text, it is not a free-for-all, and there are certainly interpretations that are more reasonable than others. It is important for researchers to understand that "[w]ays of making sense of the world aren't completely arbitrary; they don't change from moment to moment. They're not infinite, and they're not completely individual" (McKee, 2003, p. 18).

Qualitative researchers draw on the relevant context for their textual analysis to specifically understand how each text fits into the dominant worldview of a culture. It is from an emphasis on the cultural context that researchers construct their most likely interpretations of the relationships between a text and the larger society. While researchers base their analyses on theoretical and/or conceptual frameworks, it is important for them to stay open to discovering unknown possibilities that may differ from what they thought they might find.

For example, in my research example that is reprinted in the next section of this chapter, I originally wanted to look at how the practice of journalism had changed over the past century. I was interested in understanding how journalistic values and news conventions might have changed and how newspapers represented and interpreted social, political and economic change through their coverage of routine news stories. Initially I was not interested in religious changes in society or in researching the role of advertising in newspapers. However, from my textual analysis of the newspaper coverage, issues of advertising and news, and the role of religion, emerged as central themes of the coverage. Had I ignored these themes because they were not of interest to me, I would have considered my research to be ethically suspect because I would have attempted to manipulate the evidence to support my interests and concerns. While interpretation is a subjective endeavor, it is important for qualitative researchers to let the evidence guide their interpretations rather than attempting to make the evidence fit with their preconceived opinions and beliefs.

## Research Using Textual Analysis

The following research example of a critical literary textual analysis examines the print coverage of the Thanksgiving holiday from 1905 through 2005 in eleven daily urban newspapers published in the United States. My original intention was to analyze the coverage at three particular time periods, 1905, 1955 and 2005, in order to assess how newspapers covered routine news stories. For this study I wanted to understand how the newspapers represented and interpreted social, political and economic change during the past century. I chose to focus on Thanksgiving because it has been a traditional news story covered consistently by the press over the 100-year period. The research ultimately provided me with insights regarding basic routines of journalism, including specific news conventions, journalistic norms and values.

The research project is framed from a British cultural studies theoretical perspective, using Raymond Williams' concept of structure of feeling to help us understand historical changes in the newspaper coverage of the holiday. Structure of feeling focuses on the lived experiences of people at a specific place and time, and it encourages researchers to emphasize the historical context relevant to their work. The historical background that I included for the Thanksgiving holiday helped me to situate my textual analysis in the appropriate cultural, political and economic context.

In this first section I also provided a brief literature review of research that has evaluated newspaper content over time. Much of the previous research had been based on content analysis, and my commentary illustrates some of Kracauer's concerns regarding quantitative content analysis.

---

### "From Religiosity to Consumerism: Press Coverage of Thanksgiving, 1905–2005," by Bonnie Brennen

From *Journalism Studies*, *9* (1), 2008, 21–37.

### Introduction

On October 3, 1789, President George Washington (2005 [1789]) proclaimed a national Thanksgiving holiday to be held on Thursday, November 24, describing it as "a day of public thanksgiving and prayer." Washington initially conceived of Thanksgiving as a deeply religious holiday through which Americans would give thanks to God for their liberty and prosperity. Washington's religious vision for the holiday was based in part on two earlier Thanksgiving celebrations: The first observation in America, held at Berkeley Plantation on December 4, 1619, was strictly religious and did not involve feasting. The first New England Thanksgiving was held in Plymouth in 1629 after Governor Bradford proclaimed a day of holiday in gratitude for the strong harvest. Following Washington's proclamation, several states celebrated a yearly Thanksgiving holiday. However, the United States did not have an established national holiday until 1863, when President Abraham Lincoln officially proclaimed that Thanksgiving would be celebrated on the last Thursday of each November. Although President Franklin D. Roosevelt, in 1939, set the holiday one week earlier in order to lengthen the shopping period between Thanksgiving and Christmas, Thanksgiving has been celebrated each year in the United States since Lincoln's proclamation, and urban daily news-papers have consistently covered the holiday celebrations each year.

In an effort to understand routine conventions of journalism as well as changes in social, political and economic aspects of American society, this research looks at the coverage of Thanksgiving during the past 100 years in eleven daily urban newspapers published in the United States. The Thanksgiving holiday was chosen because it has been a traditional news story consistently covered each year in the press, and an analysis of the coverage may provide insights into the basic routines of journalism, including news conventions, journalistic values and norms during the past 100 years. The eleven newspapers are geographically diverse and have been chosen to represent possible regional differences within the country. While some of the newspapers' names have changed as a result of mergers and acquisitions during the 100-year period, all of the newspapers included in this research have been published continually since 1905.

A consideration of Thanksgiving coverage over time offers a perspective on journalistic routines within the larger history of urban journalism; it also provides insights into a "structure of feeling" within dominant American culture that exists at specific historical moments in US history. Raymond Williams (1988 [1977], p. 132) envisions structure of feeling as representing the culture of a time, the "living result" of a specific class or society at a particular historical moment. Within the hegemonic process, Williams distinguishes the evolving, lived experiences of individuals, classes and groups from the more formal concept of ideology and explains that a structure of feeling interacts with and reacts against formal ideological beliefs incorporating "meanings and values as they are actively lived and felt." Structure of feeling describes an ongoing tension between what is articulated and what is lived, and methodologically it offers a cultural hypothesis that may help us to understand specific material aspects of a society at a distinct historical time. For Williams, a structure of feeling can be understood from a vast variety of documentary remnants of the material culture such as newspaper articles, photographs, novels, films and fashions, all of which may offer insights into the actual dominant lived culture. From this perspective, a study of the coverage of Thanksgiving, over time, in US urban newspapers may be seen to embody, in Hanno Hardt's (2001, p. 3) words, a "rich reservoir of a living culture, a kind of public conversation that reveals what moves a nation's social, political, and economic spheres."

This research project assesses all articles published the day before Thanksgiving, Thanksgiving Day, and the day after Thanksgiving in the *Atlanta Journal-Constitution, Boston Globe, Chicago Tribune, Des Moines Register, Houston Chronicle, Los Angeles Times, New York Times, Philadelphia Inquirer, Richmond Times Dispatch, Salt Lake Tribune*, and *St. Louis Post Dispatch* in the years 1905, 1955 and 2005. Articles were obtained by reading microfilm copies of the newspapers for 1905 and 1955, and from print copies of the newspapers for 2005. Overall, a total of 431 articles were evaluated for this project: 209

articles directly related to the Thanksgiving holiday were published in the eleven newspapers during the three-day period in 2005, 143 appeared in the newspapers in 1955, and 79 Thanksgiving-themed articles were published in 1905.

In its evaluation of Thanksgiving coverage on the newspapers, this research employs critical literary methods of analysis. Stuart Hall suggests that news is defined through routines and traditions and that through its regular reporting and commentary regarding individuals and events, newspapers may be seen to reflect changing patterns in a society. The three time periods 1905, 1955 and 2005 were chosen in an attempt to assess sustained historical change that appeared in the newspapers during the past 100 years. For Hall (1975, p. 11), critical literary methods are particularly useful in understanding how through "selectivity, emphasis, treatment and presentation, the press interprets that process of social change."

Much of the research that has assessed newspaper content over time has used content analysis as a methodological tool and has focused on such elements as word usage and readability of newspapers, types of news stories, types of people in the news, front-page writing styles, and visual aspects of newspapers, including story length, page make-up, headline size, and the number and type of images. For example, Gans (1980) assessed news stories on network news and in news magazines to understand what constitutes news, while Barnhurst and Mutz (1997) purposely sampled news articles between 1894 and 1994 to illustrate how the definition of news had changed. Avery (1983) measured news content in newspapers to show a rise in domestic news content before the War of 1812, while Thompson (1991) examined sentences and words in two newspapers over a 100-year period to conclude that "oral" words were used more frequently than "print" words. Stepp's (1999) study of ten newspapers over time found fundamental changes in the visual appearance of the newspapers, and Meyer (2004) sampled 2,125 stories from forty newspapers to determine the readability of contemporary newspapers. As the previous examples illustrate, content analysis may be helpful in assessing the manifest content of a newspaper; however, critical literary methods of analysis are particularly useful in going below surface categories and distinctions to penetrate "latent meanings of a text" (Hall, 1975, p. 15). Hall explains that a consideration of the treatment of an issue, concern or topic, the tone of an article, the position and placement of a news story, the recurrence of particular themes and topics, as well as the stories that stand out as exceptions to the traditional coverage offers useful strategies of analysis that may showcase the process of social change in a society.

---

In the next section I begin my analysis with a discussion of the commonalities in the newspaper coverage during the three time periods throughout the 100 years. This part of my analysis focuses primarily on the denotative meanings of the texts, emphasizing the common themes of Thanksgiving reporting such as food preparation, weather and travel stories. At the end of the section I draw on one 2005 article as an example that offers a more nuanced understanding of the coverage. At a connotative level, this article illustrates how changes in the structure of feeling may have emerged in American society.

## Continuities in the Coverage

On a basic level, some topical aspects of the Thanksgiving coverage remained remarkably consistent throughout the 100-year period. Newspapers routinely drew on aspects of the historical context of Thanksgiving to frame their coverage. Pilgrims and Native Americans figured prominently in discussions of Thanksgiving culinary traditions, and Presidents Washington and Lincoln were remembered as central to the development of the holiday. A number of Thanksgiving-related topics including weather and travel stories, food preparations for the holiday, human interest stories on local citizens, and articles about how the president spent his Thanksgiving provided a staple of the newspaper coverage in all eleven newspapers in 1905, 1955 and 2005.

While the tone and language used in the news articles has changed over the years, weather and travel stories remained a consistent Thanksgiving mainstay during the past century. All eleven newspapers included in this study addressed the Thanksgiving weather, and many of the articles were written in conjunction with travel plans for the holiday. In 1905, with Midwest temperatures expected to drop to zero [Fahrenheit; about −18°C], the *Des Moines Register* (November 30, 1905b) noted that only "those who wish to brave the terrors of the chill blast" would be attending church and football games on Thanksgiving, while the *St. Louis Post Dispatch* (November 29, 1905a) offered a detailed description of the progress of the storm and explained that the destructive blizzard had "demoralized traffic and interrupted telegraphic communication." In a front-page news article on the day before Thanksgiving in 1955, the *Boston Globe* (November 23, 1955a) predicted good weather and "record-breaking" traffic, while on the day after Thanksgiving the *Los Angeles Times* (November 25, 1955) reported that Southern Californians experienced perfect weather for the holiday; it was clear and sunny with no smog and the temperature reached a high of 64° [18°C] with "just the right touch of fall crispness." Travel difficulties and traffic delays were reported in all of the newspapers in 2005. A *Chicago Tribune* columnist recommended moving Thanksgiving to October when the weather was better, while a news article in the *Richmond Times Dispatch* (November 23,

2005) responded to increased security travel procedures by advising travelers to "wear sensible footwear" and to avoid bringing wrapped presents on airplanes. In general, Thanksgiving travel and weather stories featured in the newspapers in 1905, 1955 and 2005 consistently offered straightforward, specific information that was intended to give readers guidance related to their holiday celebrations, and as such these news articles may be seen as print versions of public service announcements.

Not surprisingly, traditional food stories abounded in the Thanksgiving coverage over the past 100 years. For each time period considered in this study, newspaper readers were instructed on how to carve a turkey, taught what to do with leftovers and guided through family-friendly holiday recipes. While a 1905 *Philadelphia Inquirer* (November 29, 1905a) article on turkey preparation, which advised cooks to "singe the bird and cut off the legs and head. Take a clean cloth and wipe carefully, picking out the pin feathers" may be less useful to contemporary readers, the 1955 *Boston Globe*'s (November 23, 1955b) instruction to keep hot food hot and cold food cold to avoid food poisoning remains sage advice. In 2005, traditional Thanksgiving recipes were augmented with a variety of offbeat food stories. For example, the *Houston Chronicle* and the *Los Angeles Times* each included a news story on a food-eating contest during which a woman consumed an entire turkey in twelve minutes, while a columnist for the *Chicago Tribune* described in great detail why he despised Jell-O molds. Throughout the coverage, turkey was consistently showcased as the preferred Thanksgiving main course. In 1905, pigs and ducks were described as popular holiday alternatives, while in 2005, owing to fears of bird flu, the health benefits of turkey were extolled as a safer alternative to chicken. Studies on scientists' efforts to raise healthier turkeys were also included in the coverage, and as a *Chicago Tribune* (November 24, 2005) Thanksgiving day editorial explained, readers could eat turkey without any guilt because wild turkeys were vicious beasts that regularly attacked people by scratching them, chasing them and beating them with their wings. The editorial also noted that "when it comes to turkeys, it's kill or be killed."

Articles that addressed how the president spent Thanksgiving appeared consistently in the majority of the newspapers in 1905, 1955 and 2005. In 1905, news stories described the Roosevelts' Thanksgiving dinner at their country home in Virginia, complete with a 31-pound [68-kilogram] turkey, while in 1955, news articles reported on the "old fashioned" (Deakin, 1955) Thanksgiving that President Eisenhower enjoyed with his family at his farm after his two-month convalescence following a heart attack. Most of the newspapers in 2005 featured an Associated Press news article that detailed President Bush's Thanksgiving Day phone calls to servicemen as well as the holiday menu served at his Crawford, Texas, ranch, including "free-range turkey, fresh-milled cornbread dressing, pan gravy, chipotle maple whipped sweet potatoes, roasted asparagus and red peppers, green beans supreme, fruit ambrosia, fresh yeast rolls and orange cranberry relish. Dessert was two kinds of pie: Texas pecan and pumpkin" (Pickler, 2005). Throughout the coverage, the emphasis on each president's family celebrations, complete with traditional Thanksgiving feasts, may be seen as a way to humanize these leaders and to showcase common traditions and practices aligned with the majority of the American public.

Thanksgiving-themed human interest feature stories were also found throughout the newspaper coverage during the past 100 years. In 1905, feature articles detailed lavish holiday parties of the social elite and reported on how Americans visiting London and Rome celebrated Thanksgiving. Similar features appeared in the 1955 newspapers, which also included a variety of medical miracle stories in which a young child or teenager was surgically cured of a rare medical disease or defect. Such articles were consistent with a prevailing belief in the revolutionary power of technology, which framed post-World War II American consciousness. Human interest stories in the 2005 newspapers focused primarily on Hurricane Katrina survivors and holiday celebrations of movie stars and sports figures, as well as including a news brief on the fortieth anniversary of one of the most famous Thanksgiving meals in history, immortalized by Arlo Guthrie in his song "Alice's Restaurant" (*St. Louis Post Dispatch*, November 23, 2005).

While the presentation of Thanksgiving-themed topics often remained consistent throughout the coverage, a 2005 full-page human interest article in the *Philadelphia Inquirer* (November 24, 2005) titled "The Dysfunctional Family Thanksgiving" clearly illustrated that at a deeper level, Thanksgiving coverage had greatly changed during the past century. The full-page feature appeared as a "Chutes & Ladders" board game, complete with pop psychology commentary that flippantly dismissed serious medical concerns, including obsessive-compulsive disorder and Alzheimer's, and harshly judged individuals who chose not to eat meat for ethical reasons. For example, one square read: "Your annoying vegan kid brother expounds on the morality of killing turkeys. Go back 2 spaces." This full-page Thanksgiving article suggests the regularity, commonality and normalcy of discussing psychological issues, terms and conditions in contemporary society. It illustrates changes in journalistic practices regarding what constitutes news content and blurs the line between advertising and news. In an attempt to illustrate major shifts in the structure of feeling within American society, this research now assesses significant changes in the Thanksgiving newspaper coverage during the past 100 years.

When conceptualizing this study, I initially had no idea that religion would play a pivotal role in the newspaper coverage. I had considered Thanksgiving a patriotic but secular holiday and did not know that it had originated as a religious holiday. Of course, as I gathered the relevant contextual material I soon realized my error. Evaluating the coverage clearly showed how the holiday had evolved during the 100-year period and how it illustrated cultural changes taking place within American society.

## Religious Aspects of Thanksgiving

In 1905, Thanksgiving coverage in the eleven newspapers clearly continued to articulate Washington's religious vision of Thanksgiving. Newspapers boldly reminded readers of the religious meaning of the holiday and advised them to combine religious worship with family celebrations. On Thanksgiving Eve, the *Des Moines Register* (November 29, 1905a) recommended "that the confessedly religious people of Des Moines spend an hour and a half at church tomorrow," while a front-page *Philadelphia Inquirer* (December 1, 1905c) news article the day after Thanksgiving reported: "Everybody yesterday praised God, from whom all blessings flow. Thousands did it in the old conventional way, hallowed by Puritan precedent, of going to church, listening to appropriate sermons and joining in hymns of thanksgiving."

In 1905, all eleven newspapers included at least one article detailing religious services that would be held on Thanksgiving, and several of the newspapers ran follow-up articles discussing the specifics of sermons held during religious services. For example, a December 1, 1905 *Richmond Times Dispatch* news story noted: "The preacher did not overlook the evils of the day, but in eloquent words sounded a warning that in their prosperity people might forget the paths of virtue." Although much of the 1905 religious content in the newspapers focused on Christian, including Catholic, services, four newspapers, the *St. Louis Post Dispatch*, the *Houston Chronicle*, the *Atlanta Journal-Constitution* and the *Richmond Times Dispatch*, included coverage of Jewish Thanksgiving services, which also commemorated the 250th anniversary of the landing and settlement of Jews in America. Each of these four articles detailed the history of Jewish immigration to the United States and framed the coverage around Jews' contributions to the development of the wealth and power of the United States.

Religious aspects of Thanksgiving remained central to the newspaper coverage of 1955. Once again, all eleven newspapers covered Thanksgiving religious services, this time often including listings of Jewish holiday services along with Protestant, Catholic and Mormon worship services. A front-page Thanksgiving Day article in the *New York Times* outlined the offerings of a variety of religious services and included a call by the Zionist Organization of America to pray for peace, security and stability in Israel. Several of the 1955 articles situated the holiday within its religious historical context, and as a Thanksgiving Day editorial in the *Philadelphia Inquirer* (November 24, 1955) explained, the newspaper hoped that as a part of family celebrations readers did not forget the "historic consciousness of the gifts of Divine Providence."

Of particular note was the tone of three editorials that seemed to indicate a concern that some readers might need convincing to incorporate worship in their holiday celebrations. A *Salt Lake Tribune* editorial focused on the history of Thanksgiving and explained that religious observance has been tied to Thanksgiving Day since the Pilgrims first "called God to witness the first charter of democratic government in America." The editorial noted that while Thomas Jefferson lobbied for the separation of church and state,

> there is nothing wrong with a religious overtone to the observance. After all, the fact that ours is a God-fearing nation has been recognized throughout our history, from the appeal to the "Supreme Judge of the world" in the Declaration of Independence to the recent acknow-ledgment in the pledge of allegiance that this is a nation "under God."
>
> (Salt Lake Tribune, November 24, 1955)

A *Houston Chronicle* editorial urged readers to give thanks not only at the dinner table but during religious services, while a Thanksgiving Day editorial in the *Philadelphia Inquirer* (November 24, 1955) maintained that "every citizen of this Nation can take time to offer up his own humble prayer of thanksgiving for life, liberty and the God-given privilege of being an American." The word choice and tone of these editorials illustrate an acknowledgment of and a reaction to recent challenges to the traditional vision of Thanksgiving as a religious holiday. In contrast to the 1905 and 1955 Thanksgiving coverage, in 2005 newspapers primarily focused on non-religious topics and there was little indication that Thanksgiving had initially been conceived of as a religious holiday. In fact, a *New York Times* (November 24, 2005b) article on how children of immigrants encouraged their parents to celebrate the holiday described Thanksgiving as "one of the more accessible holidays for newcomers, free from religious or political affiliation." In all of the 2005 newspapers in this study the emphasis of the coverage was directed away from religiosity and focused on other aspects of the Thanksgiving holiday. During the three-day period, only eight articles were published in the 2005 newspapers that discussed any aspect of religion. The eight articles appeared in six of the papers; the other five newspapers did not publish any articles on the religious aspects of Thanksgiving. While the number of articles published alone is only a minor factor in this analysis, it is interesting to compare the content of the eight Thanksgiving articles published in 2005 that focused on religion, with the twenty-five articles in the eleven newspapers published in 1955, and the twenty-one articles with religious content published in the eleven newspapers in 1905.

No articles listed religious services for the Thanksgiving holiday in 2005, and only the *Richmond Times Dispatch* mentioned in a general news article that some Richmonders attended religious services as part of their Thanksgiving celebration. The *Times Dispatch* also reprinted George Washington's 1789 proclamation designating Thanksgiving as a religious holiday. Two newspapers, the *Philadelphia Inquirer* and the *Atlanta Journal-Constitution*, included articles reminding readers that Thanksgiving was originally conceived of as a religious holiday, while a *Chicago Tribune* human interest story on a group of Hurricane Katrina victims mentioned that one family member embraced religion after his struggles. A Thanksgiving Day article in the *New York Times* (November 24, 2005a) on the challenge of saying grace at Thanksgiving described it as "the most significant remainder of Thanksgiving's religious roots" and noted that saying grace now intimidated and confused many people. Similarly, the *Los Angeles Times* (November 24, 2005) struggled with the religious origins of the holiday and in a Thanksgiving Day editorial stated, "Thanksgiving has always posed problems for those who favor a stout wall separating church and state. Today is a fundamentally religious, Judeo-Christian holiday that was created by federal government and is deeply enshrined in its traditions." Yet, apart from this editorial, the 2005 *Los Angeles Times* Thanksgiving coverage, like that of several other newspapers in this study, was completely non-religious. The lack of religiosity in the Thanksgiving coverage clearly illustrates the secular emphasis of contemporary society. According to Stewart Hoover, the treatment of religion in the press may be seen as an indication of the larger status of religion in society. In American culture the ease with which the press has accepted "the secularization of society as a guiding principle of coverage does suggest the extent to which this idea is embedded in American social, political, and educational philosophy" (Hoover, 1998, p. 12).

---

At the beginning of the twentieth century the Progressive reform movement influenced newspaper coverage of the Thanksgiving holiday. Progressives worked to raise the social consciousness of the middle class in an effort to eliminate problems such as hunger, poverty and child labor. Note how an emphasis on the social and political issues of each era informs my analysis of the coverage.

---

## The "Needy Ones"

In the early twentieth century a Progressive reform movement opposed to waste and corruption sought change at all levels of society and fought to reduce the political power of corporate interests through government regulation. Focusing primarily on urban issues and problems, Progressives challenged dominant power relations and worked to make the US government more responsive to the needs of its citizens. During the Progressive era, investigative journalists, known as muckrakers, often focused on social, political and economic issues that targeted the public ignorance and apathy of middle-class readers and sought to arouse "a lethargic public to righteous indignation" (Weinberg & Weinberg, 1964, p. xviii). One classic 1904 study, *Poverty: Social Conscience in the Progressive Era*, by Robert Hunter (1965 [1904]), called for a sociological rather than a moralistic approach to social issues and concerns. Hunter's research posited poverty as an interconnected relationship between economic, mental, physical and emotional problems, and redefined poverty as a situation in which individuals "are underpaid, underfed, under-clothed, badly housed and overworked" (Jones, 1965, p. xix). Relying on census data, unemployment figures, pauper burials and his own observations, Hunter estimated that in 1904 no fewer than 10 million Americans, or 13 percent of the population, was in poverty and he suggested that up to 15 or 20 million people might actually be considered poor.

In line with the broader Progressive agenda, a primary focus of the Thanksgiving coverage in 1905 was on feeding orphans, the poor, the elderly, the disabled, the homeless and those in the community who were incarcerated. During the 1905 three-day Thanksgiving period, every newspaper in this study ran at least one article on efforts to feed the needy, and most of these articles were prominently placed and included long and detailed information regarding specific community service activities. For example, the *Los Angeles Times* ran an in-depth front-page news article describing the Thanksgiving activities of local civic groups and organizations to feed more than 4,000 local citizens who were referred to as "needy ones," while the *New York Times* coverage reported, in great detail, efforts to feed nearly 6,000 homeless people in the city. The *St. Louis Post Dispatch* (November 30, 1905b) described efforts of wealthy local citizens to deliver baskets of food to the poor and noted that for many families living in squalor, the holiday meant another cold day of "numbing gloveless hands and wretchedly clad feet and bodies." Coverage in the *Philadelphia Inquirer* and the *Salt Lake Tribune* emphasized efforts to feed homeless children, while a *Richmond Times Dispatch* article focused on efforts to aid African-American orphans. Newspapers also detailed Thanksgiving celebrations for those in hospitals and mental institutions, as well as community efforts to help the disabled. Overall, with descriptive language intended to showcase the plight of needy individuals, the newspapers reported how thousands of local citizens were aided through community and individual efforts.

In 1905 approximately 1 million children worked in factories, mines, tenement workshops and textile mills. Progressives who wanted "to save the children from neglect, overwork, and ignorance" (Bryant, 1969, p. 150) made ending child labor one of their primary social platforms. Muckrakers investigated child labor practices and found that within their own field, newspaper owners often exploited the labor of newsboys. At the beginning of the twentieth century, newsboys routinely bought their papers from circulation corner men and then resold the newspapers on the street; because of this practice, newspaper management considered newsboys merchants rather than employees. As young merchants, newsboys had the status of independent contractors and therefore child labor laws did not apply to them. Both the *Chicago Tribune* and the *Los Angeles Times* covered elaborate Thanksgiving dinners prepared for hundreds of local newsboys who needed assistance. In a lengthy article run the day after Thanksgiving, the *Los Angeles Times* (December 1, 1905) sympathetically described the newsboys as "ragamuffin waifs," "half-starved tatterdemalions" who fought madly to be the first in line for food and greatly enjoyed the holiday meals.

The Progressive agenda also extended to prison reform, particularly as it related to unfair labor conditions and inhuman prison conditions. Muckrakers investigated a "barbaric lease system" (Weinberg & Weinberg, 1964, p. 323) and discovered that inmates were routinely being sold to contractors who treated them like slaves. The 1905 coverage of Thanksgiving meals for those in prison clearly focused on prison reform issues and showcased the humane treatment of prisoners. Several of the newspapers noted that special Thanksgiving dinners would be held for prisoners, and some of the newspaper articles actually included the menu in the news coverage. For example, the *Chicago Tribune* reported that watching a vaudeville performance and smoking cigars was part of the festivities for 1,500 male inmates at the penitentiary, while the *Houston Chronicle* (December 1, 1905) noted that for the first time, a special Thanksgiving dinner was held in both the county and the city jails:

> The banquet table was spread with all the delicacies of the season. Turkey and cranberry sauce, oysters and the various courses down to ice cream and cigars were served. A phonograph and a violin were called into service. Games of various sorts were provided and the celebration lasted until far into the night.

By 1955, the Progressive movement was long over and a postwar conservative environment promoted patriotism, anti-communism, McCarthyism and the Cold War. After witnessing the horrors of Stalinism and the orthodoxies of the Cold

War, social critics began to reject ideological formulations and instead embraced conservatism and complacency. American popular culture extolled the virtues of conformity of opinion and showcased rigid expectations of behavior as the norm. In the meantime, as Richard Pells (1989, p. 118) explains, "the problems of poverty, racism, and urban decay simmered under the surface of middle-class affluence." In 1945, Congress had established the GI Bill of Rights, which provided educational and training opportunities as well as hospitalization for World War II veterans; Congress had also provided additional funds for veterans' housing. These actions triggered the growth of the suburbs but also contributed to the neglect of key urban issues. By 1955, nearly one-third of the public lived in suburban areas, leaving the poor, racial minorities, the old, the unemployed and the homeless in decaying urban centers, which were then commonly referred to as "skid rows" (Daly, 1996). Poverty figures calculated from population income data determined that in 1955, 32.5 million Americans—19.9 percent of the population—were poor (Barrington & Fisher, 2006).

---

The change in the concept of homelessness arose as a fascinating aspect of my analysis. I found that the coverage of this issue and the absence of coverage of homelessness in the 2005 newspaper articles on Thanksgiving were the most surprising aspects of my research.

---

## The New Homeless

Although newspapers in 1955 continued to report on efforts to feed the homeless, the sick, the incarcerated, and the disabled in their Thanksgiving coverage, feeding the needy was an issue that was sometimes conflated with religious aspects of the holiday. In several of the newspapers, such activities were downplayed and were included as secondary concerns in articles that focused primarily on other holiday activities. In 1955, only five of the newspapers—the Los Angeles Times, the New York Times, the Houston Chronicle, the Salt Lake Tribune and the Boston Globe—showcased efforts to feed the needy in separate news stories. A front-page news article and lengthy jump ran the day after Thanksgiving in the Los Angeles Times under the headline "Thanksgiving Feasts Served Unfortunates," and reported the activities of about a dozen welfare agencies and rescue missions to feed an estimated 15,000 local residents, while the New York Times detailed efforts to feed about 3,000 people living in shelters. Some of the newspapers also mentioned holiday meals at the jails: in St. Louis, Salt Lake City and Los Angeles, prison inmates ate turkey dinners, while in Houston, city jail occupants ate turkey but prisoners at the county jail ate chicken. Although poverty and homelessness remained significant urban issues in 1955, the lessening coverage of these issues during the Thanksgiving period may be seen to illustrate a changing structure of feeling specifically related to the relevance of social issues within American society.

In 1955, writers applauded the superiority of Keynesian economics and suggested that with technological developments primarily related to automation, manual labor would soon be obsolete. Mechanized agriculture, artificial photosynthesis and the use of algae and other materials from the oceans were envisioned as solutions to world hunger; pronouncements such as "the species' dependence upon nature for a steady food supply has virtually disappeared" (Rosenberg, 1957, p. 4) proliferated in books and in the popular press. Yet, larger social issues in the United States were being reflected in dramatic changes in the meaning of the term *homeless* that were occurring during the twentieth century. In his article "The Old Homeless and the New Homelessness in Historical Perspective," Peter Rossi (1990, p. 955) explains that before the 1980s, homelessness meant "living outside family units, whereas today's meaning of the term is more directly tied to the absolute lack of housing." At the beginning the twentieth century the homeless were those workers who constituted the US labor reserve. As Stuart A. Rice, former superintendent of the New York Municipal Lodging House, described:

> Homeless men are demanded to build the bridges and tunnels, the irrigation systems and railroads, to harvest our forests and embank our rivers. They are the pioneers of modern industry. They go hither and thither to the rough, unfinished, uncomfortable places of the world, to provide homes and civilized comforts for those of us who follow. Meanwhile they live in bunk houses. Homeless women are preferred to do the "dirty work" in our public institutions and to scrub and clean at night in our hotels. Generally only they are willing to accept the work and the hours demanded.
>
> (1918, p. 141)

In the 1950s, the homeless were primarily "alcoholic old men" (Rossi, 1990, p. 954) who lived alone in flophouse hotels, or mission dormitories on skid rows, located near freight yards and truck stops. Most of the homeless were Caucasian; some had physical disabilities and others were dealing with chronic mental illness and social maladjustment. Those physically able to work supplemented their pensions and social security checks with intermittent low-paid, menial work. Local shelters and mission dormitories provided housing and food to those individuals who could not work. Yet, by the 1980s a new type of homeless began to appear in the United States, with men, women and even children sleeping in cardboard boxes and in doorways, abandoned cars, parks, and other public places. According to the US Census Bureau (2005), 37 million Americans, or 12.6 percent of the population, were below the poverty level in 2005. At any given time, approximately 3.5 million Americans below the poverty level are homeless in the United States (Burt et al., 1999), and a study released by the National Alliance to End Homelessness estimates that in 2005, homelessness among families was increasing, with 41 percent of the homeless currently consisting of families with children (Philadelphia Inquirer, January 11, 2007).

Clearly, the issue of homelessness remains a serious problem in the United States, and yet in 2005 none of the newspapers in this study addressed efforts to care for the homeless of their own communities, nor was there any coverage of holiday meals served to individuals who were in hospitals, nursing homes, or prisons. However, while homelessness was not an issue addressed in the 2005 Thanksgiving coverage, some of the newspapers focused on efforts to aid Hurricane Katrina survivors. With New Orleans residents displaced after the hurricane, such an emphasis generally reported local campaigns to help Katrina survivors.

Five of the newspapers also addressed efforts to feed needy local citizens: a general news article in the *Richmond Times Dispatch* described Salvation Army efforts to serve a holiday meal to needy Richmonders; the *Des Moines Register* covered efforts to feed Iowa families displaced by recent tornadoes; and the *Boston Globe* ran several news articles on local efforts to feed the needy at Thanksgiving, including a news story about Massachusetts governor Mitt Romney serving underprivileged citizens Thanksgiving dinner. The *Atlanta Journal-Constitution* ran a list of charities with contact information and suggestions on ways local citizens could help, while news articles in the *Houston Chronicle* detailed citywide efforts to feed approximately 40,000 low-income Houston residents Thanksgiving meals. The Houston holiday effort also provided local citizens as well as some Hurricane Katrina survivors with clothing and blankets, medical checkups, and flu shots. The *Houston Chronicle* also ran an editorial column by Brian Green (2005), CEO of the Houston Food Bank, which focused on the problem of Americans who are "food insecure"; that is, unable to acquire sufficient food on a daily basis. In his column, Green noted that according to the US Department of Agriculture, in 2005 16.4 percent of Texans were food insecure and he wondered how it was possible for people to go hungry "in a society that obsesses about the consequences of overeating."

Interestingly, an obsession with weight was clearly the emphasis of a prominent news story in the *Los Angeles Times* run on the front page of its local news section the day after Thanksgiving. The lengthy news article and jump with the headline "Toning and Atoning on the Run" featured ways to burn off extra calories consumed at Thanksgiving. The news story estimated that a traditional

222 • Textual Analysis

Thanksgiving dinner consisted of about 3,000 calories and discussed strategies that Southern Californians planned to use, including cycling, hiking, running and jogging, to burn off the meal. Yet the article quoted an exercise physiologist who warned readers that their holiday celebrations could have long-term consequences: "It's futile to think you'll be able to work off your Thanksgiving meal in one day" (Horton & Ricci, 2005). This news article appears to be targeted to an affluent readership with plenty of leisure time rather than one of the "254,000 men, women and children [who] experience homelessness in Los Angeles County during some part of the year and approximately 82,000 people [who] are homeless on any given night" (Los Angeles Almanac, 2007). An obsession with weight was also apparent in the *New York Times* Thanksgiving coverage. Seemingly unaware of a 2005 report by the Coalition for the Homeless that found the number of food-insecure and homeless New Yorkers had reached an all-time high, the *New York Times* ran a Thanksgiving Day column "You Are What You Overeat" which addressed stuffing oneself at Thanksgiving, beginning with "fat-filled stuffing," as a type of "moral or civic obligation" (Klein, 2005). While the sarcastic tone of the column chides readers for overeating, it also clearly assumes that all New Yorkers (or all New Yorkers who matter) have plenty to eat each day.

Although the US Department of Agriculture reports that in 2005 35 million Americans suffered from food insecurity, apart from the *Houston Chronicle* none of the newspapers in this study mentioned this issue in any of its Thanksgiving coverage. According to the US Department of Agriculture, as well as homeless figures for the cities represented in this study, food insecurity and homelessness remain major problems in the United States. Yet, reading the 2005 Thanksgiving coverage as a whole, it is difficult not to conclude that feeding needy local citizens is no longer a news story covered by the majority of the newspapers; that is, unless people are in need as a result of a natural disaster. The lack of coverage in these newspapers may be seen to contradict the reality of larger social issues within these communities and illustrates targeted coverage of an affluent readership rather than a focus of these newspapers as papers of record for their local communities.

---

The encroachment of advertising into the news coverage emerged as a foundational theme of my research. Analyzing the articles from the three time periods illustrated major changes in the role of advertising in the newspaper coverage. By 2005 it was often impossible to differentiate news content from advertising information because advertising had been fully integrated into the Thanksgiving reportage.

---

## Advertising and News

An assessment of Thanksgiving-related news coverage over the past 100 years illustrates that during the last part of the twentieth century, advertising became a normalized and regular part of news coverage. At the beginning of the twentieth century, news and advertising departments were strictly separated in an effort to maintain the independence of journalists as well as the credibility of the news (DeLorme & Fedler, 2005). In 1905 the boundaries between news and advertising were quite firm: none of the Thanksgiving coverage in the eleven newspapers contained any advertising or promotional material. A 1905 column in the *Philadelphia Inquirer* (November 29, 1905b) on the day before Thanksgiving illustrated the care taken by newspapers to insure the separation between advertising and news. A question-and-answer column, "Womanly Answers to Womanly Questions," included a question regarding the suitability of two hotels in the Philadelphia area. While it was clear that the reader mentioned the names of the hotels in her letter, the hotel's names were omitted from the reprint of her question in the column as well as the answer to her question. The columnist responded that the first hotel mentioned was more suitable for women, as the other "entertains a number of businessmen and seems given over to them entirely." Strict boundaries between advertising and news may also be seen to illustrate the role of advertising in 1905 American society, an era before the wide-scale implementation of mass production occurred during the 1920s. At the beginning of the twentieth century, advertisements described products to the public but were not yet used, in Stuart Ewen's (1976, p. 33) words, as "a means of effectively creating consumers as a way of homogeneously controlling the consumption of a product."

By 1955 the boundaries between advertising and news had begun to blur, in part a response to a postwar commercialist environment that created the "fancied need" (Ewen, 1976, p. 35), requiring individuals to buy not only in response to their own needs but also to satisfy the needs of industrial capitalism. While the majority of the Thanksgiving coverage remained free from advertising, news articles covered Thanksgiving Day parades sponsored by Macy's and Gimbels, and a few of the newspapers mentioned gift-giving ideas for the upcoming holiday season and included actual product names and locations where the gifts could be purchased. For example, a *New York Times* article on children's toys available at local stores tied the Thanksgiving holiday to the opening of the Christmas shopping season. The article described popular toys such as a Humpty Dumpty doll that was available at Gimbels and included a selection of luxury toys that the article suggested "rich uncles" might wish to purchase: "Rocking horses covered with real pony skin priced at $115 are at Schwartz, which also has a $350 doll's house with a door bell that rings. And a small version of the Ford Thunderbird, which works on batteries is displayed at Macy's for $350" (Corrigan, 1955).

Although advertising was beginning to encroach on Thanksgiving news coverage in 1955, by 2005 the ubiquity of advertising often made it difficult to determine where news ended and advertising began. In a contemporary environment where the American way of life is described, depicted, and promoted through advertising, product placement was fully integrated into the 2005 news coverage, marking significant changes in the definition of news content. References to the Butterball Turkey Talk Line 1-800-BUTTER-BALL were included in the newspapers' Thanksgiving food coverage, and "Black Friday" business stories focused on strategies major retailers planned to lure holiday shoppers to their businesses on the day after Thanksgiving. For example, the *Boston Globe* ran two business articles on Massachusetts' blue laws that prohibited most large retailers from being open on major holidays like Thanksgiving. Both articles focused on specific retailers, Whole Foods and Wal-Mart, giving significant publicity to the retailers themselves as well as their efforts to challenge the blue laws.

A majority of the newspapers featured a lengthy obituary for Stove Top stuffing inventor Ruth Siems in their 2005 Thanksgiving coverage. Although Siems actually died on November 13, the newspapers chose to hold the obituary and feature it as part of their Thanksgiving coverage. The *New York Times* article considered Stove Top stuffing an enduring emblem of postwar convenience culture and noted that the product's advertising motto, "Stuffing instead of potatoes?" was a part of Americans' collective consciousness. However, the obituary read more like a press release for Stove Top than a news story, particularly as it explained, "Stove Top stuffing comes in a range of flavors, including turkey, chicken, beef, cornbread and sourdough" (Fox, 2005). The obituary also discussed business aspects of the product, explaining that 60 million boxes of Stove Top stuffing are sold each Thanksgiving, and lauded the role of General Mills in the development of stuffing that was quick to prepare, could be eaten at any time of the year, and spared "cooks the nasty business of having to rout around in the clammy interior of an animal" (Fox, 2005). (The *New York Times* obituary for Siems was also run in the *Des Moines Register*, the *Philadelphia Inquirer* and the *Chicago Tribune*.) Yet, as the *Los Angeles Times* obituary noted, Siems was a dominant figure in the company in her own right:

> When the billionth package of Stove Top Stuffing rolled off the assembly line in 1984, no one thought to send one of the T-shirts commemorating the occasion to Siems, a slight for which she found an appropriate response in the words emblazoned on the back of the T-shirt: "Stuff it."
> (McLellan, 2005)

Nearly every newspaper prominently covered a minor accident that occurred at the Macy's Thanksgiving Day parade in New York when the M&M balloon veered off course and slightly injured two people. The promotional references in the story offered prime publicity, which probably offset any potential damages that Macy's or M&M's parent company, Mars Food, might have incurred. More than half of the 2005 newspapers covered the pardoning, by President Bush, of two turkeys, Marshmallow and Yam. After they were pardoned, the two turkeys were flown first class to Disneyland, where Marshmallow served as grand marshal of Disneyland's Thanksgiving Day Parade. Marshmallow was dubbed "the happiest turkey on earth," an interesting play on Disneyland's advertising slogan, "the happiest place on earth."

The *Los Angeles Times* included an in-depth article in its local news section on Southern Californians who rejected the stress of traditional Thanksgiving family celebrations and instead traveled to Palm Springs for a "laid-back" (Lin, 2005) holiday. The article was a cross between a travel article and an advertisement for the La Quinta Resort and Club, describing in detail the amenities of the resort, including specifics of a holiday buffet that cost $67 per adult and $36 per child. Similarly, the *New York Times* reported on long lines for Thanksgiving shopping at Citarella, a popular Upper West Side grocery store. Although the article ran prominently on Thanksgiving Day, on the second page of the local news section, under the headline "It's 9 a.m. Do you Know Where the Turkey Line Begins?" (Steinhauer, 2005), the article's content seemed little more than a thinly veiled advertisement. The *New York Times* also included an article on the challenge of saying grace at Thanksgiving, which referenced a new book published by Tyson Foods, *Giving Thanks at Mealtime*. The *Boston Globe* bemoaned the lack of turkeys 24 pounds and larger, quoting employees at Whole Foods and Stop & Shop throughout the article, while a news article in the *Richmond Times Dispatch* discussed the Richmond Thanksgiving plans of two friends who had evacuated New Orleans during Hurricane Katrina, and showcased how the precooked turkey breasts at the local supermarket Ukrop's had solved their holiday food needs. The *St. Louis Post Dispatch* featured holiday fashions for sale at local shops, including a sweater set with ostrich feathers available for $178 at Nordstrom, while the *Richmond Times Dispatch* included an article on new Thanksgiving-themed sodas available from Jones Soda. In contrast with the clear separation between advertising and news seen in the 1905 Thanksgiving coverage, the 2005 coverage fully blended advertising, publicity and news.

---

In the conclusion, notice how I summarize key findings of the research to bring the analysis to a close. In addition, I return to my theoretical framework, specifically to the concept of structure of feeling, to showcase how it helps to explain the role of advertising in the development of contemporary consumer society.

## Conclusion

In his essay "Advertising: The Magic System," Williams (1980, p. 182) suggests that during the first half of the twentieth century, modern advertising emerged as part of an "advanced system of capitalist production, distribution and market control." Advertising developed from a simple strategy to sell products into an integral part of contemporary society, a highly organized information and persuasion system through which individuals not only buy goods but also "buy social respect, discrimination, health, beauty, success, [and] power" (pp. 188–189). For Williams, advertising's impact on the development of individuals, who view themselves as consumers rather than as product users, is a fundamental aspect of the contemporary Western capitalist structure of feeling, and it is this changing structure of feeling that has been illustrated in this assessment of newspaper coverage.

This research project focused on Thanksgiving coverage in eleven urban daily newspapers during the past 100 years in an effort to assess journalistic practices related to the coverage of routine news stories. More importantly, it has sought to go beyond analyzing or measuring distinct units or types of journalistic practice in an effort to understand how through their coverage newspapers represent and interpret social change and how an emergent structure of feeling may be read off that coverage.

American culture has changed dramatically since 1905, when a Progressive movement challenging the power elite was seeking political, economic, and social changes in the United States. Progressives fought to reduce the political power of special interest groups and challenged the government to become more responsive to the needs of its citizens. Muckrakers, the investigative journalists of the Progressive era, targeted public ignorance and apathy and encouraged the middle class to speak out about problems, issues and abuses in society. The emphasis on caring for the needy as well as other aspects of social responsibility found in the 1905 Thanksgiving newspaper coverage clearly illustrates the larger Progressive social agenda. The 1905 newspapers also adhered to strict boundaries between advertising and news, and maintained an editorial position as newspapers of record whose primary purpose was to represent the news of their community to their readership.

By 1955 a conservative and conformist social environment which extolled the virtues of technological progress, consumerism and corporate identity had begun to alter a social responsibility framework, and the separation between advertising and news began to blur. By 2005, newspaper coverage of Thanksgiving was fundamentally a-religious and devoid of any sense of social responsibility. Much of the coverage emphasized individual pursuits, targeting an affluent readership rather than extending coverage to the entire community. Although issues of homelessness and feeding the needy remained significant community issues in 2005, the majority of the newspapers in this study did not cover these important social issues, and instead the papers focused on entertainment and advertising.

In another sense, throughout the past century, articles on Thanksgiving remained a consistent story covered extensively by all of the newspapers in this study. An uncontroversial American holiday, Thanksgiving represents the type of routine reportage showcased in US daily newspapers. Such coverage may also be seen to illustrate the role of nationalism and patriotism in creating the US press culture. While there have been major social, political, religious and economic changes in the United States over the past 100 years, messages of nationalism and patriotism have consistently been promoted in urban daily newspapers. As early as 1938, sociologist O. W. Riegel (1938, p. 513) noted that the press responded to divergent economic and political interests as well as foreign and domestic conflicts by increasingly relying on popular and uncontroversial subject matter to maintain its readership. An emphasis on extensive holiday coverage, feature stories, comics and other popular trends helped to create the press as a "vehicle of nationalist propaganda" through which a confused population gained comfort and satisfaction from reading articles based on familiar patriotic images and messages. In recent years, explicit displays of the patriotism of the press are a public expectation routinely queried in press surveys and public opinion polls (see, for example, Pew Research Center Survey Report, 2005).

Finally, the 2005 Thanksgiving coverage in the eleven newspapers may be seen to illustrate successful "reality engineering" by advertisers to shape the social images depicted in popular culture. It is an accomplishment that James Karrh (1998, p. 34) suggests has resulted in citizens' acceptance of "brand images into areas of public life that were formerly 'commercial-free' and to see brands and their identifiers as a natural part of everyday life." In 1905, journalists attempted to instill a sense of righteous indignation in the minds of readers; 100 years later, newsworkers have been co-opted as handmaidens of the advertising industry, selling Thanksgiving as just another product without any understanding of the religious, moral or social foundations of the holiday.

## Textual Analysis Exercises

1. Pick a national news story and compare the coverage in three different newspapers. Consider the following questions for your analysis: How are sources used in the news stories? What is the focus of each of the articles? How are images used in the coverage? How do the headlines relate to the news story? Is the coverage similar? What (if any) differences in the coverage did you find?

2. Pick an international online news story and compare the coverage on news websites from three different countries. Consider the following questions for your analysis: How were the news stories framed? How are the sources used? What themes emerge from the coverage? Is the coverage similar? What (if any) differences in the coverage did you find? If there are differences, why do you think that the story was covered differently?

3. Conduct an ideological analysis of a print advertisement using a specific theoretical orientation to help frame your analysis. Remember to use Cormack's categories of content, structure, absence, style and mode of address to guide your analysis.

# References

Atkinson, Paul, & Coffey, Amanda. (2011). Analysing documentary realities. In David Silverman (Ed.), *Qualitative research: Issues of theory, method and practice* (3rd edn, pp. 56–75). Los Angeles, CA: Sage.

Avery, Donald. (1983). The American newspaper in the early nineteenth century: The torch-bearer? Paper presented to the Association for Education in Journalism and Mass Communication, Corvallis, OR.

Barnhurst, Kevin G., & Mutz, Diana. (1997). American journalism and the decline in event-centered reporting. *Journal of Communication, 47* (4), 27–52.

Barrington, Linda, & Fisher, Gordon M. (2006). Poverty. In Susan B. Carter, Scott Sigmund Gartner, Michael R. Haines, Allan L. Olmstead, Richard Sutch, & Gavin Wright (Eds.), *Historical statistics of the United States* (pp. 625–651). Cambridge: Cambridge University Press.

Berger, Arthur Asa. (1998). *Media research techniques* (2nd edn). Thousand Oaks, CA: Sage.

Berger, Arthur Asa. (2000). *Media and communication research methods: An introduction to qualitative and quantitative approaches.* Thousand Oaks, CA: Sage.

Boston Globe. (1955a, November 23). Vast Thanksgiving throng travels homeward today. *Boston Globe*, p. 1.

Boston Globe. (1955b, November 23). How to prepare dinner for healthy Thanksgiving. *Boston Globe*, p. 25.

Branston, Gill. (2006). Understanding genre. In Marie Gillespie & Jason Toynbee (Eds.), *Analysing media texts* (pp. 43–78). Maidenhead, UK: Open University Press.

Bryant, Keith L. Jr. (1969). Kate Barnard, organized labor, and social justice in Oklahoma during the Progressive era. *Journal of Southern History, 35* (2), 145–164.

Burt, Martha R., Aron, Laudan Y., Douglas, Toby, Valente, Jesse, Lee, Edgar, & Iwen, Britta. (1999). *Homelessness: Programs and the people they serve.* Retrieved from http://www.huduser.org/publications/homeless/homelessness (accessed January 12, 2007).

Chicago Tribune. (2005, November 24). Feast without guilt. *Chicago Tribune*, p. 18A.

Coalition for the Homeless. (2007). Homelessness in New York City: The basic facts. Retrieved from http://www.coalitionforthehomeless.org (accessed January 12, 2007).

Conroy, Pat. (2010). *My reading life.* New York: Doubleday.

Cormack, Mike. (1995). *Ideology.* Ann Arbor: University of Michigan Press.

Corrigan, Faith. (1955, November 24). Thanksgiving opens season of children's parties and toys. *New York Times*, p. 38.

Daly, Gerald P. (1996). *Homeless: Policies, strategies, and lives on the street.* London: Routledge.

Deakin, James. (1955, November 25). Eisenhower resumes work after holiday, sees White House aid. *St. Louis Post Dispatch*, p. A1.

DeLorme, Denise, & Fedler, Fred. (2005). An historical analysis of journalists' attitudes toward advertisers and advertising's influence. *American Journalism, 22* (2), 7–40.

Denzin, Norman K., & Lincoln, Yvonna S. (Eds.). (1998). *The landscape of qualitative research: Theories and issues.* Thousand Oaks, CA: Sage.

Des Moines Register. (1905a, November 29). Thanksgiving Day. *Des Moines Register*, p. 9.

Des Moines Register. (1905b, November 30). Zero expected for Thanksgiving. *Des Moines Register*, p. 6.

Ewen, Stuart. (1976). *Captains of consciousness: Advertising and the social roots of the consumer culture.* New York: McGraw-Hill.

Fox, Margalit. (2005, November 23). Ruth M. Siems, 74, inventor of a Thanksgiving mainstay. *New York Times*, p. A25.

Gans, Herbert J. (1980). *Deciding what's news.* New York: Vintage Books.

Gillespie, Marie, & Toynbee, Jason (Eds.) (2006). *Analysing media texts.* Maidenhead, UK: Open University Press.

Green, Brian. (2005, November 24). Let us never forget the victims of food insecurity. *Houston Chronicle*, p. B13.

Gripsrud, Jostein. (2006). Semiotics: Signs, codes and cultures. In Marie Gillespie & Jason Toynbee (Eds.), *Analysing Media Texts* (pp. 9–41). Maidenhead, UK: Open University Press.

Hall, Stuart. (1975). Introduction. In Anthony C. H. Smith with Elizabeth Immirzi & Trevor Blackwell (Eds.), *Paper voices: The popular press and social change, 1935–1965* (pp. 11–24). London: Chatto & Windus.

Hall, Stuart. (1980). Encoding/decoding. In Stuart Hall, Dorothy Hobson, Andrew Lowe, & Paul Willis (Eds.), *Culture, media, language: Working papers in Cultural Studies, 1972–79* (pp. 128–138). London: Hutchinson.

Hardt, Hanno. (2001). *In the company of media: Cultural constructions of communication, 1920s–1930s.* Boulder, CO: Westview Press.

Hoover, Stewart. (1998). *Religion in the news: Faith and journalism in American public discourse.* Thousand Oaks, CA: Sage.

Horton, Sue, & Ricci, James. (2005, November 25). Toning and atoning on the run. *Los Angeles Times*, p. B1.

Houston Chronicle. (1905, December 1). Thanksgiving behind bars. *Houston Chronicle*, p. 5.

Hunter, Robert. (1965 [1904]). *Poverty: Social conscience in the Progressive era.* New York: Harper Torchbooks.

Jones, Peter. (1965). Introduction to the Torchbook edition. In Robert Hunter, *Poverty: Social conscience in the Progressive era.* New York: Harper Torchbooks.

Karrh, James A. (1998). Brand placement: A review. *Journal of Current Issues and Research in Advertising, 20* (2), 32–40.

Klein, Richard. (2005, November 24). You are what you overeat. *New York Times*, p. A33.

Kracauer, Siegfried. (1952–1953). The challenge of qualitative content analysis. *Public Opinion Quarterly, 16* (4), 631–642.

Larsen, Peter. (1991). Media contents: Textual analysis of fictional media content. In Klaus Bruhn Jensen & Nicholas W. Jankowski (Eds.), *A handbook of qualitative methodologies for mass communication research* (pp. 121–134). London: Routledge.

Lin, Rong-Gong II. (2005, November 25). Desert Thanksgiving features heaping helping of relaxation. *Los Angeles Times*, p. B3.

Los Angeles Almanac. (2007). Homelessness in Los Angeles County. Retrieved from http://www.laalmanac.com/social/so14.htm (accessed July 12, 2007).

Los Angeles Times. (1905, December 1). Grim hunger put to rout. *Los Angeles Times*, p. A11.

Los Angeles Times. (1955, November 25). Perfect day here greets Thanksgiving. *Los Angeles Times*, p. 1.

Los Angeles Times. (2005, November 24). Thankful then as now. *Los Angeles Times*, p. B12.

McCormick, Neil. (2010, March 17). Lady GaGa's Telephone video: The outrageous video for Lady Gaga's release 'Telephone' has become an instant phenomenon. *Telegraph* (London). Retrieved from http://www.telegraph.co.uk/culture/music/rockandpopfeatures/7466152/Lady-GaGas-Telephone-video.html.

McKee, Alan. (2003). *Textual analysis: A beginner's guide*. London: Sage.

McLellan, Dennis. (2005, November 25). Ruth Siems, 74; Created Stove Top Stuffing Mix. *Los Angeles Times*, p. B12.

Meyer, Philip. (2004). *The vanishing newspaper: Saving journalism in the information age*. Columbia: University of Missouri Press.

New York Times. (2005a, November 24). Turkey set, guests seated. Something you want to say? *New York Times*, p. A29.

New York Times. (2005b, November 24). Children lead pilgrims of today in cultural lessons. *New York Times*, p. B1.

O'Rourke, Meghan. (2007, June 11). Diamonds are a girl's worst friend: The trouble with engagement rings. *Slate*. Retrieved from http://www.slate.com/articles/news_and_politics/weddings/2007/06/diamonds_are_a_girls_worst_friend.html.

Pells, Richard. (1989). *The liberal mind in a conservative age: American intellectuals in the 1940s and 1950s*. Middletown, CT: Wesleyan University Press.

Peräkylä, Anssi. (2008). Analyzing talk and text. In Norman K. Denzin & Yvonna S. Lincoln (Eds.), *Collecting and interpreting qualitative materials* (pp. 351–374). Thousand Oaks, CA: Sage.

Pew Research Center Survey Report. (2005). Public more critical of press, but goodwill persists. Retrieved from http://www.people-press.org/2005/06/26/public-more-critical-of-press-but-goodwill-persists/ (accessed January 12, 2007).

Philadelphia Inquirer. (1905a, November 29). To roast the turkey. *Philadelphia Inquirer*, p. 8.

Philadelphia Inquirer. (1905b, November 29). Womanly answers to womanly questions. *Philadelphia Inquirer*, p. 9.

Philadelphia Inquirer. (1905c, December 1). How a great city showed how it was thankful for year's blessings. *Philadelphia Inquirer*, p. 1.

Philadelphia Inquirer. (1955, November 24). For manifold blessings, thanksgiving. *Philadelphia Inquirer*, p. 50.

Philadelphia Inquirer. (2005, November 24). The dysfunctional family Thanksgiving. *Philadelphia Inquirer*, p. C1.

Philadelphia Inquirer. (2007, January 11). 744,000 homeless in 2005, group says. *Philadelphia Inquirer*, p. A2.

Pickler, Nedra. (2005, November 25). Bush gives thanks to GIs around world. *Salt Lake Tribune*, p. A10.

Rice, Stuart A. (1918). The homeless. *Annals of the American Academy of Political and Social Science*, 77, 140–153.

Richmond Times Dispatch. (1905, December 1). Worshippers fill churches. *Richmond Times Dispatch*, p. 12.

Richmond Times Dispatch. (2005, November 23). Infrequent fliers need to brush up. *Richmond Times Dispatch*, p. C1.

Riegel, O. W. (1938). Nationalism in press, radio and cinema. *American Sociological Review*, 3 (4), 510–515.

Romell, Rick. (2011, November 25). Why "Black Friday"? How popular term has troubled roots in Philadelphia. *Milwaukee Journal Sentinel*, pp. 1A, 7A.

Rosenberg, Bernard. (1957). Mass culture in America. In Bernard Rosenberg & David Manning White (Eds.), *Mass culture: The popular arts in America* (pp. 3–12). Glencoe, IL: The Free Press.

Rossi, Peter H. (1990). The old homeless and the new homelessness in historical perspective. *American Psychologist, 45* (8), 954–959.

Salt Lake Tribune. (1955, November 24). Checkered history of Thanksgiving Day. *Salt Lake Tribune,* p. 11A.

St. Louis Post Dispatch. (1905a, November 29). Mercury to drop to 12 above zero for Thanksgiving. *St. Louis Post Dispatch,* p. A1.

St. Louis Post Dispatch. (1905b, November 30). Lots of turkey for hungry tots. *St. Louis Post Dispatch,* p. A3.

St. Louis Post Dispatch. (2005, November 23). A Thanksgiving dinner that couldn't be beat. *St. Louis Post Dispatch,* p. L1.

Steinhauer, Jennifer. (2005, November 24). It's 9 a.m. Do you know where the turkey line begins? *New York Times,* p. B2.

Stepp, Carl. (1999). Then and now. *American Journalism Review, 21* (7), 60–79.

Stokes, Jane. (2003). *How to do media and cultural studies.* London: Sage.

Strinati, Dominic. (1995). *An introduction to theories of popular culture.* London: Routledge.

Thompson, David R. (1991). Oral history lives: A content analysis of newspapers' use of language. Paper presented to the Southwest Education Council for Journalism and Mass Communication, Corpus Christi, TX, October.

Turner, Graeme. (1997). Media texts and messages. In Stuart D. Cunningham & Graeme Turner (Eds.), *The media in Australia: Industries, texts, audiences* (pp. 293–347). St. Leonards, NSW: Allen & Unwin.

US Census Bureau. (2005). Poverty: 2005 highlights. Retrieved from http://www.census.gov/hhes/ www/poverty/data/threshld/thresh05.html (accessed June 18, 2012).

Washington, George. (2005, November 24 [1789]). Proclamation. Reprinted in: Giving thanks for the nation . . . and for the state . . . and for posterity. *Richmond Times Dispatch,* p. A22.

Weinberg, Arthur, & Weinberg, Lila (Eds.). (1964). *The muckrakers: The era in journalism that moved America to reform: The most significant magazine articles of 1902–1912.* New York: Capricorn Books.

Williams, Raymond. (1977). *Marxism and literature.* London: Oxford University Press.

Williams, Raymond. (1980). Advertising: The magic system. In *Problems in materialism and culture* (pp. 170–195). London: Verso.

# Acknowledgments

"Good Journalism: On the Evaluation Criteria of Some Interested and Experienced Actors." By Risto Kunelius. From *Journalism Studies*, Vol. 7, No. 5, 2006. 671–690. Copyright © 2006 Taylor & Francis. Reprinted by permission of the publisher, www.tandfonline.com.

"US Teenagers' Perceptions and Awareness of Digital Technology: A Focus Group Approach." By Heather L. Hundley and Leonard Shyles. From *New Media & Society*, Vol. 12, No. 3, May 2010. 417–433. Reprinted by permission of SAGE.

"Radio Utopia: Promoting public interest in a 1940s radio documentary." By Matthew C. Ehrlich. From *Journalism Studies*, Vol. 9, No. 6, 2006. 859–873. Copyright © 2006 Taylor & Francis. Reprinted by permission of the publisher, www.tandfonline.com.

Excerpts from *For the Record: An Oral History of Rochester, New York Newsworkers*. By Bonnie Brennen. Copyright © 2001 Fordham University Press. Reprinted by permission.

"The Culture of a Women-Led Newspaper: An Ethnographic Study of the Sarasota Herald-Tribune" by Tracy Everbach. From *Journalism & Mass Communication Quarterly*, Vol. 83, No. 3, September 2006. 477–493. Copyright © 2006 AEJMC. Reprinted by permission.

"Religiosity to Consumerism: Press coverage of Thanksgiving, 1905–2005." By Bonnie Brennen. From *Journalism Studies*, Vol. 9, No. 1, 2008. 21–37. Copyright © 2008 Taylor & Francis. Reprinted by permission of the publisher, www.tandfonline.com.

# Index

access to participants 31, 127, 163–4
Adams, J. 124
advertising 200–2, 205–6; of diamond
    rings 201–2; news coverage and
    222–5, 226, 227
Alinsky, S. 109–10, 118
analysis (*see also* textual analysis) 24; of
    historical evidence 102–3, 106–7; of
    interviews 37–8; of transcripts 73
Anderson, K. 130
Aristotle 205
Association for Education in Journalism
    and Mass Communication,
    Qualitative Studies division 6–7
audience response 61
*Avatar* (film), as example of participant
    observation 165–7
Avery, D. 210

background research 19; in oral history
    126–7; on respondents 30–1, 32
Barnhurst, K.G. 210
Beck, M. 152
Beck, R. 147–8
Belkin, L. 175
Black Friday, newspaper coverage 194–5
Bloor, M. 68, 73

Bluem, A.W. 107
body language 34, 66, 131
Bok, S. 17
Bourdieu, P. 55
Branston, G. 205

Carey, J. 2, 13, 14, 18–19, 22, 96–7, 105,
    119
case studies: ethnography 172–85; focus
    groups 74–89; history 105–20; oral
    history 135–56; qualitative interviews
    39–53; textual analysis 208–27
CBS 111, 113; Documentary Unit 105,
    106, 108, 114, 115–16, 117
Christians, C. 2, 16, 22
clarifying responses 64, 66
clichés, use of 48–9
Clune, H., interview with 139–40, 148
codes/coding 178, 179, 196
collaboration with participants 17, 28,
    129, 169
communication 2, 5, 200; development of
    research 5–7; history of 97–8;
    qualitative research 5, 18, 62;
    quantitative research 5, 6, 18, 62, 194,
    195; ritual view 13, 14; as social
    science 6; transmission view 13, 14

complete observer 164–5
complete participant 165; 'going native'
    165–7
conclusions 24, 88–9, 226–7
confessional style of presentation 23
confidentiality 16, 29, 71, 171
Confucius 94
consent *see* informed consent
constructivism 9, 10
content analysis 194–5; newspapers 210
context 22; for observation 161, 162, 170;
    textual analysis 199–200, 207
Cormack, M. 202–3
Corwin, N. 116, 118
Cotton, J. 111, 112
credibility of historical evidence 102
critical literary analysis 210
*Critical Studies in Mass Communication* 7
critical theories 9, 10
cultural history 95–7, 103, 104
cultural materialism 2
cultural studies 2, 161–2, 198–9, 202–3,
    208
culture, ethnography and 160, 161

Daisey, M. 104
Darnton, R. 104
Davenport, E.R. 136, 137
deception 16–17, 171
*Democrat & Chronicle* (Rochester NY)
    137, 138, 139, 149–50, 152
Denzin, N.K. 7, 8, 17, 169
Deutsch, Art, interview with 140–1, 146,
    149
Dichter, E. 114, 117–18
digital technology, teenagers' use of,
    focus group research 74–89
Dimitman, E.Z. 141
Dimitriadis, G. 62
disclosure 16, 17, 29
discourse analysis 197
dominant ideology 201–2
Douglas, S. 107

*The Eagle's Brood* (radio documentary)
    105–6, 107, 109, 110, 111, 113–20
Eastman, G. 137
Ehrlich, M.C. 105–20
Einstein, A. 100
Electronic Records Archives 99
encoding/decoding 200–1

epistemology 8
ethical issues 16–18; ethnography 170–1;
    focus groups 70–1; history 104;
    interviews 29; oral history 134; textual
    analysis 206–7
ethnography 159–61; analysis of 169–70;
    case study 172–85; ethical issues
    170–1; field notes 167–9; in media
    studies 161–3; and participant
    observation 163–5
Ettema, J.S. 119
evaluating responses 35
evaluation: of focus groups 73; of
    historical evidence 101–4
Everbach, T. 172–86
evidence (*see also* historical evidence):
    analysis of 21–2; gathering 21;
    presentation of 43–4
Ewen, S. 223
exegesis 196

facilitators *see* moderators of focus
    groups
Fedler, F. 146
feminist research: feminist-standpoint
    theory 176–7, 179–84; social 199; use
    of focus groups 62–3
Fern, E.F. 64
field notes 167–9
field theory 55
fieldwork 162, 178–9
Fine, M. 17
Finland, journalism in 39–53
Fiske, J. 21
Flynn, T., interview with 143–6, 150–1
focus groups (*see also* moderators of
    focus groups; participants) 59–61,
    62–3, 71–3; case study 74–89;
    communication strategies 64–7;
    development of 61–2, environment
    for 72; evaluation of 73; limitations of
    87–8; research objectives 72
Fontana, A. 31, 36
Fradenburgh, D. 150
framing of experience 44–5, 47
Frey, J.H. 31, 36

Gannett, F. 135, 136, 137, 138
Gannett Company 127, 129, 135–56
Gans, H.J. 173, 210
Geertz, C. 161, 169, 171–2

genre analysis 203–5
Giambrone, J., interview with 154–6
Gist, M.E. 176
Glass, I. 104
Glasser, T.L. 119
Gobo, G. 160
Gould, J. 113
government records 99
Green, B. 221
Greenbaum, T.L. 60, 67, 69, 70
Grele, R.J. 125
Guba, E.G. 8, 9
Gubrium, J.F. 27, 28, 38

Hall, S. 193, 200, 210
Hamilton, D. 8
Hardt, H. 6, 21–2, 96, 209
Hargittai, E. 74
Hearst, W.R. 137
Hebrew University of Jerusalem 100
Heller, R. 105–6, 108, 114, 116, 117
Helsper, E. 74, 85–6
historical evidence 95–6, 98; analysis of 102–3, 106–7; collection of 98, 99–100; evaluation of 101–4
historical materials 99–101, 125; accuracy of 102, 103, 104
history 93–105; case study 105–20; ethical issues 104; media 96–9; methodology 98–9; traditional versus cultural 94–6, 103–4
Holstein, J.A. 27, 28, 38
homeless, and coverage of Thanksgiving 219–22
Hundley, H.L. 74–89
Hunter, R. 217

iAsk Center 61
icebreaker questions 32–3, 65
ideological analysis 201–3
ideology 201
impressionist style of presentation 23
informed consent 16, 29, 70–1; ethnography 170; focus groups 76; oral history 128, 134
institutional history 97
International Communication Association, Philosophy of Communication Division 6–7
Internet security 89
interpretation 22, 161, 169–70, 194, 206;

context and 199–200, 207; theory and 197–9
intertextuality 199–200
interviews (see also qualitative interviews) 26–7; in-depth 177, 178; in oral history 126, 127–8, 139–45 (editing 132–3; strategies 128–30); participant observation 168, 178; skills for 34–5; structured/unstructured 27–8, 77; techniques 34–6
introductions 23–4, 105–6
iPods 75, 78, 79, 85
irony 49

Jack, D.C. 130
Jameson, F. 95
Johnson, J. 28
Jordan, A. 74, 85
Journal of Communication 7
Journal of Communicative Inquiry 7
journalism: case studies 39–53, 135–56, 172–85, 208–27; in Finland 39–53; history of 97; postmodern 52; responsibility of 49–51
journalists (see also women journalists), training of 145–6
juvenile delinquency, radio documentaries on 109–13, 118–19

Kaidy, M. 137, 138, 147
Kamberelis, G. 62
Karrh, J. 227
Keiper, E. 147, 148
Kercher, L.C. 116
Kerry, J. 62–3
King, F., interview with 141–3
Kracauer, S. 194, 201
Kunelius, R. 37, 38, 39–53
Kvale, S. 4, 30

La Ferle, C. 86
Lady Gaga 197, 198–9
language 2, 4, 14–15, 192–3, 205
Lavie, A. 175
Lazarsfeld, P. 61–2, 115, 117
leading questions 129–30
Lehman-Wilzig, S. 175
Levy, M.R. 117
Lichty, L. 107
Liebling, A.J. 32–3
Lincoln, Y.S. 7, 8, 9, 17, 169

Ling, R. 85, 86, 87
listening 28–9, 64, 128 active/passive 64; strategies for 130–2
literature review 24; ethnographic research 173–6
literature search 19
Livingstone, S. 74, 85–6
Lopes, L. 35
Lyman, S.M. 7

MacLeish, A. 108
macro-history 97–8
manipulation 16
marketing 61–2
mass communication 6, 18
Matheson, J.L. 133
Mazzarella, S.R. 75, 77
McCullough, D. 124
McFarlin, D. 179–80, 183
McKee, A. 204, 207
meanings 14, 20, 22; denotative/connotative 15; dominant 200; in textual analysis 196–7, 198–9, 200
*Media, Culture and Society* 7
media studies 5, 171; theoretical perspectives 6–7
Merton, R. 61–2
methodology 8, 24
Meyer, A. 110
Meyer, P. 210
Milgram, S. 16
moderators of focus groups 72; communication strategies 64–7; and evaluation 73; researchers as 64, 77; role of 63–4
Morgan, D.L. 71
Morley, D. 170
Morris, E. 101
Morrissey, C.T. 131
muckrakers 218, 226
Murrow, E.R. 105, 108, 111, 113, 114
Mutz, D. 210
MySpace 81, 84, 86

narrators (oral history) 127, 129, 134; access to 127; in case study 135, 136, 138, 140–56; feedback from 133; questions for 128–9
netnography 162
Neuharth, A. 139, 174

Newcomb, H,M, 31, 38
newspaper archives 99
Newspaper Guild 129
newspapers: advertising and news coverage 222–5, 226, 227; case study of ethnographic research 172–86; content analysis 210; textual analysis of coverage of Thanksgiving 207, 211–28
non-verbal communication 131; in focus groups 66, 69, 70; in interviews 34, 35
Nord, D.P. 97, 105

objectivity 8
observation (*see also* participant observation) 160, 161; context for 161; and field notes 167–9; and interpretation 161, 169–70; mental notes on 168
observer as participant 16
online focus groups 60
online risk 81–4, 87, 89
ontology 8
open-ended questions 33, 65, 128
oral history (*see also* narrators) 124–35; case study 135–56; ethical issues 134; interview strategies 128–30; technique 126–8
Oral History Association 134
Other, representations of 17
overt cynicism 49

Paley, W. 106, 109, 116
paradigms 7–11
paraphrasing responses 64–5
participant as observer 165, 167
participant observation 163–5; case study 172–86; ethical issues 170–1; 'going native' 165–7
participants (focus groups) 60, 72; in case study 75–6, 78–80; difficult 69–70; interaction with 65–6, 69; payment for 71; recruitment of 67–9, 72–3
participatory/cooperative inquiry 9, 10
Pauly, J. 5, 15, 18, 23
payment of participants 71
Pells, R. 219
Pendleton, J. 86
persuasion 205

phatic responses 35–6
political campaigns, use of focus groups 62–3
positivism 8, 9
Postman, N. 6, 14
post-positivism 9
*The Power of Words* (film) 193
power relationships, in interviews 29, 128, 130
presentation of research 22–3, 43–4
primary sources 100–1
privacy 16, 29, 171
probing responses 35
process of qualitative research 18–24
Program Analyzer 115, 117
Progressive Reform movement 226; and newspaper coverage of Thanksgiving 216–19
pseudo-history 95
Punch, M. 16

qualitative interviews 28–9, 31–4; designing a study 30–1; editing 37; ethical issues 29; taping 32, 36; transcribing 36–7
qualitative research 4, 14; development of 5–7; ethics of 16–18; methodology 4–5; paradigms 7–11; process of 18–24; terms used in 15–16, 71
quantitative research 3, 14; communications 5–6, 18, 62, 194, 195; terms used in 15–16, 71
questions (*see also* research questions) in focus groups 65–6, 73, 77; in interviews 30, 31, 32–4; oral history 128–30
quotations, use of in research reports 43–4, 45, 46–7, 79–80, 81–4, 138

radio documentaries 105–25
rapport with participants 161, 164, 176
realist style of presentation 23
reality 8, 9; social construction of 4, 14, 28, 192–3, 202, 203
recording of observations 168
*Red Channels* 116
reflecting responses 65
reflexivity 22, 169
Reisberg, S. 116
reliability 8, 38; oral history interviews 131–2

research design focus groups 72–3; qualitative interviews 41–2
research participants (*see also* narrators (oral history); participants (focus groups); respondents (interviews) 16, 17; background research on 30–1, 32, 126–7; sharing findings with 29
research questions 20–1; ethnography 168; history 98–9; oral history 126; theoretical frameworks and 10, 20, 164, 168
research reports 22–4, 38–9; use of quotations in 43–4, 45, 46–7, 79–80, 81–4, 138
research topic, choice of 18–20
respondents (interviews) 28, 29, 34, 36; access to 31; background research on 30–1, 32; in case study 41–51, 54–5; reliability of information 38
rhetorical analysis 205–6
Rice, S.A. 220
ritual view of communication 13, 14
Rochester (New York), newspapers in 127; case study 135–56
Rorty, R. 118
Rossi, P. 220
Ryan, A. 17

*Sarasota Herald-Tribune*: family-friendly policies 179–82, 184–5; female management of 172, 175–85
Saussure, F. de 196
Schudson, M. 40, 97
Second Life 60–1
secondary sources 101
Selznick, D.O. 111
semiotics 196–7
sender/message/receiver model of communication 200
Shaw, G.H. 109, 110
Shayon, R.L. 105, 108–9, 110, 111, 113, 114–15, 116, 117, 118–19
Shyles, L. 74–89
Siems, R. 224
Siepmann, C. 108–9, 114, 116
Silverstone, R. 89, 170
Skloot, R. 37
social networking 77, 81, 86, 88
social science research 6, 14
Socrates 26
*South Park* 204

238 • Index

Stanton, F. 115, 117
*Star Trek* 194
Stepp, C. 210
Stewart, D.W. 60, 67–8
structure of feeling 208, 209
summarising responses 65
survey research 27, 28
symbols 4

Tannen, D. 181, 184
taping interviews 32, 36, 128, 132–3;
    focus groups 60, 64
*Telephone* (music video), textual analysis
    of 197–9
Tennant, D. 180, 181
Terkel, S. 29, 130, 131
texts 193–4; content of 202–3, as sources
    of power 202; style of 203
textual analysis 170, 192–3; case study
    208–27; development of 194–5;
    encoding/decoding 199–201; ethical
    issues 206–7; and genres 203–5;
    ideology and 201–3; influence of
    semiotics 196–7; rhetoric analysis
    205–6; theoretical framework and
    197–9, 225–6
Thansgiving, newspaper coverage of 208,
    209–10; and advertising 223–6; food
    stories 212; and the homeless 220–1;
    human interest stories 213; and
    nationalism 227; and the needy
    217–20, 226, 227; presidential
    celebrations 212–13; religious aspects
    214–16
theoretical frameworks 10–11, 38; and
    choice of topic 19–20; ethnography
    168; and research questions 10, 20,
    164, 168; textual analysis 197–9,
    225–6
thick description 161
*This American Life* (radio documentary)
    104
Thompson, D.R. 210
Thompson, J. 102

Thompson, P. 125
Thucydides 93, 95
*Times Union* (Rochester, NY) 136–7,
    137–8, 139, 142, 143–5, 148–9,
    152–4
Tosh, J. 94
transcription 36–7, 73–4, 132; editing and
    37, 133
transmission view of communication 13,
    14
transparency 4
Tuchman, G. 173
Turner, G. 201
trust 127, 129, 177

*The Umbrella Man* (film documentary)
    101
understanding 14
understanding responses 35

validity 8; oral history interviews 131–2
Van Zoonen, L. 176
videoconferencing focus groups 60
videotaping interviews 132; focus groups
    60, 64
Vidich, A.J. 7
virtual communities 162
virtual focus groups 60–1
voice recognition software 132–3

Walters, B. 31, 32, 34
Wartella, E.A. 75
Washington, G. 208
Watts, S. 152–3
Weaver, J. 180–1, 182, 185
web ethnography 162–3, 169, 171
White, H. 95
Williams, R. 2, 135, 192–3, 209, 226
women journalists 147–56, 172–85

You Tube 160
Yow, V.R. 129, 132

Zelizer, B. 41